Studies in Australian Political Rhetoric

Studies in Australian Political Rhetoric

Edited by John Uhr & Ryan Walter

Australian
National
University

PRESS

ANU PRESS

Published by ANU Press
The Australian National University
Canberra ACT 0200, Australia
Email: anupress@anu.edu.au
This title is also available online at http://press.anu.edu.au

---

National Library of Australia Cataloguing-in-Publication entry

Title:	Studies in Australian political rhetoric / edited by John Uhr and Ryan Walter.
ISBN:	9781925021868 (paperback) 9781925021875 (ebook)
Subjects:	Rhetoric--Political aspects--Australia--History.
	Communication in politics--Australia--History.
	Politics and literature--Australia.
	Australia--Politics and government.

Other Authors/Contributors:
Uhr, John, 1951- editor.
Walter, Ryan, editor.

Dewey Number: 320.014

Cover design by Nic Welbourn and layout by ANU Press

Cover photographs:

Kevin Rudd speaking. (Photo: John Gass / APN)

Prime Minister Julia Gillard speaks during House of Representatives question time at Parliament House in Canberra, Tuesday, Oct. 9, 2012. Mr Abbott is asking the Speaker be removed from office immediately under section 35 of Constitution. (AAP Image/Lukas Coch)

A file photo of Sept. 4, 2001 of former Prime Minister John Howard speaking to eldery people at a community morning tea in Melbourne. Mr. Howard turns 70 on Sunday, July 26, 2009, relaxed and comfortable in his retirement yet still busy interpreting his own place in the political pantheon. (AAP Image/Julian Smith, files)

Coalition Leader Tony Abbott speaks during the Coalition's election campaign launch in Brisbane, Sunday, Aug. 25, 2013. (AAP Image/Dan Peled)

Contents

Introduction

Part I: Just rhetoric? Language and behaviour

Part II: Standards of rhetoric

Part III: The content of rhetoric

Conclusion

Acknowledgements

This volume represents the proceedings of a symposium, 'Australian Political Rhetoric', which was hosted by the School of Politics and International Relations, The Australian National University, in May 2013. The editors would like to thank Justine Molony for her excellent editorial assistance in preparing the manuscript, and the Australian Research Council for financial support (DP130104628).

Contributors

Editors

Professor John Uhr, Director, Centre for the Study of Australian Politics, School of Politics and International Relations, The Australian National University.

Dr Ryan Walter, School of Political Science and International Studies, University of Queensland.

Contributors

Dr Dennis Grube, School of Government and International Relations, Griffith University.

Dr Mark Hearn, Department of Modern History, Politics and International Relations, Macquarie University.

Emeritus Professor Barry Hindess, School of Politics and International Relations, The Australian National University.

Professor John Kane, Centre for Governance and Public Policy, Griffith University.

Dr Melissa Lovell, National Centre for Indigenous Studies, The Australian National University.

Dr Stephen Mills, Graduate School of Government, University of Sydney.

Jennifer Rayner, School of Politics and International Relations, The Australian National University.

Dr Mark Rolfe, School of Social Sciences, University of New South Wales.

Professor Geoffrey Stokes, Deputy Pro Vice-Chancellor (Research), College of Business, RMIT University.

Dr Ian Tregenza, Department of Modern History, Politics and International Relations, Macquarie University.

Introduction

What's at stake in Australian political rhetoric?

John Kane

Rhetoric — generally defined as the art of discourse — has been distrusted as deceptive or subversive ever since the Greek sophists made a living instructing how to make the weaker argument seem the stronger in the law courts, or how to use persuasion to win in politics. Still today, people commonly dismiss rhetoric as 'mere rhetoric' — an effusion of ineffectual words by slippery politicians, concealing more than it reveals.[1]

Yet rhetoric remains central to democratic politics, which necessarily depend more fundamentally on the power of persuasion than on the force of command. Persuasion relies crucially on explanation and argument — in Greek, the *logos*. But how are non-expert citizens to judge whether a political argument (which does not admit of mathematical demonstration) is sound or merely cleverly deceptive? Here Aristotle's amendment of sophistical cynicism remains as salient today as when he issued it millennia ago. He argued that of equal importance to *logos* in rhetorical practice were judgements of character — *ethos* — both the listeners' judgement of the character of the speaker and the speaker's judgement of the character of the audience. In the former case an audience must judge whether the speaker is a competent and trustworthy source, and in the latter the speaker must understand what matters to, and therefore will move, a particular audience. This last consideration brings up another of Aristotle's requirements of rhetoric — *pathos* — an appeal to the emotions. Even a sound argument from a reliable source is meaningless if no one cares about the issue at hand (Aristotle 2000, 1356a1–16; Bk II, Chs 2–11).

Aristotle's analysis resonated through the ages as political leaders strove to find the words and style that could move people in presumptively virtuous directions.[2] Ideal rhetoric was that capable of moving an audience by the evident wisdom of the argument and the indubitable character of the speaker. The hope of seeing this ideal realised endures, though hope is always shaded by the distrust that speech inevitably arouses in the political arena. The papers

---

1 At the opposite extreme, rhetoric may be feared as all too effectual in arousing a democratic rabble to insurrection.
2 Cicero took up the Aristotelian elements of rhetoric in his *De Oratore* (55 BCE), describing them as *probare, delectare, flectere* (to prove, to delight, to stir). This formulation is later taken up by Quintilian and becomes important in Augustine's discussion of Christian eloquence (see Kennedy 1986: 100). For a modern reassessment, see Perelman and Olbrechts-Tyteca (2003) and Garsten (2006).

in this collection afford material for contemplation of this perennial tension between ideal and actual in the Australian context, and allow us to address our leading question: what is at stake in Australian political rhetoric?

Australian political rhetoric

A general inquiry into Australian political rhetoric may be imagined to aim at one or both of two things: a) to apply a general understanding of the functioning of political rhetoric to particular Australian cases; or b) to discern what may be distinctively *Australian* in the rhetoric of our nation. Reflection on the papers collected in this volume suggests that these aims are so deeply intertwined in practice as to be scarcely separable. To be sure, Barry Hindess reports that the term 'dog-whistle politics' may (or may not) be of Australian coinage, but that marks an exception (if it is one). The profound interconnectedness across history of the Australian political system with the systems of other nations — Britain and the United States in particular, but also all other democracies — means there has been massive influence on Australian rhetoric from sources abroad, as well as a comparable set of challenges and problems that rhetorical practices must try to meet. Thus Mark Rolfe in this collection explores how political leaders in the developing Australian colonies and in the early Commonwealth looked consciously to the evolving rhetoric of US leaders to discern a style suited to their own burgeoning democracy. More recently, as Stephen Mills notes, Australian leaders have borrowed a new 'rhetoric of apology' for past official wrongs from examples set in Europe and elsewhere since the 1990s.

But for all the inherited commonalities and influences, Australian political history has followed such an idiosyncratic path that we should be surprised if Australian rhetoric had *not* acquired its own distinctive accents. Rolfe traces the general evolution of political rhetoric from a high-flown aristocratic style to a more 'middling' one that maintained some ideals of literary allusion, and then on to the more thoroughly demotic form of speech that is usual today. The example he uses of the last is that of John Howard (he might equally have mentioned Bob Hawke), fittingly I think, for few cultures have fulfilled the ideal of democratic rhetoric as thoroughly as the contemporary Australian. One has only to listen to a 1950s recording of Robert Menzies with his impeccably Anglo-Australian locution to measure how far the demotic evolution has advanced in this country. Howard was a master of Australian ordinariness, his flat accent declaring that there was no essential distance between leader and led, his low-key tone expressing the assurance that, whatever the issue, there was nothing to get in a flap about, nothing that he and his government couldn't handle. Howard would never have claimed to be an orator, but he was a clear and effective speaker who spoke to, never down to, the people.

This political expression of our famously egalitarian ethos evolved within a unique political system, a version of British parliamentarism governed by unwritten conventions modified by an American-influenced written constitution. The latter established the Senate as a supposed 'states' house' with almost coequal legislative powers as the lower House of Representatives. This system complicated parliamentary government after the introduction of proportional representation brought the Senate into serious political play by giving minor elements the balance of power. The resultant political arrangement is one that bears strong resemblances to British and American systems, but is identical to neither, a peculiarly Australian amalgam that carries within it inherent tensions. One of these results from the fact that the constitution enumerates the powers of 'the Executive' — which is to say of the Governor-General, the Queen's representative as Head of the Commonwealth — while remaining silent (in accord with British conventions) on the real agents of political power, the prime minister and cabinet. The dismissal of a sitting prime minister in 1975 by the then Governor-General dramatically revealed that the monarch's representative in the Australian system was not as safely 'constitutionalised' as was the monarch herself (a fact that may be the focus of renewed rhetorical attention if ever the subject of an Australian republic, and the presumed titular head of that republic, re-emerges for serious debate).

The principal forum for rhetorical contestation in the Australian polity remains, nevertheless, the lower house, where government is formed, the prime minister sits, and the opposition strives to call the government to account during question time. It is a curious fact, explicated in this collection by John Uhr, that the only constitutionally recognised role in this consequential assembly is that of Speaker of the House, and then only in a manner that leaves much room for interpretation and parliamentary determination. Uhr examines the controversial changeover of three Speakers under the Rudd–Gillard government and tries to determine what the rhetorical parliamentary exchanges on the issue tell us about the Speaker's role. It emerges that, despite the title, the Speaker's task is more one of listening than speaking, and listening in order to manage the chamber in a way that effectively preserves some modicum of order among the sparring parties. Uhr notes the case of Peter Slipper, a Speaker who, by general admission, provided fair and firm management but nevertheless proved unacceptable because of his out-of-chamber conduct and generally dubious character. Slipper, a former Liberal member of parliament, was appointed by Julia Gillard to deprive the opposition of a vital extra vote in a hung parliament, despite his facing criminal charges and being widely viewed as unfit for office by virtue of offensively sexist remarks. Slipper's eventual departure, says Uhr, tells us about 'the requirement for evidence of personal integrity in positions of public integrity' and 'that governments have accountability obligations when they appoint undeserving persons to high parliamentary office.'

This is a significant observation because the themes of integrity and trust and, by association, political legitimacy, echo repeatedly throughout this collection — unsurprisingly given that the central topic is political rhetoric. Distrust in leadership integrity is, as argued elsewhere (Kane and Patapan 2012), practically a defining feature of democracy, and Australians are certainly inclined toward a general cynicism regarding politics and politicians. But how deep is this distrust in the Australian political system, and how significant for its health?

Rhetoric, integrity and trust

Mark Hearn and Ian Tregenza provide a fascinating historical example of an Australian leader, Alfred Deakin, who was supremely conscious of the importance of instilling trust, and who sought to fulfil the classical rhetorical ideal. Deakin was generally recognised at home and abroad as Australia's most gifted and fluent orator. He looked to classical and contemporary models to fashion speech capable not just of convincing people on critical policy matters, but also of contributing to nation-building by fostering virtues of discipline, self-reliance and readiness to defend the new Commonwealth. In explicating the persuasiveness of a speech, Deakin noted the essential connection between a speaker's character and the words spoken, emphasising most especially the qualities of sincerity and deeply held conviction.

Australians would no doubt like to see this ideal upheld by the present generation of leaders, but seem hardly to expect it. Must it inevitably be so? The essays gathered here give us some clues to assessing this question.

It is instructive to note first that patently sincere speech has not been entirely absent from Australian politics, even over the last few turbulent years. Indeed it has been movingly witnessed in a sequence of official apologies by Australian prime ministers and ministers: to Aboriginal Stolen Generations, to people forced to migrate to Australia as children, to sexually abused members of the defence forces, and to individuals caught up in the practice of forced adoption. Though this rhetoric of apology may have been modelled on precedents set abroad, it has proved, as Mills argues, an effective instrument of public leadership for governments concerned, after decades of avoidance, to admit and allay old offences of Australian officialdom. The road to deploying such rhetoric has been long and contested, centrally at issue being questions of historical continuity and enduring responsibility. Howard expressed 'sincere regrets' and 'deep sorrow' over the treatment of Aboriginal children in the past, while denying that the present generation could be held collectively responsible for the public acts of previous generations — a view that sat in curious contradiction to his desire to see an affirmative ('non-black armband') account of Australian history taught in schools. We were entitled, it seemed, to take pride in the positive achievements of our forebears, in the sacrifices of our soldiers at Gallipoli and so on, but could not assume responsibility, through outright apology, for past wrongs in which we were not personally implicated. Kevin Rudd, in his apology to the Stolen Generations, asserted to the contrary that the necessary continuity was provided, not by individuals, but by the enduring institutions of the Commonwealth, most particularly the Parliament, which was the author of past policies and thus the locus of current responsibility for their amendment.

The rhetoric of apology is, however, the exception that proves the rule, a special form to be distinguished from the normal political rhetoric used, for example, to defend a policy, explain a budget or attack an opponent. Mills writes that it is rather a 'constitutive' form of performative speech act that 'transforms the polity' and allows it 'to address and deal with … profound questions of national reconciliation and identity.' The various issues that have been addressed are part of the mixed but distinctive Australian story, ones that could be effectively addressed only by a government authorised to speak on behalf of the whole Australian people. It is this 'speaking for the nation' that places the apologies in a higher, more sacred political realm than day-to-day politics, where the sincerity of speakers is usually much harder to judge and is in fact frequently questioned.

Distrust of leadership rhetoric is a theme that has played long and loud in recent Australian politics, and many essays in the present collection expressly address the period of the Rudd–Gillard Labor governments in order to explore the connection between rhetoric, trust and legitimacy. Jennifer Rayner, for example, tries to show how closely leadership legitimacy is tied to the rhetoric that leaders deploy to explain themselves; in Gillard's case to explain her sudden assumption of prime ministerial office. Rayner's method is to contrast Gillard's rhetorical failure with the success of Paul Keating, a generation earlier, when he defeated Hawke without being regarded as an illegitimate usurper. At issue was not the (then) right of the Labor caucus to change the leadership, which was unquestioned in both cases. Keating, however, came to power after a prolonged struggle and as though 'to the manor born', while Gillard came suddenly, like an assassin in the night. Her earliest words as prime minister seemed, as Rayner argues, to confirm her own doubts about her legitimacy, describing herself as a reticent conscript to the role, refusing to move into the Lodge until she had an election in which she 'fulsomely earned the trust of the Australian people to be prime minister', and tying her right to leadership to promises to deliver on key policies better than Rudd had done. Rayner also contrasts the words of the defeated leaders: Hawke accepting (genuinely if reluctantly) the validity of Keating's win; Rudd claiming that factional leaders (the notorious 'faceless men') had overthrown a prime minister elected by 'the people of Australia', a theme that was ever after reflected in press commentary describing the event as a 'coup' or a 'putsch'.

Rayner claims that this initial failure by Gillard to convincingly assert her legitimacy as prime minister was more important than, and in fact set the scene for, the furore over her broken promise not to introduce a carbon tax. Yet the latter shift of policy — again poorly defended by Gillard — gave reasonable cause for the unrelenting attacks by Tony Abbott's opposition on Gillard's honesty and trustworthiness. Further rhetorical missteps gave more ammunition to the opposition, particularly the promise made and oft-repeated by Treasurer Wayne Swan and Gillard herself to bring the budget into modest surplus in 2013. The latter case is carefully explored by Ryan Walter in this collection, again using an historical contrast, this time with the Howard–Costello administration and its failure to produce a surplus in 2002. Little damage was done to the credibility of Howard and Peter Costello because they had rhetorically framed the issue as one of aspiration ('we don't like budget deficits') and of reasonable forecasting that was inevitably at the mercy of external economic conditions. Labor's blunder was to frame the matter as a solemn promise, which as Walter argues, fatally 'shifted the rhetorical contest from the terrain of economic management to trustworthiness'. As the 2013 election neared, Abbott and shadow Treasurer Joe Hockey could repeatedly charge that nothing '*this government*' said could be believed, and that the Australian people should not trust it with another three years.

The Gillard period undoubtedly dramatised as seldom before the central importance of maintaining a level of reasonable trust among voters, as well as the difficulties of achieving and maintaining trust in a democratic environment. The fractious debates, ad hominem attacks and relentless negativity that characterised political rhetoric between 2010 and 2013 may have been peculiarly bitter and desperate given the circumstances of a hung parliament and an unusually insecure government, but they emphasised an obvious point — one sometimes neglected by people longing for the Deakinite ideal to be realised in Australia — that democratic politics is, with rare exceptions, a politics of dissent and opposition. Democratic rhetoric must aim to persuade an always doubting populace of one's general competence and legitimacy, as well as the wisdom of one's own policies, while calling into doubt the wisdom and competence of the opposition. One must at the same time meet the challenge of a vociferous, ever clamorous, and often hostile media.

This generally agonistic political environment presents inescapable challenges for every democratic politician. No doubt each would like to be seen as realising the ideal of speaking plainly from the heart, thus inspiring trust and respect if not necessarily agreement. This is far from easy to accomplish while trying to survive in the political bearpit, where others have a vested interest in undermining one's credibility at every point. Speech is the essential tool of offence, defence and justification, but political speech, in a world where an ill-chosen word can invite censure or even calamity, must be carefully judged and sometimes carefully crafted. Walter criticises the Gillard government in this respect for failing to understand even basic points of rhetorical strategy, but this is to remind us of the importance of *having* a rhetorical strategy and implementing it well. The irony is that the demand for democratic speech to be open, honest and straight-shooting can be met only by careful (and not too blatant) calculation (see Kane and Patapan 2010).

This artless art is doubly difficult because room for rhetorical manoeuvre is constricted, not just by one's own missteps, but by history, specifically the history of political rhetoric itself. Walter traces the shift in rhetoric after Costello's charter of budget honesty in 1998 from a concern with 'social justice' to a central concern for 'responsible economic management', and its associated term 'fiscal discipline'. We are reminded, as so often in this collection, that the rhetorical contest is to a large extent fought over the issue of who can successfully 'frame' debate, so that one's opponents have little option but to fight on conceptual grounds favourable to one's own cause. Although Rudd defeated Howard in 2007 by reassuring Australians that he was an 'economic conservative', ultimately the victory belonged to the conservatives who had made this framing necessary, and who could point the finger at Labor profligacy in its response to the global financial crisis. They had also, of course, set the budget surplus trap that the Gillard–Swan team obligingly fell into.

This general theme is theoretically elaborated here by Dennis Grube, who applies the idea of path dependency to political rhetoric in the Australian context. He notes that one may often see path dependency in policy — as, for example, when the coalition parties felt constrained by already sunk costs to adopt their own version of Rudd's National Broadband Network plan, despite having condemned it as bad policy — but claims that it is also observable in rhetorical practice. The history that matters in the examples Grube provides is the more immediate one of politicians' past pronouncements, which once spoken entrap them in a 'gilded cage' of their own making. One hears much about 'narrative' in politics these days, and the need for politicians to craft a convincing one. Grube accepts that politicians have no choice but to define central policy imperatives aimed at realising some vision of national advancement, but notes that in so doing they also necessarily define *themselves* politically and, having done so, inevitably constrict their space for future manoeuvre and change. Thus when Rudd called climate change 'the greatest moral, economic and social challenge of our time', one demanding firm and unflinching leadership that he would provide through the introduction of an emissions trading scheme, he laid down a test of his own leadership, commitment and sincerity that it would prove extremely damaging to squib — as he eventually did, starting the decline in his hitherto remarkable public approval ratings that led to his downfall.

It is at such times that people are likely to say a politician's words have proved to be 'just rhetoric', yet this case and the others Grube provides (Gillard's 'no carbon tax' promise and Abbott's 'turn back the boats' policy) show that one's own rhetoric can pose a considerable danger to one's political fortunes. To be sure, electorates are generally patiently long-suffering, their judgement of leaders being normally cumulative over repeated experience of leadership talk and performance. Moreover, their scepticism about the typically evasive speech of politicians surely provides a margin of toleration by perennially suppressing expectations — especially during election campaigns when an implicit bargain seems to exist between candidate and people: 'I'll pretend to be sincere in what I promise if you pretend to believe me.' But there are promises and 'core' promises, the latter creating public perceptions and expectations that, when upset by policy U-turns, can only with great difficulty be successfully renegotiated. The lesson is that *speech matters* in politics, and matters in consequential ways. Politicians will eventually be judged for good or ill according to their *ethos*, that is to their character as publicly assessed through a combination of their words and deeds.

But if perceptions of character are important, then political rivals inevitably have a keen interest in influencing those perceptions. If, as noted, trust was a dominant theme of the Rudd–Gillard years, it was always one closely related to character. Unprecedented personal attacks were mounted, not only between government and opposition, but in Labor's intra-party disputes over the leadership. Whatever Rudd's public persona, his alleged private character as revealed in interactions with colleagues and administrators was, after his fall and to forestall his return, savagely condemned by members of his own party. This gave opportunity to Abbott's strategy team during the 2013 election, who reportedly received a psychiatric evaluation of Rudd as a 'grandiose narcissist' that they used to target his supposed Achilles heel — overconfidence (Williams 2013). Gillard for her part was, despite her stiff public persona, generally reported to be warm and personable in private, but her political character was constantly impugned, particularly after her broken promise on the carbon tax when enemies began cruelly to label her 'Ju-liar'. She hardly helped her own cause, after her ascent, by promising to reveal 'the real Julia', as though her former self-presentation had been a sham. Labor members nevertheless believed, despite their travails, that they had an ace-in-the-hole with Abbott's perceived character as former 'attack dog' of Howard's coalition, his crude style seeming to disqualify him for leadership and render him 'unelectable'. Rudd returned to lead the charge against Abbott conscious of the widespread public disgust and dismay at the tone and manner of recent politics. He promised a return to the rhetorical ideal of dignified civil debate over policy issues, eschewing 'negative' campaigning, but after a week of flailing he desperately resumed the character attacks. The Australian people were told not to trust Abbott, a man who would 'cut to the bone' people's entitlements and, despite his denials, restore punitive labour laws, a man who was misogynistic, out-of-touch and a social conservative (*sotto voce*, Catholic). Rudd's reversal was interpreted as a capitulation to the reality that, whatever people profess to want, they are susceptible to negativity. The rhetorical ideal inevitably succumbed to the pressing exigencies of a politics of competition in which winning is all and honourable defeat meaningless.

Ideals and ideologies

Was this period atypical of Australian politics over the long run? After reading the astute analyses in this collection one may indeed think that political rhetoric hit some new low during the years of fractured Labor government. The historical contrasts of Rayner and Walter seem to suggest things were better done in the past (and indeed, in recent years, the Hawke–Keating years of reform have acquired something of an exemplary status across the political spectrum, while the Howard years appear more and more as an era of firmness and stability).

Rolfe's essay, however, argues that the general tendency to imagine a golden age of rhetoric is, like all golden ages, largely an exercise in myth-making. Rolfe argues that we rightly expect (or hope) that our leaders will possess the self-mastery and judgement necessary to make prudent choices on our behalf, and that the apparent lack of these qualities during the Rudd–Gillard years naturally tempted us to look longingly to a lost ideal.[3] He relates how Australians have traditionally looked to masterful rhetoricians from British and American as well as Australian political history. He also notes, however, that old heroes were hardly venerated by their contemporaries, as they were by posterity, but rather suffered and struggled in the usual rough-and-tumble of political contest. Rolfe does not dismiss mythologising, which he says is intrinsic to political experience and provides a ground of community for leaders and their constituents that can give rhetoric its essential purchase. A tradition of great leaders whose words and deeds have put a distinctive stamp upon history forms a common bond, a reference point that is both a regulative ideal and an enduring rhetorical resource for everyday politics, though arguments over the standards these ideals embody are simply a part of the ongoing contest that is a permanent feature of liberal democracy.

This is no doubt true, for traditions themselves are open to reinterpretation and critique, as the reference to Howard's 'history wars' above suggests. Deakin,

---

3   Or to a current fictional one, specifically to the characters in *The West Wing* who are described in Rolfe's essay.

the exemplary Australian rhetorician whom Rolfe references in passing, put his talents to the service of a nation with which many contemporary Australians, despite inheriting it, would not wish to identify. As Hearn and Tregenza explain, Deakin's ideal was of his time, mixing liberal values of equality and class accommodation with masculinist assumptions about gender roles as well as with racially informed xenophobia. The Deakinite rhetoric of white Australia has long since been repudiated by the rhetoric, first of assimilation, and then of multiculturalism, but the legacy of decades of the White Australia policy can hardly be so easily sloughed off. The 'cage' within which acceptable rhetoric may occur shifts its shape and boundaries over historical time, imposing new imperatives and making different demands on rhetoricians trying to achieve their political ends or advantages. It is impossible now, except on extremist fringes, to deploy the frank racialism of Deakin, although one may employ the 'dog-whistle' rhetoric that Hindess analyses: 'a way of sending a prejudicial message to certain potential supporters in such a way as to make it inaudible to others whom it might alienate.'

Hindess, to be sure, reclassifies dog-whistling as just a particular species within the genus 'coded message' that forms the normal currency of political rhetoric. One of the targets of his critique is Robert Goodin who talks of the 'perniciousness' and 'fundamental perversity' of dog-whistle politics. It is perverse because it allegedly undermines democratic deliberation and destroys any sense of a democratic mandate (Goodin and Saward 2005; Goodin 2008). The argument here is between the hopeful idealist — who would see political rhetoric purified, stripped of ulterior intentions and devoted to reasonable discussion of good policy — and the realist who believes that political rhetoric will never be anything but political. If there is an advantage to be gained, politicians can be expected to craft their rhetoric to appeal to our baser feelings as much as to the better angels of our nature. And those who condemn such practices, Hindess says, will generally find they are indulging in coded messages of their own (for example about 'those benighted people who fall for this stuff').

Hindess's other contribution to this collection points to the difficulty of managing rhetoric, even when one is conscientiously aiming at our better angels and striving to achieve laudable goals in appropriate language. The problem is that we may be caught by our linguistic heritage, a case of Grube's path dependency writ large. Hindess analyses the *'Little children are sacred'* report into child sexual abuse in Aboriginal communities, which he claims, despite its good intentions, inadvertently gave the Howard government an excuse to send troops to police Indigenous communities in the Northern Territory. He takes particular issue with the linguistic contrast between 'modern' and 'traditional' and the residue this carries of the West's rhetoric of progress, with its inherent assumptions of superiority versus inferiority. The report's authors, he says, despite striving to be neutral do not manage to avoid this trap. We normally think of rhetoric as words spoken with intention, but in such cases our language seems to speak us, with unintended consequences. The rhetorical ideal proves hard to grasp even when we mean to.

Melissa Lovell traverses the same territory, bringing the tools of Foucauldian critical theory to bear on the question of how coercive approaches to Aboriginal governance became 'normalised' in Australian political discourse, particularly by proponents of neoliberal politics who object to government intervention in other circumstances (notably in the provision of welfare services). In examining the idea of Aboriginal 'development', Lovell shows how neoliberal rhetoric linked a market economy and 'proper' jobs with the production of capable citizens and functional communities, factors that were ignored by the old land rights legislation that aimed at preserving spiritual links between Aboriginal people and their land. The justifications for coercive governance, she says, depended on a particular population being identified as incapable of self-discipline and a simultaneous explanation of why more facilitative processes would not succeed. Lovell's aim is to 'destabilise the authority' of such discourses by pointing out their incoherence and contingency, and thus open up the possibility of alternative and presumably more benign discourses.

Neoliberalist discourse (under its original Australian moniker, economic rationalism) is also the subject of the paper by Geoffrey Stokes, painted on the much wider canvas of the entire political economy. Here the rhetorical ideal finds expression in the language of free markets, efficiency, deregulation, anti-protectionism and so on. This rhetoric is peculiarly effective because it presents itself under the banner of neutral science — specifically economic science — whose policy admonitions it would be irrational to defy, thus closing down debate and effective opposition. It is a case of rhetorical capture of the field on a grand scale, forcing even Labor leaders, as we noted, to adopt the language of 'responsible economic management'. In this regard, one might note how the Aristotelian categories — *logos*, *ethos*, and *pathos* — apply to the understanding of economic rationalism when viewed as a form of rhetoric: the *logos* is economic free market theory; its *ethos* or character is embodied in its claim to being a value-free science untainted by politics, rendering it deserving of our trust; its *pathos*, or ability to motivate an audience, lies in its promise to deliver individual and national prosperity more surely than any other system. It is an intrinsic presumption of rhetoric as persuasion that alternative choices must exist from which one needs to be *dis*suaded. A rhetoric that pretends not to be rhetoric, but scientific fact, tries to be maximally persuasive by informing you that (as Margaret Thatcher famously said) 'There is no alternative!'

The stakes of political rhetoric

It may seem a long way from an analysis of Gillard's defence of her leadership to a discussion of the dominant contemporary ideology of neoliberalism, yet all these essays fall under the rubric of rhetoric. Moreover there is a close connection between the microcosm of party politics and the macrocosmic context of a globalised economy. For one thing, when Australian parties come into government their central challenge is to 'manage' the little corner of the global system that is Australia with far fewer levers of control, following deregulation, than parties had in former times. Abbott and Hockey, having gained the glittering prize, are most sensitively conscious of this fact as they face the uncertainties of the global economy.

The problem is perhaps even more pressing for Labor in opposition. The question of character bears not just on individuals, but on the organisations to which they belong and, as Labor tries to heal its wounds and regroup, there has been much comment on what the party now stands for, if anything. Despite repeated hoary references to 'true believers' and 'Labor values', it is manifestly not the party it once was. It does not even pretend any longer that socialism is a valid goal, or one that it aspires to, but merely promises to manage the economy better and perhaps more fairly than its rivals. But here it is very much playing an away game on its opponents' home ground. The task for Bill Shorten and his team is not just to devise policies and oppose the government, but to rebuild an organisation that has heart and soul enough to convince present and future generations of Australians that it deserves support. This is a rhetorical task of the first order and it will require considerable imagination, courage and political skill to accomplish.

The stakes for Australian rhetoric are therefore very high. To be sure, politics is more than rhetoric — it is also policy and action — but rhetoric remains fundamental. One of the lessons emerging from this collection is that, in politics, words are never innocent. Words have power, both to create and destroy. Political speakers know the possibilities and the dangers; they are acutely aware of the power of words — their own and others — to do them either harm or good. Having always a vested interest in the success or failure of their rhetorical intentions, they must continuously weigh, calculate and choose each word. They cannot afford an unguarded moment.

This makes the Deakinite ideal of political rhetoric, in which no gap exists between the sincere belief of the speaker and the speech delivered, a difficult one to realise. Democratic people may hope for frank truth telling from their leaders, who are after all their servants, but frankness will not always serve in a fiercely competitive environment. Moreover the sovereign people, like all sovereigns, must occasionally be flattered, and flattery and frank truth telling are mutually exclusive. No doubt Mitt Romney spoke the truth to his well-heeled audience when he dismissed the 47 per cent of ordinary Americans who would not vote for him, but it was not a truth that endeared him to the mass of people when it leaked out, and in fact it damaged his electoral chances. This is not to say that politicians never tell the truth — or never *can* tell the truth, the whole truth, and nothing but the truth — but you can bet that when they do they have carefully calculated beforehand the political consequences of doing so. And so they must if they are to survive and succeed.

Rhetoric, therefore, is vital but perennially problematic. Even the apparently most sincere, straightforward example of political speech must be scrutinised, analysed and contextualised in order to reveal the layers of its meaning and political intention. This is the task of political scientists, theorists and commentators. It requires considerable acuity and some subtlety to perform it well, and it has been performed well in the diverse but always enlightening papers of this excellent collection.

References

Aristotle 2000. *The art of rhetoric*. Trans. John Henry Freese. Cambridge MA: Harvard University Press.

Garsten, B. 2006. *Saving persuasion: A defense of rhetoric and judgment*. Cambridge, MA: Harvard University Press.

Goodin, R.E. 2008. *Innovating democracy: Democratic theory and practice after the deliberative turn*. Oxford: Oxford University Press.

Goodin, R.E. and Saward, M. 2005. Dog whistles and democratic mandates. *The Political Quarterly* 76(4): 471–76.

Kane, J. and Patapan, H. 2010. The artless art: Leadership and the limits of democratic rhetoric. *The Australian Journal of Political Science* 45(3): 371–89.

—— 2012. *The democratic leader: How democracy defines, empowers and limits its leaders*. Oxford: Oxford University Press.

Kennedy, G. 1986. *Classical rhetoric and its Christian tradition from ancient to modern times*. Chapel Hill: The University of North Carolina Press.

Perelman, C. and Olbrechts-Tyteca, L. 2003. *The new rhetoric: A treatise on argumentation*. Notre Dame: Notre Dame University Press.

Williams, P. 2013. How Kevin Rudd's campaign unravelled. *Financial Review* 9 September. URL: http://www.afr.com/p/national/how_kevin_rudd_campaign_unravelled_MUATc7semL7gLrK69U2OvN (last accessed 26 November 2013).

Part I: Just rhetoric? Language and behaviour

1. 'I am sorry': Prime ministerial apology as transformational leadership

Stephen Mills

The apology to the Stolen Generations delivered by Prime Minister Kevin Rudd in the House of Representatives in February 2008 remains a distinctive landmark in Australian political life.[1] Yet, viewed from a distance of five years, Rudd's speech emerges as but one, albeit a significant one, in a sequence of apologies made by Australian politicians. Before Rudd, state and territory parliaments delivered apologies recommended by the *Bringing them home* (1997) report of the Australian Human Rights Commission inquiry into the forced removal of Aboriginal and Torres Strait Islander children from their families. Following his apology to the Stolen Generations, Rudd apologised again, in November 2009, to the Forgotten Australians — those who, as children, were removed from their families and institutionalised, including children forced to migrate to Australia.[2] In November 2012, the Defence Minister Stephen Smith apologised in parliament to members of the Australian Defence Force who had been sexually abused. In March 2013, Prime Minister Julia Gillard apologised to mothers and children caught up in the practice of forced adoptions.[3]

This wave of Australian political apologies has followed in the wake of apologetic speeches by national leaders elsewhere, notably in Europe, which arise from diverse circumstances including the Holocaust, the destruction of indigenous populations by colonial invaders, and acts of violence during civil wars and regional conflicts (Celermajer 2009; Nobles 2008). The gathering tempo and range of political apology from the 1990s has led Danielle Celermajer to refer to the 'apology phenomenon' (2009: Chpt 1) while other scholars, more ambitiously, have asserted the existence of an 'age of apology' (Gibney et al. 2008). Over the

---

1 Parliament of Australia 2008. Apology to Australia's Indigenous peoples. House Hansard. 13 February. URL: http://parlinfo.aph.gov.au/parlInfo/search/display/display.w3p;db=CHAMBER;id=chamber%2Fhansard r%2F2008-02-13%2F0003;query=Id%3A%22chamber%2Fhansardr%2F2008-02-13%2F0000%22. Consulted November 2013.
2 Rudd's speech is at: http://www.heraldsun.com.au/archive/news/transcript-of-kevin-rudds-apology-to-forgotten-australians/story-e6frf7l6-1225798255277. The National Museum of Australia maintains a site on this issue at: http://www.forgottenaustralianshistory.gov.au/apology.html. Consulted November 2013.
3 Gillard's speech is at: http://parlview.aph.gov.au/mediaPlayer.php?videoID=190367#/3. The Attorney-General's Department maintains a site on this issue at: http://www.ag.gov.au/ABOUT/ForcedAdoptionsApology/Pages/default.aspx. Consulted November 2013.

same period, apologies for collective or institutional failure have been expressed by non-state actors, such as church (Marrus 2008) and business leaders (Hearit 2006; Grebe 2013).

Despite the manifestly central role that leaders play in them, apologies have not to date received significant attention from leadership scholars. The three necessary elements of apology — a speaker apologising on behalf of a community, the recipient of the apology, and the wrong for which the apology is offered — reflect the tripartite focus of leadership studies: leaders who possess various attributes of personality and power, their relationship with followers, and the common enterprise of leaders and followers to achieve shared goals (Wills 1994; Bennis 2007). If public leadership requires the performance of distinctive, strategic functions that are necessary in order for a polity to govern itself effectively and democratically, but which are not performed spontaneously or routinely by the polity's other institutions or actors ('t Hart and Uhr 2008), then apology may have emerged as a new instrument of public leadership. Further, in line with the canonical distinction set out by James MacGregor Burns (1978, 2003), the question may be asked of apology whether, with its language of offer and acceptance, it represents transactional leadership or whether, with its language of justice and reconstitution, it seeks transformational goals.

In dealing with such issues, further questions arise around the language of leadership and the significance of speech as a form of political action — and, indeed, about the merits of focusing on speech as a means of understanding politics. Some forms of political speech — for example, a budget announcement or policy launch — can be understood as largely representational, standing for actors and ideas that exist separately from the speech act itself. On other occasions, however, political speech takes on a constitutive, not merely representative, role. An electoral promise does more than describe some possible future executive action; it creates, at the time of the speech, an enduring obligation and expectation. A concession speech on election night constitutes the acceptance of defeat and the passage of authority witnessed by the national television audience. From a leadership perspective, speeches in which political leaders mobilise followers, articulate visions or delineate community boundaries constitute the performance of political leadership. Prime ministerial apology may likewise be thought of as performing a constitutive function, operating not as a speech 'about' a historical circumstance, but as an act whose performance itself transforms the polity and creates new circumstances and relationships within it.

James Curran has explored how prime ministers have used the past to engage in 'the shaping of Australian national ideals and the voicing of national aspirations'. Curran noted that for prime ministers Gough Whitlam, Malcolm Fraser, Bob Hawke, Paul Keating and John Howard, the evocation of history was 'no idle glance backwards', but instead 'affected the way they have performed as leaders and given substance to how they have conceived Australia' (Curran 2004: 1). Consideration of prime ministerial apology builds on Curran's themes by presenting a new instrument for political engagement with the past (Celermajer 2009: 47), and extends his project to include the post-Howard Labor prime ministers. More importantly, where Curran was concerned with the leaders' individualised conceptions of Australian history, apology entails a collective understanding by a community of its own past, albeit articulated and crystallised on its behalf by its political leader. Indeed, where Curran's leaders adopted an essentially educative relationship with their audiences, prime ministers can apologise only if authorised to do so by their community. On the lips of a prime minister, then, the words 'I am sorry' have shed much of their traditional association with retrospective admission of failure at the personal or executive policy levels. Instead they have taken on a collective and more positive, forward-looking and even transformational character. Notably, in the case of the Stolen Generations apology, the uttering of these words has allowed the Australian polity to address and deal with, after decades of avoidance and failure, profound questions of national reconciliation and identity.

The first and essential consideration in understanding prime ministerial apology is to understand the nature of the wrongs to which apology responds. The wrongs experienced by the Stolen Generations, Forgotten Australians, and victims of forced adoptions constitute a special category of wrongs, whose unusual characteristics have the effect of making difficult the attribution of responsibility for them.

At their core all involve a violation of the fundamental human relationship between parents and children, which as a consequence caused vulnerable people to experience physical pain and psychological suffering. These hurtful acts were not directed externally at a foreign enemy or alien people, but were, in each case, directed internally, against members — albeit marginalised members — of the community responsible for them. In the language of apology, the vulnerability of these individuals bestows an incontrovertible status of innocence or blamelessness upon them.[4] While the argument has been made that the removal of Indigenous children constituted an act of genocide, these violations did not constitute an act of war as legally understood, and were not carried out solely or even largely by uniformed agents of the state. Rather, institutions of civil society (hospitals, churches, orphanages, so-called 'homes' for children) were critical actors seeking, with the at least implicit permission of

---

4   As Rudd put it in his Apology to Forgotten Australians: 'The protection of children is the sacred duty of us all'. A recurrent element in the apologies is the reassurance provided to the wronged of their innocence: 'The valley of tears was not of your making' (Rudd, Apology to Forgotten Australians) or, more prosaically, Gillard's declaration that 'these mothers did nothing wrong'.

the state, to intervene in and destroy the parent–child relationship.[5] Critically, all these events occurred in the past, continuously over periods of time measured in decades; some of the behaviours they represent — notably, the destruction of Indigenous society — can be traced to the earliest period of settler society.[6] All of the wrongdoing behaviours have now ceased, and the former official sanction for them has been withdrawn. Yet many of their victims remain members of the contemporary community. In summary, the wrongs were perpetrated and experienced collectively, by diverse groups through time.

Parliamentary democracies are reasonably well equipped to deal with the exposure and punishment of individual fault. The doctrine of ministerial responsibility provides, however imperfectly, an enduring process of accountability to Parliament for policy failures of the executive and individual failings of the minister. Question time, committee inquiries, censure motions, confidence motions, and the ultimate sanction of ministerial resignation or dismissal provide a flexible range of means to test accountability. Beyond the legislature, the courts also provide forums to expose and punish actions found to be illegal. But such accountability mechanisms provide little assistance in dealing with wrongs whose cause cannot be sheeted home to identifiable individuals. It is this space that is being occupied by the practice of apology.

In 2002, New South Wales became the first jurisdiction to provide legislative protection for apologies: under the *Civil Liability Act 2002*, an apology by a member of the community for any harm they have done does not constitute an admission of liability and is not admissible in civil proceedings. Full apologies, it is argued, encourage individuals to take responsibility for their actions, and to make recipients of an apology feel their grievance has been taken seriously (Wheeler 2011). At the Commonwealth administrative level, the 2005 discovery of the illegal immigration detentions of Cornelia Rau and of Vivian Solon led the minister, Amanda Vanstone, to issue a written statement in which 'the Government' apologised to the two women for the treatment they received and provided ex gratia assistance to them (Vanstone 2005). More recently, the family of two Afghan boys killed in a military action involving the Australian Defence Force led, in March 2013, to an apology and payment

---

5 Gillard made the link explicit in her apology: 'This story has its beginnings in a wrongful belief that women could be separated from their babies and it would all be for the best. Instead, these churches and charities, families, medical staff and bureaucrats struck at the most primal and sacred bond there is: the bond between a mother and her baby.' In the case of the Australian Defence Force, similar issues of institutional neglect and abuse are apparent although victims are adults.

6 Where the wrongs have not definitely ceased taking place, apology may be a premature or incomplete response and is typically preceded by a process of formal investigation. The current Royal Commission into Institutional Responses to Child Sexual Abuse perhaps offers an example of this. URL: http://www.childabuseroyalcommission.gov.au.

of cash compensation (Australian Broadcasting Corporation (ABC) 2013). Here, collective or organisational malpractice and misadventure towards identified individuals have been addressed through a collective apology.

Attributing responsibility for the wrongs for which Rudd and Gillard have apologised raises more difficult questions of attribution. Which historical individuals and institutions of the state and civil society were responsible? To what extent can those historical actors be identified in contemporary society and, in a kind of reverse-grandfathering, responsibility attached to them? And can responsibility properly be attached to any of those actors while the broader societal norms that permitted them escape censure? As Celermajer (2009: 4) puts it, in relation to what she calls the systematic nature of the atrocities of the twentieth century, it is simply not viable to attribute responsibility to those who wielded machetes or drove the children away; the massive body of the society that condoned the violence, albeit perhaps silently, stands in the shadows. The only statement about responsibility that can be made with certainty concerns the innocence of those who suffered.

The *Bringing them home* report, which documented the harrowing personal stories of the Stolen Generations and the legal frameworks that permitted them, was clear in identifying that governments were responsible for the denial of common law rights, breaches of human rights and other instances of victimisation. Relying on the UN-authorised van Boven principles (van Boven 1996), the report recommended that the 'first step in any compensation and healing for victims of gross violations of human rights must be an acknowledgement of the truth and the delivery of an apology'. For governments, this would involve official acknowledgement by 'all Australian Parliaments' of the responsibility of their predecessors for the laws, policies and practices of forcible removal (Australian Human Rights Commission (AHRC) 1997: Chpt 14, 5a). State and territory governments responded with formal parliamentary apologies. Yet the Commonwealth Government resisted the call.

Bringing them home did not specify a mechanism for parliamentary apology. Leadership theory however is emphatic in requiring that statements on behalf of any organisation must come from a person, usually the most senior officer, with unfettered authority to speak on its behalf and to take responsibility for its actions. In the case of the Stolen Generations, Howard refused to apologise — but in doing so he implicitly accepted that, as prime minister, he was responsible for making that decision. Conceivably, an apology by the Governor-General could have been made on behalf of the Australian state, though this could not have carried any parliamentary authority. Less likely still, a parliamentary apology could have been issued by the presiding officers (Speaker of the House of Representatives and President of the Senate), but this would have lacked appropriate political accountability. In other contexts outside Australia, attempted apologies by public officials below prime ministerial rank have tended to fail.[7]

In refusing to heed the call for apology, Howard was apparently deterred by the complex collective and inter-temporal character of the wrong: he asserted that responsibility could not be taken by one collective (the present generation) for the acts of another (a previous generation) and, implicitly, that responsibility could not — and would not — be taken by an individual (himself as prime minister) for a collective of which he was not a part (previous Australian generations). Moreover, he believed that apology implied the acceptance of guilt for actions which may have been, in the circumstances of the time, properly based and sincerely intended; apology could in turn have carried some form of collective liability. Thus he told the Australian Reconciliation Convention in 1997 that 'Australians of this generation should not be required to accept guilt and blame for past actions and policies over which they had no control' (Howard 1997). Howard was willing only to express his 'deep sorrow' for the injustices brought about by past generations and the hurt and trauma that contemporary indigenous people may continue to feel as a consequence. Likewise in 1999, Howard moved a Motion of Reconciliation in the House of Representatives which expressed 'deep and sincere regret' for the injustices but rejected an Opposition amendment seeking an unqualified apology.[8]

Rudd's apology to the Stolen Generations vaulted such hurdles by accepting, and dramatically elaborating, parliament's enduring responsibility for its prior actions as well as his own capacity to issue apologies on their behalf. In his speech he apologised for 'the pain and suffering that we the parliament have caused you by laws that previous parliaments enacted' and for 'the indignity, the degradation and the humiliation these laws embodied'. That is, Rudd asserted that the Commonwealth was the original author of the policies and practices at issue and, as an enduring institution, was capable of accepting contemporary responsibility for its previous acts. He implied further that, as a representative

---

7   For example, the Canadian Federal Minister of Indian Affairs formally apologised in 1998 to the Aboriginal people of Canada for the government's policies of assimilation, yet this statement was largely discounted coming as it did from a junior minister. In 2008 Canadian Prime Minister Stephen Harper made a full apology (Celermajer 2009: 30–32).

8   This position captured the well-known distinction between *feeling sorry* that your window broke while not *saying sorry* for breaking it. That Howard deliberately carved out this niche of non-apologetic regret was made clear in a different policy context when, during the 2007 election campaign, the Reserve Bank of Australia announced an increase in interest rates. Howard told a press conference: 'I would say to the borrowers of Australia who are affected by this change, that I am sorry about that. And I regret the additional burden that will be put upon them as a result'. The following day he was asked by another reporter: 'Mr Howard, if you are not responsible for the interest rate rise, why did you apologise for it?' Howard replied: 'Well I said that I was sorry they had occurred. I don't think I actually used the word apology. I think there is a difference between the two things. I think we have been through that debate before, haven't we?' (See www. abc.net.au/worldtoday/content/2007 for 7 and 8 November 2007).

elected institution, the Commonwealth Parliament embodied the social attitudes of the Australian community — those of the past, which had permitted the removal of children, and of the present, with its preparedness to apologise and reconcile. A narrow apology might have focused on the Commonwealth's historic responsibility for laws of the Northern Territory up to self-government in 1978, while rejecting responsibility for the legislative acts of sovereign parliaments in the states. Rudd instead took the largest course, claiming to speak on behalf of 'we the parliaments' — that is, of state and territory parliaments as well as the Commonwealth Parliament.[9] Indeed Rudd's apology, while largely focused on the Stolen Generations issue, is actually framed as an apology 'to Australia's Indigenous Peoples' and addresses, in its opening words, their 'past mistreatment' in general.

Like Howard, Rudd felt sorry for the pain and suffering of the Stolen Generation, and he expressed this in powerful, empathetic language. But unlike Howard, Rudd also felt equipped to say sorry for it. Moving a parliamentary resolution of apology, Rudd did so by drawing on a powerful multi-layered authorisation:

> To the stolen generations, I say the following: as Prime Minister of Australia, I am sorry. On behalf of the government of Australia, I am sorry. On behalf of the parliament of Australia, I am sorry. I offer you this apology without qualification.

In this triple apology, Rudd spoke in an individual capacity as prime minister — that is, as leader of the majority party in the House of Representatives; in an executive capacity as leader of the national government; and, in a representative capacity 'on behalf of' the Parliament (which came into effect with the passage of the resolution). Rudd's triple formulation demonstrated that an appropriately authorised prime minister can, through the institution of parliament, effectively address complex historical wrongs.[10]

Rudd's identification of parliament as the responsible institution made it highly appropriate, of course, that the apology be delivered in this location and during — indeed, at the beginning of — a parliamentary sitting. Moreover, the

---

9   Rudd's words on this point were as follows: 'The uncomfortable truth for us all is that the parliaments of the nation … enacted statutes and delegated authority under those statutes that made forced removal of children on racial grounds fully lawful … Put simply, the laws that our parliaments enacted made the Stolen Generations possible. We the parliaments of the nation are ultimately responsible, not those who gave effect to our laws, the problem lay with the laws themselves.' Rudd may have overreached in this claim; nor did he acknowledge the apologies that had already been made by state and territory parliaments. Likewise, Rudd also blurred state-Commonwealth boundaries in apologising to the Forgotten Australians with the broad claim: 'These children, both from home and abroad, were placed in care under the auspices of the state, validated by the law of the land'.

10   Rudd's apology had also been facilitated, as Celermajer has pointed out (2009: 190–93), by the reframing of the apology debate away from connotations of guilt, for which punishment of the specifically guilty is the appropriate response, towards feelings of shame, which can be expiated by non-punitive atonement and apology.

presence of members of the Stolen Generation in the galleries of the chamber effectively meant Rudd presented his apology face-to-face to (some of) those who had suffered from these parliamentary wrongs. A live television broadcast allowed people around the country — outside the parliament in Canberra, in Redfern, in Federation Square, Melbourne, and in public and private spaces generally — to participate in this event.[11] These locational considerations form a key element in determining whether the apology can, in the language of scholars and practitioners, be deemed 'effective'. Ineffective apologies include those that express regret without taking responsibility ('sorry that' rather than 'sorry for'), that use passive language to avoid responsibility ('mistakes were made'), and that impose conditions on the other party ('If you were offended then I am sorry'). By contrast, 'effective' or 'full' apologies are performed in an appropriate context (in the parliament, in this case, rather than, for example, in a television studio). In an effective apology, the speaker explicitly acknowledges wrongdoing and accepts responsibility for it; the apology is truthful, sincere, and voluntary; the apologiser shows identification with injured stakeholders, asks them for forgiveness, seeks reconciliation with them and offers corrective action and appropriate compensation (Hearit 2006). In a similar vein, the New South Wales deputy ombudsman suggests an effective apology should recognise the wrong, take responsibility, explain the reasons, express regret, implement redress and seek release.[12] The apologies by Rudd and Gillard fulfil most of these criteria, suggesting linkages between the requirements for effective apology and the deliberate construction of performative leadership. A familiar trope of their apologies, for example, is the way in which both prime ministers drew evidence from the reports of formal investigations into the wrongs and, further, recounted their personal meetings with individual victims. In so doing they confronted the reality of the collective wrongs while also establishing the authenticity of their own understanding of and responses to them.

Some criteria for effective apology are inherently problematical. In relation to Hearit's emphasis on timeliness, it is noted that apologies rediscover past events with a contemporary awareness of them as wrong. Apology cannot precede the emergence of that awareness, but must not be delayed once it is complete. Leaders must also wait until they have authority to proceed. Howard could have made an apology following the release of *Bringing them home*, but delayed for a decade. Rudd needed to wait until he became prime minister after the election, but then moved promptly to apologise in Parliament on its

---

11   The subsequent apologies by Rudd and Gillard varied the staging in a significant way. Both these speeches were delivered in the Great Hall immediately prior to a session of Parliament. Neither speech, therefore, forms part of Parliament's formal record of proceedings and they serve only to foreshadow the 'actual' apologies, which were moved and passed later, in Parliament. The trade-off for loss of parliamentary authenticity was that more people could participate in the larger spaces of the Great Hall, thereby receiving their apology face-to-face from their political leader.

12   The NSW Ombudsman (2009) has published a useful and wide ranging 'practical guide' to apologies.

first sitting day. More problematic still is the requirement for compensation as part of an effective apology. Howard apparently regarded an apology as potentially exposing the Commonwealth to the risk of claims from individuals for loss or damage (Celermajer 2009: 173–74). Rudd dealt with the issue through proposing a collective form of compensation — initiatives to 'close the gap' in living standards between Indigenous and non-Indigenous Australians, which have so far failed to deliver on their promise; in the later apologies, collective compensation assumes largely symbolic forms such as the provision of funding for memorial exhibitions.

Any discussion of the performative aspects of apology must acknowledge partisan calculation. Acting and speaking as a national leader, as opposed to a mere political executive, is always politically attractive to prime ministers, who have increasingly ascended a platform that, in earlier periods, might well have been occupied by the Governor-General. International forums such as the United Nations or G20, national disasters such as a bushfire or terror attack, celebrations or commemorations such as Australia Day or Anzac Day, provide opportunities for a prime minister to express and reinforce the nation's identity, elevating his or her personal authority to that of *parens patriae* (Mills 1996). Meanwhile the Opposition leader is rendered — temporarily at least — irrelevant and virtually unable to oppose. Prime ministerial apology must now be added to this genre.

Further aspects of prime ministerial leadership through apology can be discerned through consideration of the critically important leadership function of providing direction: that is, formulating and articulating the organisation's vision. This is not a process in which the leader selects a personal preference and imposes it on followers; instead, the leader identifies a goal that is mutually shared with followers and the attainment of which would serve their best interests. Leaders must then communicate the vision within and beyond the organisation and mobilise and coordinate followers so as to facilitate its attainment. Leaders need the 'ability to communicate their mission in ways that generate intrinsic appeal' (Conger 1991). Understanding of the diverse suite of leader mobilisation practices continues to evolve. Marshall Ganz, for example, speaks of social movement leaders needing a number of strategies to overcome or catalyse barriers to purposeful action by followers; for example, urgency to overcome inertia and hope to overcome fear (Ganz 2010). It appears that in setting out to achieve reconciliation of Indigenous and non-Indigenous Australians, to 'remember' the Forgotten Australians, and to recognise the victims of forced adoption, prime ministers are indeed performing these goal-setting roles. Having recognised a community preparedness to reach a just settlement with its violated members, a goal that would serve the best interests of the Australian community, the prime ministers delivered formal apologies in ways that mobilised their followers to reconcile. Ganz's list of catalysing communications strategies could be extended by positing apology as a means of overcoming the barriers of shame or guilt.

Burns' distinction between transactional and transformational leadership (Burns 1978, 2003) provides a useful frame for addressing prime ministerial goal-setting in the context of apology. For Burns, transactional leadership is a reciprocal process of mutual benefit based on modal values such as fairness and honesty. There are clearly important transactional elements in these apologies: the apology to the Stolen Generations represented the transactional fulfilment of an election promise; compensatory measures, however symbolic, can also be seen as good-faith attempts to lay out a modally commensurate transaction between the parties. Most fundamentally, the nature of apology itself is a transaction: an offer by one party that can be either accepted or rejected by the other. In Burns, transformational leadership transcends the existing motives and values of followers by mobilising them towards end values such as justice, liberty and equality. The language of the prime ministerial apologies provides many such transformational aspirations. Rudd spoke of the need for a new beginning, turning a new page, crafting a new future, and embracing a new partnership between Indigenous and non-Indigenous Australians; likewise, to the Forgotten Australians, he urged 'us' to go forward with confidence as 'equal, valued and precious members of this one great family that we call Australia'. Gillard spoke of a profound act of moral insight that would right an old wrong. Transformation is here seen taking place both as the apologiser acknowledges shame and as the recipient of the apology moves from rejection to acceptance and from injury to wholeness. Importantly, to achieve this transformation, the prime minister speaks both on behalf of the society that has committed a wrong and to the victims of that wrong — victims who are not, as noted earlier, foreigners or aliens but members of the same society. Apology is expressed on behalf of 'us' and also directed to 'us' or, perhaps, to 'the others within'. Here, then, transformation occurs in the constitution and identity of the community as a whole: the leader articulates the apology of his or her existing followers and then, where the apology is accepted, enrols the marginalised as full members of a restored community. Thus the apology for past deeds becomes the basis for a national future-oriented project (Celermajer 2009: 172).

Conclusion

Prime ministers can refuse to apologise; attempted apologies can fail; and, the practice of apology might degenerate into ritual or partisan manoeuvring. There may, in a happier future perhaps, be fewer societal wrongs for which to apologise. It is argued here, at least in relation to the category of the profound social wrongs under discussion, that apology is a new and distinctive mode of prime ministerial leadership. Delivered in the chamber of the House of Representatives, in the presence of the victims of parliamentary wrongdoing, witnessed by a national television audience of millions, the prime ministerial speech act, which is often dismissed as a transient and contingent representation, is here correctly seen as an act of social construction and transformation, bringing into being a new set of relationships among and between citizens and their political leaders. This emergence has coincided with evidence of an apparent intensification of the authority exercised by individual prime ministers (Strangio 2012; Kefford 2013; Dowding 2013), of increasingly tangled relationships between political leaders and the media (Savage and Tiffen 2007), of rising public dissatisfaction with politicians (Young 2000), and of the exhaustion of the Australian polity's repertoire for problem-solving and innovation (Marsh 1995; Marsh 2012). It is all the more striking, then, that prime ministerial apology has operated as an effective and innovative, though still problematic, leadership tool in addressing hitherto unresolved issues of historical responsibility and national identity. Indeed, the transformative impact of apology would be practically impossible were it not for the mutual affection of media and political leadership and their shared capacity to include a national audience in a profound moment of respect, recognition and reconciliation.

References

Australian Broadcasting Commission (ABC) 2013. Australia takes responsibility for death of Afghan boys. *ABC News* 5 March. URL : http://www.abc.net.au/news/2013-03-05/australia-takes-responsibility-for-incident-where-boys-killed/4553320. Consulted 26 November 2013.

Australian Human Rights Commission (AHRC) 1997. *Bringing them home: Report of the National Inquiry into the Separation of Aboriginal and Torres Strait Islander Children from Their Families*. URL: http://www.humanrights.gov.au/publications/bringing-them-home-stolen-children-report-1997. Consulted 26 November 2013.

Bennis, W. 2007. The challenges of leadership in the modern world. *American Psychologist* 62: 2–5.

Burns, J.M. 1978. *Leadership*. New York: Harper & Row.

—— 2003. *Transforming leadership: A new pursuit of happiness*. New York: Grove Press.

Celermajer, D 2009. *The sins of the nation and the ritual of apologies*. Cambridge: Cambridge University Press.

Conger, J. 1991. Inspiring others: The language of leadership. *Academy of Management Executive* 5: 31–45.

Curran, J. 2004. *The power of speech*. Carlton: Melbourne University Press.

Dowding, K. 2013. Presidentialisation again: A comment on Kefford. *Australian Journal of Political Science* 48: 147–49.

Ganz, M. 2010. Leading change: Leadership, organisation and social movements. In N. Nohria and R. Khurana eds. *Handbook of leadership theory and practice*. Boston: Harvard Business Press.

Gibney, M., Howard-Hassmann, R., Coicaud, J.-M. and Steiner, N. eds. 2008. *The age of apology: Facing up to the past*. Philadelphia: University of Pennsylvania Press.

Grebe, S.K. 2013. The importance of being genuinely sorry when organisations apologise: How the Australian Wheat Board (AWB Limited) was damaged even further by its response to a corporate scandal. *Journal of Public Affairs* 13: 100–10.

Hearit, K. 2006. *Crisis management by apology: Corporate responses to allegations of wrongdoing*. Marwah, N.J.: Lawrence Erlbaum Associates.

Howard, J. 1997. Opening address to the Australian Reconciliation Convention, Melbourne. Indigenous Law Resources. Australasian Legal Information Institute. URL: http://www.austlii.edu.au/au/other/IndigLRes/car/1997/4/pmspoken.html. Consulted 29 May 2013.

—— 1999. Motion of reconciliation. Media release, 26 August. URL: http://parlinfo.aph.gov.au/parlInfo/search/display/display.w3p;query=(Id:media/pressrel/23e06);rec=0. Consulted 29 May 2013.

Kefford, G. 2013. The presidentialisation of Australian politics? Kevin Rudd's leadership of the Australian Labor Party. *Australian Journal of Political Science* 48: 135–46.

Marrus, M. 2008. Papal apologies of Pope John Paul II. In M. Gibney, R. Howard-Hassman, J.-M. Coicaud and N Steiner eds. *The age of apology: Facing up to the past*. Philadelphia: University of Pennsylvania Press.

Marsh, I. 1995. *Beyond the two party system: Political representation, economic competitiveness, and Australian politics*. Melbourne: Cambridge University Press.

—— 2012. *Democratic decline and democratic renewal: Political change in Britain, Australia and New Zealand.* Cambridge: Cambridge University Press.

Mills, S. 1996. The making of a prime minister's speeches. In J. Disney and J.R. Nethercote eds. *The house on Capital Hill: Parliament, politics and power in the national capital.* Sydney: Federation Press.

NSW Ombudsman 2009. *Apologies. A practical guide.* URL: http://www.ombo. nsw.gov.au/news-and-publications/publications/guidelines/state-and-local-government/apologies-2nd-ed. Consulted 26 November 2013.

Nobles, M. 2008. *The politics of official apologies.* New York: Cambridge University Press.

Savage, S. and Tiffen, R. 2007. Politicians, journalists and 'Spin': Tangled relationships and shifting alliances. In S. Young ed. *Government communication in Australia.* Melbourne: Cambridge University Press.

Strangio, P. 2012. Prime ministerial government in Australia. In R. Smith, A. Vromen and I. Cook eds. *Contemporary politics in Australia.* Melbourne: Cambridge University Press.

't Hart, P. and Uhr, J. 2008. Understanding public leadership. In P. 't Hart and J. Uhr eds. *Public leadership: Perspectives and practices.* Canberra: ANU Press.

van Boven, T. 1996. Revised set of basic principles and guidelines on the right to reparation for victims of gross violations of human rights and humanitarian law, prepared by Mr Theo van Boven pursuant to Sub-Commission resolution 1995/117, UN Doc: E/CN4/Sub 2/1996/17, 24 May 1996. UN Sub-Committee on Prevention of Discrimination and Protection of Minorities.

Vanstone, A. 2005. Report of Palmer Inquiry into Cornelia Rau matter. Media Release, 14 July. URL: http://parlinfo.aph.gov.au/parlInfo/search/display/ display.w3p;query=Id%3A%22media%2Fpressrel%2F9JPG6%22. Consulted 26 November 2013.

Wheeler, C. 2011. The power of apology: An effective form of remedy in dispute resolution, Speech at the Public Sector Litigation and Dispute Management Forum, Canberra, 6 September. URL: http://www.ombo.nsw.gov.au/__ data/assets/pdf_file/0020/6239/SP_The_Power_of_Apology-Canberra-6_ Sept_2011.pdf. Consulted 30 May 2013.

Wills, G. 1994. *Certain trumpets: The nature of leadership.* New York: Simon and Schuster.

Young, S. 2000. Why Australians hate politicians: Exploring the new public discontent. In D. Glover and G. Patmore eds. *For the people: Reclaiming our government*. Annandale, NSW: Pluto Press.

2. Economic management, rhetorical tactics, and the cost of promises

Ryan Walter

This chapter is concerned with the language that is used to legitimate governmental action and the dynamics that can arise between divergent tactics for legitimation. The focus is those actions that are normally referred to as fiscal policy, the high moment of which is the annual presentation of the federal budget, for which spending priorities are identified, new programs announced, and the fate of older policy initiatives is often sealed. Public political speech in relation to budgets has typically been a prized site for discerning the ideological orientation of political parties and individual politicians, especially regarding the purported diminution of the state's role in the economy. The research presented here occupies a related but distinct terrain to the study of ideology,[1] as the language around budgets is examined with an eye for the competition between the major parties for control of the normative force that derives from applying appraisive descriptions to their actions. In other words, language is not studied for insight into the realm of ideas, but as holding resources for legitimation and delegitimation that are the subject of partisan contest. Politicians dispute the meanings of the words that rival politicians use, along with the phenomena to which their rivals attempt to apply disputed terms. The implication is that the contests over language use are so messy that they need to be clarified *before* the ideological significance of a given piece of political speech can be established.

In recent years, the dominant description that leaders of the Australian Labor Party have sought to apply to their fiscal policy is that its budgeting behaviour evinces 'fiscal discipline' and thus represents 'responsible economic government'. Terms such as 'economically responsible', 'fiscal discipline', 'budget prudence', and their antonyms, such as 'economically wasteful' or 'irresponsible', are special because at the same time they describe and normatively evaluate behaviour. We can follow Quentin Skinner in referring to this class of words as 'evaluative–descriptive terms' (2002a: 148).[2] Skinner's key idea is that these terms evoke accepted principles, in this case, that the economy should be managed in a responsible manner. To claim that the government's fiscal action is economically responsible is to justify both the action (which is good because it is responsible) *and* the motive for which it is performed (which is good because it is done from a sense of responsibility and obligation). To assert that the same behaviour is

---

1   For a fuller discussion see Walter and Uhr (2013).
2   See also Skinner (2002b: Chpt 13).

wasteful is, conversely, to criticise the action (as hurtful to the Australian economy) and impugn the underlying motive (the government acted irresponsibly, or negligently). It is this legitimating power that explains why this class of terms is the subject of such intense rhetorical and intellectual contest regarding the range of behaviour to which they can be applied (Skinner 2002a: 149).

Using the phrase 'responsible economic' to qualify nouns such as 'government',[3] 'policy',[4] 'strategy',[5] and 'course'[6] can be dated to at least the 1970s and 1980s. The same holds for qualifications such as 'responsible fiscal'[7] and the qualified noun 'fiscal discipline'.[8] Yet the current pattern of use of these and similar appraisive terms in relation to budgets roughly coincides with the passage of the *Charter of Budget Honesty Act 1998* (Cth), which the Howard Coalition government (1996–2007) introduced as a legislative accompaniment to its rhetorical attack on Labor for purportedly concealing its fiscal profligacy before losing office in 1996. The chapter begins by sketching this context and the use of this language by both major parties in relation to fiscal policy. Attention then turns to observe a rhetorical stumble from the Coalition, one caused by a forecast budget surplus that was not achieved. This is also where Labor fell down a decade later, when the government was obliged to concede in December 2012 that a surplus in 2013 would be impossible. The key difference in the rhetoric of the parties is that the Coalition largely succeeded in maintaining the status of the budget surplus as a forecast that would change with economic conditions, while Labor converted its forecast into a solemn promise, and this shifted the rhetorical contest from the terrain of economic management to moral fitness, allowing the Coalition to continue an assault that was already well established regarding the Prime Minister's trustworthiness as a former deputy leader who deposed her prime minister and then broke her election promise not to introduce a carbon tax. To these rhetorical consequences we might add those likely electoral costs that arose from the sensitive cuts Labor made — for example, to university funding (Emerson 2013) and family payments (Macklin 2013)[9] — in an attempt to align its behaviour with its rhetoric. Taken together, this was a costly blunder, seemingly made because Labor's leaders possess a limited understanding of the meaning and history of the words they use.

---

3 See, for example, House of Representatives (1981: 1809).
4 See, for example, House of Representatives (1971).
5 See, for example, House of Representatives (1986: 2380).
6 See, for example, House of Representatives (1978).
7 See, for example, House of Representatives (1973).
8 See, for example, House of Representatives (1976).
9 For the negative response among voters to these cuts, see Kenny (2013) and Joyce (2013).

The language of responsible economic government

The use of terms such as 'fiscal discipline' and 'responsible economic management' as we are familiar with them today can be approximately dated to Peter Costello's first budget as Treasurer in 1996. Consider, by contrast, the 1994 budget delivered by Treasurer Ralph Willis, the penultimate under Prime Minister Paul Keating (1991–96). Willis listed amongst the foremost aims of his budget reducing the deficit to one per cent of GDP by the 1996–97 budget, and then reaching surplus shortly thereafter. While this action was said to represent a 'rigorous fiscal consolidation' (House of Representatives 1994: 587), the language of responsible economic management is absent. In fact, the merits of deficit reduction are held to lie in a technical fact — that declining government expenditure reduces the demand on national savings and overseas borrowings. From today's perspective, it is easy to imagine such behaviour being portrayed as responsible economic government. But when Willis's budget speech is examined for legitimations of the budget in non-technical language, the leading term is 'social justice' (House of Representatives 1994: 587). The spending commitments embodied in the government's workfare scheme, Working Nation, were clear evidence of the 'Government's commitment to social justice' (House of Representatives 1994: 587).

As Leader of the Opposition, John Hewson saw this invocation of social justice as important enough to warrant a sustained disagreement. Hewson began his attack by denying that the budget reflected an 'economic strategy', as it was bereft of 'sensible and honest economic policies in the interests of all Australians' (House of Representatives 1994: 869). The budget was merely a 'political exercise' intended to preserve the Labor government in office through spending (House of Representatives 1994: 869). Hewson then combined this attack with his denial that Labor's budget could be claimed to have realised social justice:

> I reckon you ought to go and tell the one million Australians who have been put out of work by your policies your ideas on social justice … They are human beings and they want a job, and this budget does not provide it for them. What sort of social justice is that? … your talk about social justice is absolute tripe; it is absolute nonsense. You do not even understand it, judging by the permanent underclass you have created in this country. Real social justice is about restoring full employment … This budget has nothing to do with social justice and has everything to do with trying to appease particular interest groups. (House of Representatives 1994: 869)

Note that Hewson did not deny the validity or desirability of attempting to achieve social justice through budget decisions; his attack is instead based on denying that the government's actions can rightly enjoy this characterisation. Note also that Hewson acknowledged the importance of deficit reduction for the same reason Willis gave in his budget speech — 'to leave more of our savings in Australia' (House of Representatives 1994: 869) — but the size of the reduction was inadequate. As with Willis's comments, Hewson evidently felt no need to construe deficit management as either responsible or irresponsible, neither a mark of discipline nor of laxity.

A similar pattern emerged the following year. Willis proudly announced that the budget was in surplus for 1995–96, three years earlier than forecast. Once again, this was not treated as evidence of responsibility or prudence, but as necessary to enable growth by reducing public demands on national savings. Taken together, the budget represented a 'creative and decisive' response to Australia's needs, and raised the level of 'social justice' (House of Representatives 1995: 68). The Leader of the Opposition, now John Howard, undermined Willis's claim to have produced a surplus by questioning the inclusion of asset sales in the surplus figure and insisting that the underlying deficit figure of $8.2 billion was the figure that should have been the centre of attention (House of Representatives 1995: 400). Howard promised that his government would create a charter of budget honesty 'which will not allow this to happen again' (House of Representatives 1995: 400). Once more, while the surplus is clearly positioned as desirable, this is not because it is an obvious mark of 'responsible economic government' or similar, but primarily because it was thought to relieve pressure on the current account deficit. Howard's attack in response declared that the Prime Minister had 'gone to sleep on the job of economic modernisation … the process of micro-economic reform' (House of Representatives 1995: 400).

The example set by Peter Costello's first year as Treasurer illustrates a clear link between budget surpluses and the notion of responsible economic government. Costello generated rhetorical momentum before his budget speech by insisting that Labor had not, in fact, delivered the Coalition government a budget in surplus, as Labor had claimed during the election campaign, but that Labor had been 'running such a lax fiscal policy' that the balance was in deficit to the amount of some $8 billion (House of Representatives 1996: 173). It therefore fell to the new Coalition government to restore the budget to a true balance, since Labor was 'addicted to deficit and debt' (House of Representatives 1996: 286). The switch to a government that was not so afflicted was therefore crucial, according to Costello, because his budget 'changes the conduct of fiscal policy in this country' (House of Representatives 1996: 3269). The new focus was savings, understood as the key part of a 'responsible economic strategy' (House of Representatives 1996: 3269). Such an approach was to be guaranteed by the innovation Howard signalled in his budget reply the previous year, a charter of budget honesty, which was intended to 'entrench this Government's commitment to responsible and accountable fiscal policy' (House of Representatives 1996: 3269).

The second reading of the Charter of Budget Honesty Bill, which took place later in 1996, reveals how Costello sought to realise this aim. The first point to note is that Costello linked the aims of the bill with the goal of deficit reduction, claiming that the 'improvement of the fiscal position will only be achieved through greater discipline, transparency and accountability in government fiscal policy' (House of Representatives 1996: 8183), and this was exactly what the charter was to achieve through the reporting requirements it imposed on government. The second key point is that the bill was to underwrite '[f]iscal discipline' by 'requiring government fiscal policy to be formulated according to principles of sound fiscal management' (House of Representatives 1996: 8183). This prescriptive aspect of the bill aroused controversy because the pretension to establish 'principles of sound fiscal management' was interpreted by Labor politicians as an attempt to insert ideology into legislation that would then bind future governments of a different political stripe (House of Representatives 1996: 8183). The general nature of the principles being prescribed was also criticised, and this quality of the principles can be seen in the charter's injunction that the government 'ensure that its fiscal policy contributes: (i) to achieving adequate national saving; and (ii) to moderating cyclical fluctuations in economic activity' (*Charter of Budget Honesty Act 1998* (Cth) s5(1)(b)).

Gareth Evans's protests, then Deputy Leader of the Opposition, regarding the bill's framing related to both its perceived ideological character and the commodious nature of its precepts. The principles, Evans maintained, reflect 'a view of the nature and purpose of fiscal policy, which is frankly quite out of touch with current community needs and realities'. The true purpose of fiscal policy was 'to get the economy right for the people who inhabit it' (House of Representatives 1997: 136), and this must include 'the income distribution implications of a particular fiscal regime' (House of Representatives 1997: 136). In short, the principles were 'a dream come true for the so-called economic rationalists' (House of Representatives 1997: 136). At the same time, these prescriptions were so general that they only amounted to 'a rather bland and meaningless set of motherhood statements ... these kinds of principles are essentially meaningless in statutory guise' (House of Representatives 1997: 136). Labor's protests regarding the charter went unheeded and it was passed into law, providing a legislative requirement that government construe their budget actions in relation to its principles. As we will see, the term 'responsible' was well suited to conveying the general virtue resulting from budgeting that followed the charter's precepts.

Costello's language continued in the pattern he had established in 1996. In an address to the Economic Society of Victoria, for example, Costello happily claimed that after 'two responsible budgets ... we have now cut the deficit in half to around $4.9 billion'. Low interest rates and a 'concrete and responsible fiscal plan' were the key to Australia's economic success (Costello 1997). In an equivalent address the following year, Costello claimed that the government's economic decisions had been 'in Australia's economic interest. They have been responsible and they have been right', despite Labor's protests regarding the government's deficit reduction, which Costello saw as evidence of Labor's 'irresponsibility', along with their 'ignorance and incompetence' (1998). Costello's 1999 budget speech similarly spoke of 'sound economic management and sound institutions', and the government's economic strategy as 'responsible, fair and prudent' (House of Representatives 1999: 5047).

In his budget reply as Leader of the Opposition, before the charter's fruition, Kim Beazley did not accept Costello's emphasis on 'responsible' and 'irresponsible' fiscal behaviour as central to his terms of debate. Beazley instead focused on developing criticisms of the Howard government in unabashedly moral terms, especially in relation to Howard's infamous distinction between 'core promises and non-core promises' (House of Representatives 1996: 3619), and the creation of an 'unfair Australia' (House of Representatives 1996: 3619). Beazley made similar attacks in his next two budget replies. He portrayed the government's 1997 budget as exhibiting the 'instinctive cruelty of a government bereft of vision and purpose', a budget 'intent on creating division in our society' (House of Representatives 1997: 3825). When the Coalition delivered its first budget surplus, in 1998, Beazley decried the outcome as an 'accountant's surplus' created by a 'government that has long since ceased caring' (House of Representatives 1998: 3443). In particular, Beazley trained his rhetoric on the Treasurer's personal indifference to the fate of the unemployed and his tendency to make 'glib analogies about real lives'. Beazley did, however, concede that his government understood the need for 'fiscal restraint' in the context of the Asian financial crisis, and he also promised that, if elected, Labor would deliver 'three underlying surpluses' in its first term (House of Representatives 1998: 3443).

This second pattern of language use from Beazley stabilised in his following two budget replies. In 1999 Beazley declared that one of the essentials of a federal budget was 'a commitment to fairness for future generations which demands strong fiscal discipline' (House of Representatives 1999: 5436). The core of this discipline was the 'golden rule that governments do not borrow to finance current spending and save in the good times so that over the cycle the budget balances' (House of Representatives 1999: 5436). Beazley went further in the following year and declared that bipartisan support existed over the core of Australian economic policy: 'We all now largely agree on the old agenda:

the need for fiscal discipline, an independent monetary policy, deregulation of financial markets, the floating of the dollar, low inflation and a more open economy' (House of Representatives 2000: 16348). Beazley's comments represent *prima facie* evidence that the appraisive vocabulary the Coalition used in relation to budgets had gained a significant degree of bipartisan acceptance.

The Howard government and budget surpluses: Pragmatic not promissory

The next wrinkle to add to the story is the Howard government's language use regarding its ability to deliver a surplus in 2002, in the context of deteriorating economic conditions. The rhetorical tactics that Howard and Costello adopted were to treat the forthcoming surplus as a forecast and a policy intention — with one or two slips — and decline requests to promise or guarantee a surplus. When the surplus did not eventuate, the political costs were minimal, not least because the government had already established the claim that budget positions move up and down with the economic times, and because their record of budget surpluses protected their fiscal policy against serious damage from Labor's allegations of irresponsibility. These tactics establish a baseline against which to judge Labor's tactics under prime ministers Kevin Rudd and Julia Gillard.

To the first tactic: avoid promises. In Costello's 2001 budget address, he announced a surplus of $1.5 billion for the 2001–02 year, which would have been the Treasurer's fifth consecutive budget surplus. The Treasurer validated this behaviour in the terms we have now come to expect. Costello said of his budget, 'I think it's responsible … A fifth consecutive surplus … since the Government was elected and I think that's consistent with good economic management' (2001d). It was 'a Budget which is from a prudent Government, responsible economic management … I think that's responsible economic policy management' (Costello 2001b). Later in the year, however, the Treasurer was confronted with a line of questioning that sought to understand how firm the government's commitment was to delivering a surplus, and how likely a surplus was in view of a slowing world economy and rising government expenses from military commitments in Afghanistan. One journalist, for example, pressed the Treasurer with 'how important is that Budget surplus to you?' Costello's response was wan: 'Well, we would like to return a Budget surplus this year. It would be the fifth consecutive Budget surplus' (2001c). On another occasion, a journalist asked '[t]here will be, presumably, problems for you balancing a Budget, or delivering a surplus, given the increased costs that we will now be facing … Will you still be aiming for a surplus?' Costello evaded, but his questioner pursued him a second time, to which Costello simply replied by listing the sources of pressure on the surplus without addressing the nature of his government's commitment. The journalist tried one more time with '[b]ut you still think you'll get a surplus?', and Costello finally relented: 'we are still budgeting for a surplus, yes we are … we want to keep the Budget in surplus' (2001a). Note how no promise or guarantee is offered in Costello's responses — the surplus is merely an aspiration based on the intrinsically provisional act of budgeting.

Costello's emphasis on the process of budgeting leads to the second tactic: to underline the point that fiscal policy was a pragmatic affair that needed to change with circumstances. As international prospects weakened further, Costello was asked, '[i]s the outlook so grim that you need to look at more fiscal involvement to a point of even putting the Budget in deficit?' Costello again refused to answer in the affirmative and instead insisted on his prerogative to wait and see what happens, 'I am not going to proclaim that now because I can't tell you when the world will turn … What I'm saying to you, is, as we look back in retrospect in 2001–02, fiscal 2001–02, which we laid down in May of last year, I think fiscal policy was right.' He then continued, and concluded with a pedagogical tone, 'You are asking me what my strategy for 2002–03 will be, it will be to so pitch fiscal policy that it will be right for the times as well. You are asking me what it will be, I'll tell you at the time' (2001e). After further questions, the Treasurer gave an answer that is worth quoting at length:

> We don't like deficit Budgets, no. We don't … we've, look, we haven't worked so hard to put Australia back in the black and to repay debt, just to go back into deficits. But what I am talking to you about, is the size of surpluses. … I think there still is a role to play in fiscal policy. It is a longer term thing, the time lags are longer, it requires legislation, and that is why monetary policy is much more easily moved, it does not have to go through the Parliament … I think there is still a place for fiscal policy, and the way in which we have used fiscal policy, is we have used it to build up large surpluses in growth times so we can run small surpluses in difficult times. (2001e)

In this passage Costello is using the press conference forum for a pedagogical purpose, to explain that fiscal policy is used by the government as a tool for smoothing the economic cycle subject to maintaining surpluses. The lesson prepares the ground for 'responsible economic management' to be used to signify economic management that responds to the times, while keeping in view the Coalition's preference for surpluses.

Similar rhetorical tactics were used by Howard, although he was less adroit at avoiding committal language. When asked if he was confident that a surplus would be delivered, Howard replied that the government was 'very confident, they're [the budget targets] based on the advice we have from the Treasury …

They're Treasury estimates. We believe them ... We'll know a bit more about that next month' (2001b). Likewise, when asked how committed he was to a surplus, Howard replied that the government was 'committed to running a surplus ... The times have changed, and both sides of politics will have to take that into account. ... We will have a lower surplus this financial year and we will project a lower surplus next financial year from that projected at Budget time. But we will still project a surplus' (2001d). In these comments we see that Howard underlined the nature of a surplus as dependent on projections while he also emphasised his government's commitment to achieving surpluses as a principle. Projections and principles do not make a promise; perhaps the closest Howard comes to making a promise is with formulations such as the following: 'There'll be surpluses but they will be lower' (2001c), '[w]e're going to have a balance in our Budget in May, we're not going back into deficit' (2001a). This latter statement was then immediately qualified: 'But you don't need to run a big surplus particularly if you have only 6.4% of GDP as government debt. So once again it's a question of keeping things in perspective' (2001a).

When a journalist closely pressed the Prime Minister on the issue, asking if Howard could 'categorically rule out running a budget deficit', Howard responded that 'it is not the policy of the Coalition, it is not my policy to run a budget deficit in any year' (2001e). Neither is a policy a promise. As with Costello, Howard attempted to establish the principle that fiscal policy is obliged to respond to circumstances. The Prime Minister explained to ABC journalist Kerry O'Brien, for example, the negative economic effects of the terrorist attacks of 11 September 2001:

> The surpluses in the out years will be greater but they will not be as great as might otherwise have been the case. Now that is a fact of economic life, it has happened through circumstances not within our control so we obviously have to tailor our commitments according to those circumstances. (Howard 2001f)

The final result was not a surplus, however, at least not according to the underlying cash balance, which showed a modest deficit for the financial year ended 30 June 2002 (Reserve Bank of Australia 2002). The Labor party seized the deficit as a prize. The Shadow Minister for Employment, Education, Training and Science, Jenny Macklin, moved a second reading amendment that the House condemn the government for 'its failure to deliver a budget surplus in 2001–02 after a decade of growth' (House of Representatives 2002: 2754). The Member for Fraser, Robert McMullan, intoned that the government's 'claims of fiscal prudence are not supported by actions', accused the Treasurer of 'budgetary incompetence', and bemoaned the 'failure to live up to proper standards of prudent management by going into deficit' (House of Representatives 2002: 2760). He also linked the charge of incompetence with promise-breaking, and portrayed the Prime Minister as having made the surplus a solemn promise. As we have seen, the Prime Minister presented a small target in this respect,[10] yet Mark Latham, the Shadow Assistant Treasurer and Shadow Minister for Economic Ownership, similarly described 'a budget of broken promises' (House of Representatives 2002: 2768).

The Labor party's attacks did not intensify through the media and, when they did, the government did not find them hard to parry. When Costello was asked if he was embarrassed by the deficit, for example, he explained that '[t]he principal reasons why it has changed are that we have had additional expenditure in relation to the war against terrorism and tax receipts in the early part of 2002 were weaker than expected' (2002a). In addition, he could plausibly claim that the government was 'still running a very, very strong fiscal policy. And if there were ever a time to allow fiscal policy to take some slack it is probably during an economic global slowdown when you have got substantial defence commitments' (2002).[11] The same line was argued by economics commentator Ross Gittins when he wrote that it was 'important to the future good management of our economy for Mr Costello to finish this week believing that, no matter what silly things you've said in the past, the political penalty for having the Budget lapse into deficit isn't high' (2002). More instructively, Gittins attempted to clear away the political mist for his readers, writing that:

> It's important to understand that the significance of this Budget deficit is purely political, not economic. It's an embarrassment to Mr Costello because he's spent the past six years tirelessly convincing ignorant punters that avoiding Budget deficits is the *sine qua non* of good economic management … From an economic perspective, however, whether the Budget balance is a billion or two above or below zero is of little consequence. (2002)

Political and economic commentators also later attempted to dispel the political myths regarding surpluses in the context of the Labor surplus in 2012, making the same distinction between economic (good) and political (bad) arguments. While assistance from the media was no doubt welcomed by the Howard government, it was hardly essential, since the government had been returned to office in the 2001 election, and because it was able to return to comfortable surpluses before the October election in 2004. In sum, two points have been established here. First, good government came to be equated with budgeting for surpluses, but it was also regarded as responsible to allow the budget to adjust

---

10   McMullan's evidence is the following quotation from the Prime Minister: 'I have made that commitment, I will repeat it to you this morning, I do not believe that we should go into deficit, and we won't go into deficit if we are re-elected' (House of Representatives 2002: 2760).

11   See also the defusing treatment on the *7.30 Report* (Costello 2002b). By contrast, a more hostile response came from the *Age* (Davidson 2002).

to circumstances — such as deteriorating economic conditions or unexpected defence expenditures. Secondly, one virtue of this rhetorical strategy is that a small target is presented to political opponents for, even though a deficit is presented as undesirable *prima facie*, it is also defendable as the unexpected outcome of contingent events.

Labor's blunder: The 2010–12 surplus debate

As Leader of the Opposition in 2007, Rudd promised in his budget reply that, '[i]f elected, the government I will lead will be grounded in the discipline of not spending more than we earn' (House of Representatives 2007: 129). This maxim and the Reserve Bank's independence in pursuing its inflation target were the 'disciplines' of economic management that enjoyed 'bipartisan consensus' (House of Representatives 2007: 129). As Treasurer, Wayne Swan claimed that the government had realised this discipline in the Rudd government's first budget in May 2008, for the budget represented the 'disciplined spending' and 'responsible economic management' necessary for Australia to meet the challenges facing the economy. In fact, Swan not only proclaimed his budget as 'the responsible budget our nation needs', but he even ventured that it opens 'a new era of responsible economic management' (House of Representatives 2008: 2600). The new era was evidenced by the government's preparedness to act on its assessment that there was 'an economic case for cutting government spending' (House of Representatives 2008: 2600), and this action yielded the budget's centrepiece — a projected surplus of over $21 billion, almost two per cent of GDP (Swan 2008).

Brendan Nelson, giving his budget reply in 2008 as Leader of the Opposition, rejected Labor's claims to be 'good economic managers' and instead asserted the continuation of 'old Labor': Swan's budget was a 'high-taxing, high-spending Labor budget' (House of Representatives 2008: 2997). Australia was, therefore, right to be nervous regarding Labor's economic competency, since the 'sound economic strategy' of the Coalition had been consistently demonstrated during its term in government, and yet it had been opposed by the Labor party while in opposition (House of Representatives 2008: 2997). The proximate reason was that Rudd's claim to be an 'economic conservative' was spurious, as he lacked the necessary 'philosophical conviction and character' (House of Representatives 2008: 2997).

Swan's second budget had a different quality to his first: it was a budget 'forged in the fire of the most challenging global economic conditions since the Great Depression' (House of Representatives 2009: 3532), the Global Financial Crisis (GFC). A program of 'responsible borrowing' was intended to stimulate the economy through 'nation-building' initiatives (House of Representatives 2009: 3532), such as road and railway building, broadband, and ports. Swan assured his audience that while the budget met the challenge posed by the GFC it still bore the marks of 'discipline' and 'hard choices', and so represented a 'responsible course' (House of Representatives 2009: 3532). The Leader of the Opposition, Malcolm Turnbull, was unconvinced. He accused Labor of 'reckless borrowing and spending' and of failing to develop a 'credible or convincing plan for economic recovery' (House of Representatives 2009: 3973). Australians who were 'prudent and thrifty' would pay for 'reckless and spendthrift Labor' (House of Representatives 2009: 3973), who were taking the nation on an 'irresponsible, dangerous course of high deficits', instead of evincing 'discipline and more responsibility' (House of Representatives 2009: 3973).

The crucial point to underline from these two sets of exchanges is that, regardless of whether Labor announced a surplus or a deficit, the legitimating and delegitimating claims are the same — responsible economic management was the cloak that Labor draped over itself and that the Opposition claimed to see through. The reason would seem to be that responsible economic management, fiscal discipline, budget prudence and so on are not types of action that can be clearly demarcated from their antonyms. To invoke this action is therefore to make a safe claim, since it is always defendable and seemingly unfalsifiable. This observation amounts to the point made by Evans that the principles of sound fiscal management set out in the Charter were 'essentially meaningless' (House of Representatives 1997: 136).

The following year saw claims and counterclaims made that could have been substituted with the previous year, only this time with a new Leader of the Opposition, Tony Abbott. Swan portrayed the budget as manifesting 'the highest standards of responsible economic management' thanks to its 'responsible fiscal strategy' (House of Representatives 2010: 3134). In his reply to Swan's budget speech, Abbott called the budget a 'typical old-fashioned tax-and-spend Labor budget' (House of Representatives 2010: 3593), and he insisted that the government was not entitled 'to claim prudent economic management' (House of Representatives 2010: 3593). In fact, Abbott's rhetoric included a 'particular message for the Prime Minister … this reckless spending must stop' (House of Representatives 2010: 3593).

This pattern of speech continued into 2011. Early in the year, when Swan was detailing the government's response to that summer's floods in Queensland with an eye for their likely economic effects, the Treasurer explained that the government's response would be conditioned by 'the economic discipline that has been a hallmark of this government', for '[f]iscal responsibility is about keeping our budget in a position where it can deal with surprises like the floods in the future', and the key manifestation of this condition was Swan's introduction of the flood levy (Swan 2011b). Finance Minister Penny Wong extolled the government's 'tough choices' (2011a), and the toughest choice of all was to run a budget surplus, 'it is responsible for the Government to be committed to budget surpluses' (Wong 2011a).

The government's assurances that its projected budget surplus constituted responsible economic management were met with straightforward counter-characterisations by Opposition politicians. In response to Swan's flood levy, for example, Abbott railed that if the government had not 'recklessly squandered the surplus left to it by the Howard government … it would now be in a position to respond effectively to the floods without a new tax' (2011a). Abbott added that, while in general '[s]pending cuts might be unpopular', they are nevertheless 'the necessary tough decisions that a responsible government would be prepared to take' (2011a). The Shadow Treasurer, Joe Hockey, disputed the government's capacity to meet its own standards for 'fiscal rectitude' and instead prophesied a path of 'fiscal expansion and running deficit Budgets' (2011a).

Attention naturally focused on the May 2011 budget. In one of his numerous speeches detailing the budget, Swan approvingly quoted his own words describing the previous year's budget, which purportedly instantiated 'the highest standards of responsible economic management' (2011a), by limiting spending in an election year. The 2011 budget continued 'the hard slog back to surplus' (Swan 2011a), which involved unpopular cuts to spending, but Swan and the government took 'comfort from knowing they are the right and responsible thing to do for the economy' (Swan 2011a). Wong also assured the public that 'the Government will do what is responsible' (2011a), and made full use of the concept's capaciousness:

> Responsible economic management is also about making room within the budget for important investments that reflect the economic challenges we face, and improve the long term prosperity of the nation (2011b).

Abbott continued to develop his counter-characterisations of the government's behaviour. The government's 'badge of economic virtue' was a 'wafer thin surplus' and, if realised, would only be the result of favourable economic conditions and not 'tough-minded economic reform or serious spending cuts' (House of Representatives 2011: 3905). What the government had not been able to evidence was 'the capacity to bring its own spending under much tighter control' (Abbott 2011d). Hockey was more strident, saying that it was a 'fairytale story' that the government would 'bring the budget back to surplus with fiscal discipline' (House of Representatives 2011: 3607). The government was said to be engaged in 'fiscal recklessness' as they pursued 'politics and not policy' (House of Representatives 2011: 3607); '[r]esponsible economic management is not in Labor's DNA', 'Labor is addicted to spending' (Hockey 2011c).

With this contest between Labor's claim to be evincing responsible economic government and the Opposition's counter-characterisation of Labor as fiscally irresponsible, we have one of the two key strands of the budget surplus debate under the Labor government. The second strand to now bring into focus is Labor's shift from presenting the surplus as a contingent forecast to transforming the surplus into a solemn promise, diverging from the tactics of the Howard government. The effects of Labor's rhetorical conversion were severe, and this change in language should be seen as a strategic blunder. Consider, for example, how Abbott consistently underlined that achieving a surplus by the promised date of 2013 was 'looking increasingly implausible' (2011b), and it was widely perceived that 'government revenues are under great pressure' (Abbott 2011c). Given the Treasurer's open avowal of Keynesian countercyclical policy, and that the terms of the Coalition's Charter stipulated 'moderating cyclical fluctuations in economic activity' (*Charter of Budget Honesty Act 1998* (Cth) s5(1)(b)(ii)) as a principle of sound finance, allowing the budget to fall into deficit would have been eminently construable as a straightforward exercise in macro-stabilisation and responsible fiscal policy. Yet the government could not produce a deficit and use this justification because the surplus was no longer a projection or intention, but had become a promise. The rhetorical contest over responsible economic discipline, characterised by weak predicates and covering the divergent behaviours of producing deficits and surpluses, had become entangled with a contest over trustworthiness.

If we move back in time from 2011 to 2010, when Rudd was still prime minister and Labor leader, then we find a revealing response to the following Dorothy Dixer asked by Labor backbencher Michael Symon: 'Will the Prime Minister explain the importance of responsible economic management to secure economic growth and prosperity for all Australians?' (House of Representatives 2010: 4747). Rudd's response was to align responsible economic management with the government's stimulus package by claiming that it saved the Australian economy from recession. This is one of the meanings of responsible economic management that we have already encountered — countercyclical spending. The Prime Minister then claimed that 'through prudent financial management the government will return the budget to surplus in three years time, three years ahead of time' (House of Representatives 2010: 4747). The shift in the adjective — from economic to financial — is less important than the implied relationship between the end (surplus) and the means (prudent management). For the surplus is simply treated as the happy result of prudent financial management; the surplus is not a promise or a guarantee. Just two days later, however, the logic shifts in Rudd's answer to a similar question, in which he said of his government '[w]e stand for returning this budget to surplus in three years' time, three years ahead of time; those opposite refuse to nominate the date at which it will be returned' (House of Representatives 2010: 5219). In this phrase what is being positioned as virtuous governmental action is not simply prudent financial management that yields a surplus as a positive by-product, but the act of nominating a date is now the virtuous behaviour. Later in the same month this logic was cemented when Rudd said '[t]he government is committed to keeping the economy strong … That is why we are committed to bringing the budget back to surplus in three years time' (House of Representatives 2010: 5304). The virtuous act (keeping the economy strong) has been redefined as meeting a deadline. There is a now a clear test, a falsifiable claim, against which the invocation of virtuous behaviour can be measured: meeting a deadline.[12] It was a version of this type of falsifiable claim that Gillard repeated in her leadership acceptance speech less than ten days later: 'And today I can assure every Australian that their Budget will be back in surplus in 2013' (2010a). Only a few days after Gillard's acceptance speech, the Treasurer embraced the same timeframe. When asked by a journalist if he was 'still committed to a surplus in 2012/2013?', Swan replied, '[t]oo right we are' (Swan 2010a).

The shift in the logic of government's language from responsible and pragmatic economic management to promise-making became increasingly explicit over the two months following Gillard's acceptance of the leadership in June 2010. Consider these statements from Gillard: 'my commitments to the Australian people are clear and I'm happy to restate them. We'll bring the budget to surplus in 2013' (2010b); 'I'm determined Laura, to see the budget returned to surplus in 2013 as we've promised' (2010c); 'we will acquit our obligations to bring the budget back to surplus in 2013' (2010d); 'we are obviously looking each and every day of the campaign to make sure that we acquit our promise that the budget comes to surplus in 2013' (2010e). The Treasurer's word use in the same period is equivalent: 'the Government is absolutely committed to bringing this budget back to surplus in 2013' (Swan 2010b); 'that essential commitment of coming back to surplus in 2013' (Swan 2010b).

Political rhetoric that positions promise-keeping as virtuous behaviour is logically incompatible with rhetoric that holds adjusting to circumstances as virtuous. Either one is steadfast or one is flexible. Given that one of the primary meanings of 'responsible economic management' is to indicate adjusting fiscal policy to the needs of the economy, such as deficit spending to avoid recession after the GFC, the government's commitment to reach a surplus by a specified date suggests a failure to understand even basic points of rhetorical strategy. Consider an address by Gillard to the Sydney Institute in early 2011. Gillard told her audience that '[w]e will keep a tight rein on spending to return the Budget to surplus. Fiscal responsibility is something we have long been committed to'

---

12 Although it should be noted that the difference between a surplus and a deficit is not such a clear matter given the under-prescription of how government accounts are to be presented — see Wines and Scarborough (2006).

(2011). So far these comments remain on the terrain of economic management. Yet just a few sentences later the logic of economic exigency is tied to the divergent logic of political promises:

> Some have described our commitment to achieving a surplus as a political commitment. Of course, this is true — my commitment to a surplus in 2012–13 was a promise made and it will be honoured. But this political commitment was given and will be honoured because that's what prudent economic management now demands. When the private sector was in retreat, the government stepped forward to fill the gap and over coming years as the private sector recovers strongly, it is the right time for the government to step back. (Gillard 2011)

In these words one sees the mistake clearly: the temporary and the permanent are shackled together by the assumption embodied in the final sentence — that there will be a strong private sector recovery. In hindsight, we can see that this is exactly what did not happen.

The inflexibility of a promise was targeted consistently by the Opposition. In the lead-up to the budget speech in May 2012, the Shadow Treasurer told a Business Council of Australia audience that the 'only way to impose some fiscal discipline' on the government was to 'force them to return the budget to surplus' (Hockey 2011b). The challenge here is clear: if the government does not produce a surplus then it has failed to evince fiscal discipline. In addition, Hockey also insisted that a failure to return to surplus would impugn the government's trustworthiness:

> For the government to break its promise of a budget surplus next year would be yet another broken commitment to the Australian people. It would drive a nail into their integrity coffin. (Hockey 2011b)

The Treasurer's budget maintained the forecast of a surplus by 2013, but Hockey was quick to seize on how 'precariously balanced' it was in terms of the assumptions built into the forecast (House of Representatives 2012: 4335). Abbott referred to 'the great fraud of Tuesday night's Budget' (2012a), which Hockey later elaborated as the 'Treasurer's extraordinary shuffling of money' that saw spending on the National Broadband Network kept 'off budget' by being financed through government borrowing (Hockey 2012). This idea of dubious accounting practices nicely complemented the earlier attack on the government's trustworthiness, which Hockey repeated and linked with the consistent denial that the government was fiscally disciplined: 'the history of broken promises and the lack of genuine commitment to fiscal consolidation make me doubt the Treasurer's new promise of a surplus' (2012). This sentence conveys the combined challenge being made to the government, as a deficit would be evidence of untrustworthiness and fiscal irresponsibility.

There was a different type of criticism from media sources, at times of limpid acuity. Consider this editorial from the *Age*, just over a month before the budget:

> The government locked itself into a politically loaded promise, but the exact timing of a surplus is of no great economic consequence. What matters to Australians is a healthy economy. (*Age* 2012)

The economist Graham White, writing on *The Drum*, lamented that the government was 'ignoring the dangers of too fast a return to surplus for fear of giving the Opposition a political free-kick' (2012). Mike Seccombe diagnosed the situation at greater length for the *Global Mail*. Persisting with the surplus was, he wrote, 'inexplicable in economic terms', but perfectly understandable in 'political terms' (2012). The government had arrived at a 'position where to abandon the promise of a Budget surplus ... would come at a great political cost', because it was still trying to shrug off its reputation for economic mismanagement acquired more than a decade earlier (Seccombe 2012).

The Treasurer confronted the issue more or less directly in a Press Club address, saying that the government would 'return to surplus only if we were satisfied we could do it without imposing too great a burden on households and businesses' (Swan 2012c). That is, this was a 'surplus for the right reasons, and not at any cost' (Swan 2012c). Note how this assessment only refers to economic calculations, but having decided that the economic conditions still supported a return to surplus, it was not necessary to break the government's promise and it was conveniently unnecessary to mention this additional motive for delivering a surplus. Gillard similarly assured a minerals industry audience that 'the surplus is right for the domestic economy' because it was 'designed to maintain sustainable, low-inflation growth' (2012a). Just as was the case with Swan's reply, the economic and promissory have been presented as if they were uncoupled for the purposes of decision-making, only to then point happily in the same direction *ex post facto*.

The pressure built throughout the year as further economic data became available, while the government stayed with these lines of defence. In an interview, for example, the journalist Peter van Onselen pursued the Finance Minister with the germane question: 'why is it so important that we still try to find a way to get to what is, at the end of the day, a wafer-thin surplus? ... That's purely a political thing, surely?' (Wong 2012d). It certainly was, yet, as we have seen, only the Australian media was prepared to call a spade a spade. As a result, Wong persisted in providing an economic rationale, claiming that the decision was 'grounded in the economy' (2012d), which was returning to trend growth and this mandated 'putting fiscal policy back on a more normal setting' (2012d), as this was 'the right thing to do for the economy' (2012b), the 'right fiscal strategy for the economic circumstances' (2012c). Swan and Gillard followed this pattern of tautological reasoning, respectively describing the budget as 'appropriate' (Swan 2012b) given a return to trend growth and 'the right economic statement for the Australian economy' (Gillard 2012c). We can treat this decay in argumentative quality as a symptom of the government's contextual difficulty. As the close of the year approached, interviewers and Opposition politicians alike were asking the Prime Minister if the surplus was a promise or a goal, and her responses were evasive. In one case, Gillard was only prepared to say that her government 'stand by that Treasury Forecast' and avoided choosing between 'guarantee or an aspiration' by saying 'we're very determined to bring the budget to surplus' (2012b). Statements of this type might be read as preparation to concede the issue, or as symptomatic of the argumentative weakness of the position.

This weakness was easily exploited by the Opposition. Abbott claimed to identify 'a government which is preparing the ground to abandon yet another solemn commitment to the Australian people' (2012c), while Hockey made the same accusation when he inquired in parliament, '[w]hen did the Treasurer decide to start crab-walking away from his solemn commitment — his honest promise — to deliver a surplus in 2012–13?' (House of Representatives 2012: 12546). Perhaps the most brutal moment came in late October, when Hockey brought to the attention of the House of Representatives that the Treasurer had made a commitment to achieving a surplus more than 150 times since May 2010 (House of Representatives 2012: 12547).

When the time finally came to concede defeat on the 2013 surplus, it is instructive to note that Wong did not flinch in appealing to the value that for three years had justified pursuing a surplus regardless of the political and social costs: 'we have to put jobs and growth first and we want to continue the responsible economic management that's seen Australia weather the GFC' (2012a). The interviewer immediately pointed out the apparent redefinition of what was responsible, since until that day only a surplus was responsible. In typical style, Wong bit the bullet, replying that the 'key to this decision today is responsible economic management … We don't believe it's responsible for us to continue to make cuts to offset this revenue downgrade if that is bad for jobs and bad for growth' (2012a). It was the recent data that her office had just released, Wong said, that made it clear that the latest revenue downgrades could not be offset through further cuts without crossing the threshold of irresponsible economic management (2012a). The point is eminently reasonable: budgets are made with forecast numbers and, when the actual numbers diverge, the budget's bottom line must change. But Labor's ill-considered language had changed the test from responding to circumstances to keeping a promise. Abbott and Hockey called a joint press conference to claim their prize. The charge of economic mismanagement was to the fore as Abbott described a government that 'fails to understand any of the fundamentals of economic management. We know this because we know its record' (2012d). The more prominent accusation, however, was of untrustworthiness:

> this is a government which you simply can't trust. You can't trust it on anything. You can't trust it on the Budget, you can't trust it on borders, you can't trust it with the truth. You simply cannot trust this government. You simply cannot trust this Prime Minister. (Abbott 2012d)

This attack on the Prime Minister's trustworthiness was launched on the back of a government statement regarding its fiscal policy. That the budget had become this litmus test for Gillard's character was lamentable for Labor, because the Prime Minister was already exposed on this front, and because a statement regarding the budget should have been a moment for political speech protected by that impregnable phrase, 'responsible economic government'.

Conclusion

The preceding usefully depicts how Labor arrived at this awkward position. It arose from the interaction between the two dynamics that drove the claims and counterclaims made regarding the budget surplus debate during 2010–12. The first dynamic was the attempt by Labor to legitimate its behaviour as economically responsible and Opposition efforts to deny that the government's behaviour was consistent with this value. The second dynamic arose from the mistake to convert what was essentially a forecast — that returning the budget to surplus in 2013 was economically feasible and judicious — into a promise. The result was to transform a revisable, technical claim into an immobile test of morality and confront the government with an invidious choice. On the one hand, the government could have made further deep and unpopular cuts to keep its promise and, in doing so, endanger its claim to responsible economic government with expert and civil opinion. On the other hand sat the government's choice: to break its promise and face attacks on its trustworthiness.

Labor's rhetoric was unsuccessful in at least two respects. Firstly it failed to evince a basic understanding of the words it leaders use, not in the sense of their propositional content, but in the sense of the rhetorical effects and dynamics that they create. Tying together the contingent and the inflexible is illogical; an action is good either because it is flexible or because it is steadfast. Worse, this promise, which tied the government's hands to a set course on fiscal policy, was made in the midst of a continuing GFC, that is — as the government repeatedly claimed — the worst economic crisis since the Great Depression. Labor's second failure relates to historical sense. The lines of attack and defence regarding a broken promise to produce a surplus in the context of sustained claims to responsible economic management were played out in miniature under the preceding government when Labor was the Opposition. During that episode, Howard and Costello modelled the superior tactics to deploy regarding budget rhetoric: avoid promises and explain the cyclical nature of budget balances.

The cliché chiding those who do not learn from history is near at hand, especially when the Coalition has demonstrated its ability to learn from history. During the National Press Club debate just over a week before the 2013 election, between the Treasurer Chris Bowen and the Shadow Treasurer Joe Hockey, the Treasurer committed to a date for returning the budget to surplus, 2016–17. Hockey did not, and instead gave the strategically optimal answer to a question on fiscal policy: 'We will get to surplus when it is reasonable, responsible to do so' (Hockey 2013). But the part of Hockey's reply that followed is more satisfying:

> We are not going — I am not going to make the mistake that Labor made of making big heroic promises and never delivering because I stood at this chair, at this table 3 years ago with another Labor treasurer and he promised that he would deliver a surplus in the next term of government. (Hockey 2013)

Those who learn from the mistakes of the past are destined to triumph over those who do not.

References

Age 2012. First fix the economy and surplus will follow. 30 March.

Abbott, T. 2011a. Spending cuts better than levy. *Herald Sun* 29 January.

—— 2011b. Address to the Committee for Economic Development of Australia. n.d. URL: http://www.tonyabbott.com.au/LatestNews/Speeches/tabid/88/articleType/ArticleView/articleId/8278/Address-to-the-Committee-for-Economic-Development-of-Australia-Melbourne.aspx. Consulted 9 August 2013.

—— 2011c. Address to the Opposition Leader's breakfast. n.d. URL: http://www.tonyabbott.com.au/LatestNews/Speeches/tabid/88/articleType/ArticleView/articleId/8459/Address-to-the-Opposition-Leaders-Breakfast-Financial-Services-Council-Political-Series-2011-Sydney.aspx. Consulted 11 August 2013.

—— 2011d. Address to the Victorian Employers' Chamber of Commerce. n.d. URL: http://www.tonyabbott.com.au/LatestNews/Speeches/tabid/88/articleType/ArticleView/articleId/8046/Address-to-the-Victorian-Employers-Chamber-of-Commerce-and-Industry-Industry-House-Melbourne.aspx. Consulted 18 August 2013.

—— 2011e. Address to the WA Liberal Party State Conference. n.d. URL: http://www.tonyabbott.com.au/LatestNews/Speeches/tabid/88/articleType/ArticleView/articleId/8253/Address-to-the-WA-Liberal-Party-State-Conference-Perth.aspx. Consulted 4 August 2013.

—— 2012a. Address to Federal Budget reply luncheon. n.d. http://www.tonyabbott.com.au/LatestNews/Speeches/tabid/88/articleType/ArticleView/articleId/8711/Address-to-Federal-Budget-Reply-Luncheon-Sydney.aspx. Consulted 30 July 2013.

—— 2012b. Address to the Melbourne Institute/The Australian 2012 Economic and Social Outlook Conference. n.d. URL: http://www.tonyabbott.com.au/LatestNews/Speeches/tabid/88/articleType/ArticleView/articleId/8958/Address-to-the-Melbourne-Institute-The-Australian-2012-Economic-and-Social-Outlook-Conference.aspx. Consulted 3 August 2013.

—— 2012c. Doorstop Interview. n.d. URL: http://www.tonyabbott.com.au/LatestNews/InterviewTranscripts/tabid/85/articleType/ArticleView/articleId/8951/Doorstop-Interview-Canberra.aspx. Consulted 31 July 2013.

—— 2012d. Joint press conference. n.d. URL: http://www.tonyabbott.com.au/LatestNews/InterviewTranscripts/tabid/85/ArticleType/ArticleView/ArticleID/9019/Default.aspx. Consulted 20 August 2013.

Costello, P. 1997. Address to the Economic Society of Victoria Forecasting Conference. URL: http://searcha.beta.capmon.com/pdfdisplay/data/repository/pressrel/p0731050_5.pdf. Consulted 14 August 2013.

—— 1998. Address to Committee for the Economic Development of Australia. *Peter Costello*. 28 January. URL: http://www.petercostello.com.au/speeches/1998/2004-address-to-committee-for-the-economic-development-of-australia-ceda. Consulted 14 August 2013.

—— 2001a. *3AW with Neil Mitchell*. Transcript of interview. 20 September. URL: http://searcha.beta.capmon.com/pdfdisplay/data/repository/pressrel/p0920083.pdf. Consulted 11 August 2013.

——2001b. *7.30 Report* with Kerry O'Brien. Transcript of interview. *Peter Costello*. 22 May. URL: http://www.petercostello.com.au/transcripts/2001/2360-older-australians-budget-surplus-growth-forecasts-welfare-reform. Consulted 11 August 2013.

—— 2001c. Interview with Katherine McGrath. Transcript. *Peter Costello*. 22 May: 8 am. Consulted 11 August 2013. URL: http://www.petercostello.com.au/transcripts/2001/2307-singtel-optus-takeover-kim-beazley-health-budget.

——2001d. Interview by Katherine McGrath. Transcript. *Peter Costello*. 22 May: 8.22 pm. URL: http://www.petercostello.com.au/transcripts/2001/2361-budget-election-building-industry-surplus-self-funded-retirees-child-care-pensioners-motor-industry-unemployment. Consulted 11 August 2013.

—— 2001e, Press conference: National accounts. *Peter Costello*. 5 December. URL: http://www.petercostello.com.au/transcripts/2001/2280-national-accounts-interest-rates-budget-petrol-excise-world-economies-border-protection-credit-card-debt-productivity-commission-reports. Consulted 12 August 2013.

—— 2002a, Budget Lock-up Press Conference. *Peter Costello*. 14 May. URL: http://ministers.treasury.gov.au/DisplayDocs.aspx?doc=transcripts/2002/028.htm&pageID=004&min=phc&Year=2002&DocType=2. Consulted 12 August 2013.

—— 2002b, 'Mr Surplus' becomes 'Mr Deficit'. Television program. *7:30 Report*. 14 May. URL: http://www.abc.net.au/7.30/content/2002/s555622.htm. Consulted 15 August 2013.

Davidson, K. 2002. The bottom line on Costello's 'surplus'. *Age* 15 September.

Emerson, C. 2013. Statement on higher education. URL: http://capitalmonitor.com.au/LeftMenu.aspx. Consulted 11 August 2013.

Gillard, J. 2010a. Joint press conference. Transcript. *Treasury Portfolio Ministers*. 24 June. URL: http://ministers.treasury.gov.au/DisplayDocs.aspx?doc=transcripts/2010/079.htm&pageID=011&min=wms&Year=2010&DocType=2. Consulted 19 August 2013.

—— 2010b. Transcript of doorstop interview, Richmond. 20 July. URL: http://searcha.beta.capmon.com/pdfdisplay/data/repository/pressrel/p100720306.pdf. Consulted 2 September 2013.

—— 2010c. Transcript of 2010 election debate. 25 July. URL: http://searcha.beta.capmon.com/pdfdisplay/data/repository/pressrel/p100726150.pdf. Consulted 2 September 2013.

—— 2010d. Transcript of joint press conference with Member for Leichhardt, Jim Turnour, Cairns. 4 August. URL: http://searcha.beta.capmon.com/pdfdisplay/data/repository/pressrel/p100804335.pdf. Consulted 3 September 2013.

—— 2010e. Transcript of press conference, Packenham, Victoria. 11 August. URL: http://searcha.beta.capmon.com/pdfdisplay/data/repository/pressrel/p100811307.pdf. Consulted 2 September 2013.

—— 2011. The dignity of work. Address to the Sydney Institute Annual Dinner. 13 April. URL: http://searcha.beta.capmon.com/pdfdisplay/data/repository/pressrel/p110414159.pdf. Consulted 14 August 2013.

—— 2012a. Minerals industry parliamentary dinner, Parliament House, Canberra. 30 May. URL: http://searcha.beta.capmon.com/pdfdisplay/data/repository/pressrel/p120531151.pdf. Consulted 3 August 2013.

—— 2012b. Transcript of interview with Keiran Gilbert, Sky News. 29 October. URL: http://searcha.beta.capmon.com/pdfdisplay/data/repository/pressrel/p121029224.pdf. Consulted 7 August 2013.

—— 2012c. Transcript of interview with Sabra Lane, ABC AM. 23 October. URL: http://searcha.beta.capmon.com/pdfdisplay/data/repository/pressrel/p121023208.pdf. Consulted 9 August 2013.

Gittins, R. 2002. Please, for all our sakes, don't mention the deficit. *Sydney Morning Herald* 30 September.

Hockey, J. 2011a. Address to the Trans Tasman Business Circle. *The Hon Joe Hockey MP*. 29 March. URL: http://www.joehockey.com/media/speeches/details.aspx?s=50. Consulted 4 August 2013.

—— 2011b. Benchmarking the budget. Address to the Business Council of Australia annual forum. *The Hon Joe Hockey MP*. 13 April. URL: http://www.joehockey.com/media-files/speeches/ContentPieces/105/download.pdf. Consulted 31 July 2013.

—— 2011c. Budget 2011: Labor fails Australian families. Press release. *The Hon Joe Hockey MP*. 10 May. URL: http://www.joehockey.com/media/media-releases/details.aspx?r=94. Consulted 2 August 2013.

—— 2012. Address to the National Press Club. *The Hon Joe Hockey MP*. 16 May. URL: http://www.joehockey.com/media/speeches/details.aspx?s=99. Consulted 1 August 2013.

House of Representatives 1971. Question: Economy: Reductions in Commonwealth expenditures. *Debates*. 18 February. URL: http://parlinfo.aph.gov.au/parlInfo/search/display/display.w3p;query=Id%3A%22hansard80%2Fhansardr80%2F1971-02-18%2F0127%22. Consulted 15 August 2013.

—— 1973. Financial Corporations Bill 1973: Second reading. *Debates*. 11 December. URL: http://parlinfo.aph.gov.au/parlInfo/search/display/display.w3p;query=Id%3A%22hansard80%2Fhansardr80%2F1973-12-11%2F0156%22.

—— 1976. *Debates*. 20 May. URL: http://parlinfo.aph.gov.au/parlInfo/search/display/display.w3p;query=Id%3A%22hansard80%2Fhansardr80%2F1976-05-20%2F0225%22. Consulted 15 August 2013.

—— 1978. Government economic policy. *Debates*. 6 June. URL: http://parlinfo.aph.gov.au/parlInfo/search/display/display.w3p;query=Id%3A%22hansard80%2Fhansardr80%2F1978-06-06%2F0106%22. Consulted 15 August 2013.

—— 1981. *Debates*, 24 September: 1809. URL: http://parlinfo.aph.gov.au/parlInfo/search/display/display.w3p;query=Id%3A%22chamber%2Fhansardr%2F1981-09-24%2F0144%22. Consulted 15 August 2013.

—— 1986. *Debates*. 16 April: 2380. URL: http://parlinfo.aph.gov.au/parlInfo/search/display/display.w3p;query=Id%3A%22chamber%2Fhansardr%2F1986-04-16%2F0026%22. Consulted 15 August 2013.

—— 1994. *Debates*. 10 May: 587. URL: http://parlinfo.aph.gov.au/parlInfo/search/display/display.w3p;query=Id%3A%22chamber%2Fhansardr%2F1994-05-10%2F0093%22. Consulted 23 August 2013.

—— 1994. *Debates*. 12 May: 869. URL: http://parlinfo.aph.gov.au/parlInfo/search/display/display.w3p;query=Id%3A%22chamber%2Fhansardr%2F1994-05-12%2F0130%22. Consulted 23 August 2013.

—— 1995. *Debates*. 9 May: 68. URL: http://parlinfo.aph.gov.au/parlInfo/search/display/display.w3p;query=Id%3A%22chamber%2Fhansardr%2F1995-05-09%2F0079%22. Consulted 23 August 2013.

—— 1995. *Debates*. 11 May: 400. URL: http://parlinfo.aph.gov.au/parlInfo/search/display/display.w3p;query=Id%3A%22chamber%2Fhansardr%2F1995-05-11%2F0130%22. Consulted 23 August 2013.

—— 1996. *Debates*. 1 May: 173. URL: http://parlinfo.aph.gov.au/parlInfo/search/display/display.w3p;query=Id%3A%22chamber%2Fhansardr%2F1996-05-01%2F0094%22. Consulted 16 August 2013.

—— 1996. *Debates*. 20 August: 3269. URL: http://parlinfo.aph.gov.au/parlInfo/search/display/display.w3p;query=Id%3A%22chamber%2Fhansardr%2F1996-08-20%2F0070%22. Consulted 16 August 2013.

—— 1996. *Debates*. 22 August: 3619. URL: http://parlinfo.aph.gov.au/parlInfo/search/display/display.w3p;query=Id%3A%22chamber%2Fhansardr%2F1996-08-22%2F0128%22. Consulted 15 August 2013.

—— 1996. *Debates*. 11 December: 8183. URL: http://parlinfo.aph.gov.au/parlInfo/search/display/display.w3p;db=CHAMBER;id=chamber%2Fhansardr%2F1996-12-11%2F0005;query=Id%3A%22chamber%2Fhansardr%2F1996-12-11%2F0002%22. Consulted 4 August 2013.

—— 1997. *Debates*. 5 February: 136. URL: http://parlinfo.aph.gov.au/parlInfo/search/display/display.w3p;query=Id%3A%22chamber%2Fhansardr%2F1997-02-05%2F0017%22. Consulted 7 August 2013.

—— 1997. *Debates*. 15 May: 3825. URL: http://parlinfo.aph.gov.au/parlInfo/search/display/display.w3p;query=Id%3A%22chamber%2Fhansardr%2F1997-05-15%2F0134%22. Consulted 14 August 2013.

—— 1998. *Debates*. 14 May: 3443. URL: http://parlinfo.aph.gov.au/parlInfo/search/display/display.w3p;query=Id%3A%22chamber%2Fhansardr%2F1998-05-14%2F0187%22. Consulted 14 August 2013.

—— 1999. *Debates*. 11 May: 5047. URL: http://parlinfo.aph.gov.au/parlInfo/search/display/display.w3p;query=Id%3A%22chamber%2Fhansardr%2F1999-05-11%2F0074%22. Consulted 9 August 2013.

—— 1999. *Debates*. 13 May: 5436. URL: http://parlinfo.aph.gov.au/parlInfo/search/display/display.w3p;query=Id%3A%22chamber%2Fhansardr%2F1999-05-13%2F0134%22. Consulted 14 August 2013.

—— 2000. *Debates*. 11 May: 16348. URL: http://parlinfo.aph.gov.au/parlInfo/search/display/display.w3p;query=Id%3A%22chamber%2Fhansardr%2F2000-05-11%2F0143%22. Consulted 14 August 2013.

—— 2002. *Debates*. 30 May: 2754. URL: http://parlinfo.aph.gov.au/parlInfo/search/display/display.w3p;query=Id%3A%22chamber%2Fhansardr%2F2002-05-30%2F0037%22. Consulted 11 August 2013.

—— 2002. *Debates*. 30 May: 2760. URL: http://parlinfo.aph.gov.au/parlInfo/search/display/display.w3p;query=Id%3A%22chamber%2Fhansardr%2F2002-05-30%2F0039%22. Consulted 11 August 2013.

—— 2002. *Debates*. 30 May: 2768. URL: http://parlinfo.aph.gov.au/parlInfo/ search/display/display.w3p;query=Id%3A%22chamber%2Fhansardr% 2F2002-05-30%2F0041%22. Consulted 11 August 2013.

—— 2007. *Debates*. 10 May: 129. URL: http://parlinfo.aph.gov.au/parlInfo/ search/display/display.w3p;query=Id%3A%22chamber%2Fhansardr% 2F2007-05-10%2F0162%22. Consulted 17 August 2013.

—— 2008. *Debates*. 13 May: 2600. URL: http://parlinfo.aph.gov.au/parlInfo/ search/display/display.w3p;query=Id%3A%22chamber%2Fhansardr% 2F2008-05-13%2F0101%22. Consulted 17 August 2013.

—— 2008. *Debates*. 15 May: 2997. URL: http://parlinfo.aph.gov.au/parlInfo/ search/display/display.w3p;query=Id%3A%22chamber%2Fhansardr% 2F2008-05-15%2F0126%22. Consulted 17 August 2013.

—— 2009. *Debates*. 12 May: 3532. URL: http://parlinfo.aph.gov.au/parlInfo/ search/display/display.w3p;query=Id%3A%22chamber%2Fhansardr% 2F2009-05-12%2F0119%22. Consulted 18 August 2013.

—— 2009. *Debates*. 14 May: 3973. URL: http://parlinfo.aph.gov.au/parlInfo/ search/display/display.w3p;query=Id%3A%22chamber%2Fhansardr% 2F2009-05-14%2F0177%22. Consulted 18 August 2013.

—— 2010. *Debates*. 11 May: 3134. URL: http://parlinfo.aph.gov.au/parlInfo/ search/display/display.w3p;db=CHAMBER;id=chamber%2Fhansardr %2F2010-05-11%2F0078;query=Id%3A%22chamber%2Fhansardr% 2F2010-05-11%2F0077%22. Consulted 16 August 2013.

—— 2010. *Debates*. 13 May: 3593. URL: http://parlinfo.aph.gov.au/parlInfo/ search/display/display.w3p;query=Id%3A%22chamber%2Fhansardr% 2F2010-05-13%2F0150%22. Consulted 17 August 2013.

—— 2010. *Debates*. 1 June: 4747. URL: http://parlinfo.aph.gov.au/parlInfo/ search/display/display.w3p;query=Id%3A%22chamber%2Fhansardr% 2F2010-06-01%2F0023%22. Consulted 15 August 2013.

—— 2010. *Debates*. 3 June: 5219. URL: http://parlinfo.aph.gov.au/parlInfo/ search/display/display.w3p;query=Id%3A%22chamber%2Fhansardr% 2F2010-06-03%2F0086%22. Consulted 15 August 2013.

—— 2010. *Debates*. 15 June: 5304. URL: http://parlinfo.aph.gov.au/parlInfo/ search/display/display.w3p;query=Id%3A%22chamber%2Fhansardr% 2F2010-06-15%2F0016%22. Consulted 15 August 2013.

—— 2011. *Debates*. 11 May: 3607. URL: http://parlinfo.aph.gov.au/parlInfo/search/display/display.w3p;query=Id%3A%22chamber%2Fhansardr%2Fec6 310df-bafa-4bec-a4a5-53f05d4fef3e%2F0115%22. Consulted 11 August 2013.

—— 2011. *Debates*. 12 May: 3905. URL: http://parlinfo.aph.gov.au/parlInfo/search/display/display.w3p;query=Id%3A%22chamber%2Fhansardr%2Ff4bf7791-17d5-4b7a-b906-c3b3ab0f734a%2F0217%22. Consulted 4 August 2013.

—— 2012. *Debates*. 9 May: 4335. URL: http://parlinfo.aph.gov.au/parlInfo/search/display/display.w3p;query=Id%3A%22chamber%2Fhansardr%2Ffd ab017b-97a3-4480-a3f7-e214d5c068b2%2F0118%22. Consulted 31 July 2013.

—— 2012. *Debates*. 30 October: 12546. URL: http://parlinfo.aph.gov.au/parlInfo/search/display/display.w3p;query=Id%3A%22chamber%2Fhansa rdr%2Ff3460e8f-bde4-4fc5-8d67-52fdc5190016%2F0081%22. Consulted 6 August 2013.

—— 2012. *Debates*. 30 October: 12547. URL: http://parlinfo.aph.gov.au/parlInfo/search/display/display.w3p;query=Id%3A%22chamber%2Fhansa rdr%2Ff3460e8f-bde4-4fc5-8d67-52fdc5190016%2F0084%22. Consulted 6 August 2013.

Howard, J. 2001a. Transcript of the Prime Minister the Hon. John Howard MP address at the 500 Club luncheon, Perth. *PM Transcripts*. 11 April. URL: http://pmtranscripts.dpmc.gov.au/browse.php?did=12292. Consulted 25 August 2013.

—— 2001b. Transcript of the Prime Minister the Hon. John Howard MP interview with Georgie Gardener and Mark Beretta, *Seven Sunrise*. *PM Transcripts*. 23 May. URL: http://pmtranscripts.dpmc.gov.au/browse.php?did=11941. Consulted 25 August 2013.

—— 2001c. Transcript of the Prime Minister the Hon. John Howard MP press conference, Parliament House. *PM Transcripts*. 5 October. URL: http://pmtranscripts.dpmc.gov.au/browse.php?did=12065. Consulted 25 August 2013.

—— 2001d. Transcript of the Prime Minister the Hon. John Howard MP press conference, Sydney. *PM Transcripts*. 2 October. URL: http://pmtranscripts.dpmc.gov.au/browse.php?did=11906. Consulted 25 August 2013.

—— 2001e. Transcript of the Prime Minister the Hon. John Howard MP questions and answers at the National Press Club, Canberra. *PM Transcripts*. 8 November. URL: http://pmtranscripts.dpmc.gov.au/browse.php?did=12447. Consulted 26 August 2013.

—— 2001f. Transcript of the Prime Minister the Hon. John Howard MP television interview with Kerry O'Brien *7:30 Report*, ABC. *PM Transcripts*. 5 October. URL: http://pmtranscripts.dpmc.gov.au/browse.php?did=12067. Consulted 25 August 2013.

Joyce, Y. 2013. Single mothers need education, not welfare cuts. *The Conversation* 1 April.

Kenny, M. 2013. One in four reject uni cuts to pay for Gonski reforms. *Sydney Morning Herald* 3 June.

Represe, J. 2013. Interview with Leon Byner. URL: http://capitalmonitor.com.au/LeftMenu.aspx. Consulted 8 September 2013.

Reserve Bank of Australia 2002. Government finance: Statistical tables. URL: http://www.rba.gov.au/statistics/tables/index.html#govt_finance. Consulted 19 August 2013.

Seccombe, M. 2012. Surplus to requirements. *Global Mail* 16 March.

7.30 Report 2002, television program, ABC, 14 May.

Skinner, Q. 2002a. *Visions of politics: Volume I*. Cambridge: Cambridge University Press.

—— 2002b. *Visions of politics: Volume II*. Cambridge: Cambridge University Press.

Swan, W. 2008. Budget 2008–09. Transcript. 13 May. URL: http://www.budget.gov.au/2008-09/content/speech/html/speech-01.htm. Consulted 19 August 2013.

——2010a. Doorstop interview. Transcript. *Treasury Portfolio Ministers*. 30 June. URL: http://ministers.treasury.gov.au/DisplayDocs.aspx?doc=transcripts/2010/086.htm&pageID=011&min=wms&Year=2010&DocType=2. Consulted 22 August 2013.

—— 2010b. Interview with John Stanley and Sandy Aloisi. Transcript. 1 July. URL: http://searcha.beta.capmon.com/pdfdisplay/data/repository/pressrel/p100701293.pdf. Consulted 4 September 2013.

—— 2011a. The 2011 budget and a tale of two booms. Address to the Queensland Media Club, Brisbane 20 April. URL: http://ministers.treasury.gov.au/DisplayDocs.aspx?doc=speeches/2011/010.htm&pageID=010&min=wms&Year=2011&DocType=1. Consulted 7 August 2013.

———— 2011b. The impact of the floods on our patchwork economy. Address to the CEO Institute (Queensland), Brisbane 28 January. URL: http://ministers. treasury.gov.au/DisplayDocs.aspx?doc=speeches/2011/001.htm&pageID=01 0&min=wms&Year=2011&DocType=1. Consulted 31 July 2013.

———— 2012a. Mid-year economic and fiscal outlook. n.d. URL: http://ministers. treasury.gov.au/DisplayDocs.aspx?doc=pressreleases/2012/099.htm&pageID =003&min=wms&Year=2012&DocType=0. Consulted 11 August 2013.

———— 2012b. Press conference: MYEFO. n.d. URL: http://ministers.treasury.gov. au/DisplayDocs.aspx?doc=transcripts/2012/106.htm&pageID=011&min=w ms&Year=2012&DocType=2. Consulted 31 July 2013.

———— 2012c. The budget and the fair go in the Asian Century. Address to the National Press Club, Canberra. n.d. URL: http://ministers.treasury.gov.au/ DisplayDocs.aspx?doc=speeches/2012/010.htm&pageID=010&min=wms& Year=2012&DocType=1. Consulted 30 July 2013.

Universities Australia 2013. Multi-billion dollar university budget hit the biggest since the 1990s. n.d. URL: http://capitalmonitor.com.au/LeftMenu. aspx. Consulted 7 September 2013.

Walter, R. and Uhr, J. 2013. Budget talk: Rhetorical constraints and contests. *Australian Journal of Political Science* 48(4): 1–14.

White, G. 2012. Budget surplus: Economic or political imperative? *The Drum* 2 April.

Wines, G. and Scarborough, H. 2006. Behind the headlines: An analysis of Australian commonwealth, state and territory budget balance numbers. *Accounting, Accountability and Performance* 12(2): 82–122.

Wong, P. 2011a. CEDA 2011 economic and political overview. URL: http://www. financeminister.gov.au/speeches/2011/sp_180211.html. Consulted 1 August 2013.

———— 2011b. ORD Minnett post budget luncheon. n.d. URL: http://www. financeminister.gov.au/speeches/2011/sp_130511.html. Consulted 7 August 2013.

———— 2011c. Per CAPITA public forum. n.d. URL: http://www.financeminister. gov.au/speeches/2011/sp_030511.html. Consulted 1 August 2013.

———— 2012a. ABC 7:30 with Chris Uhlmann. Transcript. *Senator Penny Wong*. 20 December. URL: http://www.pennywong.com.au/transcripts/abc-730-with-chris-uhlmann/. Consulted 7 August 2013.

—— 2012b, ABC AM with Alexandra Kirk. Transcript. *Senator Penny Wong*. 22 October. URL: http://www.pennywong.com.au/transcripts/abc-am-with-alexandra-kirk/. Consulted 31 July 2013.

—— 2012c. ABC PM with Sabra Lane. Transcript. *Senator Penny Wong*. 22 October. URL: http://www.pennywong.com.au/transcripts/abc-pm-with-sabra-lane/. Consulted 4 August 2013.

—— 2012d. Sky Australian agenda with Peter van Onselen and Judith Sloan. Transcript. *Senator Penny Wong*. 21 October. URL: http://www.pennywong.com.au/transcripts/sky-australian-agenda-with-peter-van-onselen-and-judith-sloan/. Consulted 30 July 2013.

3. Leaders and legitimacy: Lessons from two Labor leadership transitions

Jennifer Rayner

In modern Australian political history, few events have generated as much comment and controversy as the sacking of first-term prime minister Kevin Rudd. With its dramatic mid-winter setting and colourful cast of conspirators, Rudd's replacement by his then-deputy, Julia Gillard, captured the public imagination in a way that few other political events have since the Dismissal.

The level of public, media and scholarly attention paid to this event is perhaps not surprising, given at that time only one other Labor prime minister — Bob Hawke — had ever been forced from the party's leadership while still occupying the Lodge. The circumstances surrounding his 1991 replacement by Paul Keating bear many similarities to the more recent political drama: an acrimonious leadership tussle between a popular prime minister and his ambitious deputy, significant global financial uncertainty, and a re-energised and outwardly disciplined Opposition on the attack. Yet the two cases are also distinctly different, as Keating was able to quickly put the leadership issue behind him and move forward to govern for four more years. By contrast, Gillard struggled to shake off questions about her leadership and establish clear authority for her government, before ultimately succumbing to the same party processes that had elevated her to the prime ministership in the first place.

Why was this so? Some have suggested that Gillard's problems have their roots in discomfort with her gender (Hall and Donaghue 2012), or the presidential-style election campaign of 2007, which fostered an extreme attachment to Rudd within the Australian electorate (Robinson and Lowe 2012). As Gillard has acknowledged, these factors undoubtedly played some role in the public's response to her as prime minister (Gillard 2013). Close examination of these two cases also demonstrates, however, that there were significant differences in the rhetoric used to communicate and justify these leadership changes to the Australian people, offering an alternative explanation for the origins of Gillard's legitimacy deficit.

As authors such as Christopher Hood (2004), David Zarefsky (2004) and Ronald Krebs and Patrick Jackson (2007) acknowledge, rhetoric is more than verbal window dressing: the way in which public actors describe and define their actions is vital in shaping how the public understands them. Rhetoric constructs meaning by linking real-world events to abstract norms or ideals, providing a context and a set of criteria for evaluating such events, and closing off alternative narratives or explanations (Nelson 2004). It is a form of 'persuasive speech' and therefore a 'formidable means of wielding power' (Kane and Patapan 2010). Given its ability to shape public perceptions and mould the public narrative about politics, rhetoric has a direct relationship with political legitimacy, which David Beetham suggests rests upon:

> the degree of congruence, or lack of it, between a given system of power and the beliefs, values and expectations that provide its justification … When we seek to assess the legitimacy of a regime, a political system, or some other power relation, one thing we are doing is assessing how far it can be justified in terms of people's beliefs, how far it conforms to their values or standards, how far it satisfies the normative explanations they have of it. (1991: 11)

In other words, political legitimacy depends — at least in part — upon the public's perception that the exercise of power is 'desirable, proper, or appropriate within some socially constructed system of norms, values, beliefs and definitions' (Suchman 1995: 574). A political leader may possess extensive formal powers and have a range of coercive means at their disposal, but to lead effectively they must also 'convince everyone else that they "deserve" to rule and make decisions that influence the quality of everyone's lives … authorities find governance easier and more effective when a feeling that they are entitled to rule is widespread within the population' (Tyler 2006: 377). As rhetoric is an important tool for constructing and maintaining this perceived right to rule, it should therefore be seen as a fundamental building block of political legitimacy itself.

This chapter explores how Keating and Gillard explained the decision to sack a sitting prime minister and worked to convince the public of their entitlement to the nation's highest elected office. These two events serve as a useful case study because the sudden removal of one leader and their replacement by another would usually be expected to trigger some crisis of legitimacy, but this only appears to have happened in the case of the 2010 leadership spill. The differing fortunes of these two replacement leaders were significantly influenced by differences in rhetoric both leading up to, and at the time of, these leadership transitions. Specifically, where the rhetoric of Keating's rise served to legitimate him as replacement prime minister from the moment of his elevation to the top job, the rhetoric of Gillard's ascension gave the public multiple reasons to question her right to the role.[1]

---

1   The rhetoric surrounding Gillard's 2013 deposition by Rudd is not discussed here as, at the time of writing, these events were very much still unfolding.

A tale of two transitions

The background to the sackings of Hawke and Rudd has been extensively canvassed in both popular and academic works, but it is worth briefly recapping these events to emphasise the parallels between these cases.[2] Hawke was the Labor hero who returned his party to government in 1983 after the collapse of Gough Whitlam's government and the ensuing eight years of conservative rule, and went on to become Australia's longest-serving Labor prime minister. Throughout his eight years in office Hawke led an ambitious agenda of economic reform, which was primarily conceived and driven by his Treasurer, Paul Keating (Mitchell and Bassanese 2003). The combination of Hawke's populist appeal and Keating's policy nous was hailed as one of the great pairings of modern Australian politics, but it was always balanced on Keating's ambition to be prime minister and the personal tensions this created between the two (Hawke 1994). On two occasions — in 1980 and 1988 — Hawke reportedly promised to hand the leadership over to Keating at an agreed time, but reneged on both deals because he believed that Keating lacked electoral appeal and put policy purity above the interests of working people (Australian Broadcasting Corporation (ABC) 1993: episode 4). Fed up with waiting, Keating launched his first challenge at a meeting of the Australian Labor Party (ALP) Caucus on 3 June 1991, but lost the ballot and spent the next six months on the backbench while a series of political missteps caused Hawke's authority as leader to ebb away (Edwards 1996). On 19 December 1991 Keating mounted a second challenge, and this time defeated Hawke to become Australia's 24th prime minister.

Like Hawke, Rudd was hailed as Labor's messiah after bringing an end to the era of John Howard's conservative government at the 2007 election. 'Kevin 07' and Hawke share the distinction of having the highest personal approval ratings ever recorded by Newspoll (Coorey 2009) and, like Hawke, Rudd embarked on an ambitious reform agenda which encompassed major health, education, Indigenous, environment and communications initiatives. Unlike Hawke, however, Rudd came to Labor politics without a connection to the union movement or the party's factions, and relied on a unity ticket with his deputy, Gillard, to secure Caucus support for his leadership (Wanna 2007). Throughout 2008 and 2009 issues emerged with the implementation of Labor's complex policy agenda, and this led to a decline in both polled support for the party, and Rudd's personal popularity (Stuart 2010). Concerns about the party's electability under Rudd eventually caused members of the ALP's right faction to withdraw

---

2   For more detailed accounts see d'Alpuget 2010; Hawke 1994; Carew 1992; Edwards 1996; Tanner 2012; McKew 2012; Gordon 1993; Stuart 2010.

their support for his leadership, and precipitated a formal challenge by Gillard on 23 June 2010 (Coorey 2010). Caucus elected Gillard unopposed and she was sworn in as Australia's first female prime minister on 24 June 2010.

It is indisputable that, on both occasions, the Labor party had the formal power to replace its leader, and that this process was carried out according to established Australian parliamentary convention. It is also true, however, that replacing the nation's highest elected official with little more than a show of hands behind closed doors is an exceptional and contentious move, and one that raised questions about the legitimacy of the replacement leader. The following sections explore three key differences in the rhetoric of these transitions, which may have shaped the perceptions of Keating and Gillard as prime ministers: their prior discussion of desire for the role, their explanation of the reasons for taking it, and the response from the leaders they deposed.

Who wants to be prime minister?

The first, and perhaps most critical, difference in rhetoric surrounding these transitions was that, where Keating explicitly positioned himself as an alternative prime minister over a period of years leading up to his eventual challenge, Gillard consistently denied that the leadership of her party needed to change — or that she wanted Rudd's job — right up until the evening she replaced him.

Almost since entering the Parliament in 1969, Keating was identified as a potential future prime minister, with big ambitions and a big ego to match (Carew 1992: 2–3). At various points throughout the Labor government's first four terms in office (1983–1990) there were suggestions of an orderly transfer of leadership from Hawke to Keating (Gordon 1993: 76–77; Mills 1993: 214), but as the 1990s unfolded without any sign from the incumbent that he would willingly step aside, Keating began a more active public campaign laying out his claim to the job. This rested upon two pillars. The first was his possession of a big vision for Australia and the capacity to make hard decisions to see it implemented, characteristics that he implied Hawke no longer possessed. The second was the fact that Hawke had publicly anointed him as his successor and privately agreed to hand over the leadership after the 1990 election.

Keating launched the first of these narratives in his leaked speech to the National Press Club in 1990.[3] Supposedly delivered off the cuff and in an emotional moment following the sudden death of the head of Treasury, Chris Higgins,

---

3   For a more detailed discussion of this speech and its impact see Carew 1992; Gordon 1993.

the speech was loaded with such persuasive and evocative language about his vision for Australia and the nature of leadership that it came across as a public application for the nation's highest office. Keating stated:

> I think we can do a lot of things better in Australia. Even though this government is ten years old, it's still only scratching the surface of the enormous changes I think Australians will accept and which Australians will embrace … we're now gathering our pace and we're gathering our people in, and we're a more interesting society and we're well placed in the world. So we have this chance to pull Australia into one of the preferred countries of the nineties and beyond. We really do have this opportunity; it's not beyond us. (1990)

Keating explicitly emphasised that his vision went beyond securing the economic future of Australia — the task that had occupied him as Treasurer — and encompassed nothing less than the creation of a wholly modern, wholly independent nation 'that can truly be the envy of the world'. Moving to the question of how Australia would seize the opportunities of this bright new decade, Keating argued:

> It just requires a national will and a national leadership to have a go and do it … leadership is not about being popular. It's about being right and being strong. And it's not whether you go through some shopping centre, tripping over the TV crews' cords. It's about doing what you think the nation requires, making profound judgements about profound issues. (1990)

With this speech, Keating subtly countered long-running suggestions from Hawke and others that he lacked the breadth of vision required from a national leader (Edwards 1996: 391–92). He also presented himself as someone champing at the bit to make that vision a reality, in implied contrast with the ageing Hawke. Furthermore, although Keating never explicitly mentioned Hawke in the speech, his description of the necessary characteristics for leadership clearly favoured himself as someone willing to make 'profound judgements about profound issues', compared with the populist Hawke shaking hands in shopping centres. Similarly, he undermined Hawke's major remaining claim to the prime ministership — his enormous personal popularity — by unfavourably contrasting being popular with 'being right and being strong'. Although Keating subsequently denied that he intended the speech to be a direct challenge to Hawke's leadership, he clearly fired the opening salvo in what turned out to be a year-long march towards the Lodge.

In the lead-up to Keating's first challenge to Hawke in June 1991, he also gave an exclusive live interview on Laurie Oakes's *Sunday* program, during which he returned to the key themes of the Press Club speech and explicitly stated that he could offer renewed leadership in neglected areas such as foreign policy, superannuation and the future design of Australia's cities (Carew 1992: 292). He took pains to frame his challenge to Hawke in terms of the national interest, rather than his personal interest, saying:

> I don't resile from the fact that I have personal ambitions but they're nothing like the ambitions I have for Australia. It is the ambitions I've always had for Australia that have kept me running and they still do. I think, obviously, I think I can provide better government. That is, in terms of direction, strategy, *esprit de corps*, enthusiasm and, dare I say it, where necessary, a touch of excitement. (1991a)

In the interview, Keating also emphasised the second of his claims to the prime minister's role: the fact that Hawke himself had promised to hand it over to him in the now-public Kirribilli agreement of 1988:

> I made arrangements with Bob ... for a smooth, effective, sympathetic transition of both leadership and power within the party and to continue to regenerate ideas for the government, and that's what I was hoping would be the case.

The subtext of this interview was the same as that of the Press Club speech: Keating was the man for the future, a new leader for a new decade. This time, however, the contrast with Hawke was overt rather than implied, as Keating outlined the ways he would provide 'better government' and highlighted Hawke's concurrence with the idea of a need for regeneration at the top of the government, as evidenced by the Kirribilli agreement. Collectively, these rhetorical efforts fostered a perception that Keating had a right to lead on the grounds of both expertise and fairness — two criteria that are argued to be important underpinnings of leadership legitimacy (Tost 2010). Significantly, too, this foundation for legitimacy was laid long before Keating actually seized the prime ministership.

By contrast, some of the most vivid and engaging rhetoric employed by Gillard during her political career was used to downplay suggestions that Rudd's leadership was under threat and deny that she had any personal designs on the prime minister's office. As deputy prime minister during the period of Rudd's declining popularity, media speculation naturally turned to Gillard's intentions and the possibility of a challenge to restore the ALP's fortunes. While she initially batted away this speculation with the standard lines about being happy in her current role and having plenty of challenges to meet as deputy, when the speculation showed no sign of dying down, she began to resort to more colourful characterisations.

In a Sydney radio interview in early May 2010, Gillard denied that there were any moves afoot to replace Rudd, and made an unqualified commitment that she would not be in the prime minister's role by the time of the forthcoming federal election:

> Gillard: I'll make the following comments. I always expected that this year as we came into election day we would have a tough, close contest … so I'm happy to go into that tough, close contest, side by side with Kevin Rudd …
>
> Interviewer: So will you promise you will not be leader at the next federal election?
>
> Gillard: I can, completely. Neil, this is, you know, it makes good copy for newspapers but it is not within cooee of my day to day reality. You may as well ask me am I anticipating a trip to Mars. No, I'm not, Neil.
>
> Interviewer: After the next election? There's nothing wrong with ambition.
>
> Gillard: I'm ambitious to continue as Deputy Prime Minister doing some very special portfolios I absolutely love.
>
> (Gillard 2010a)

In three separate interviews that month Gillard reiterated this position with increasing exasperation, telling interviewers:

> This is all silly hypotheticals. I mean, if Steven Spielberg rang me from Hollywood and asked me to star opposite Brad Pitt in a movie, would I do it? Well, I'd be a little bit tempted. But you know what, I don't reckon Steven Spielberg is going to give me a call. So there's no point worrying about these sorts of hypotheticals. No-one is talking about it so let's not talk about all these fanciful things …
>
> (Gillard 2010b)
>
> There's more chance of me going round the world sailing solo a dozen times than this chatter in the media becoming anything more than that.
>
> (Gillard 2010c)
>
> There's more chance of me becoming the full-forward for the Dogs than there is any change in the Labor Party.
>
> (Gillard 2010d)

Gillard's rhetoric went far beyond simply denying that a leadership challenge was ahead; it framed the concept as fanciful and poured scorn on the very idea of her becoming prime minister, making this appear to be a ridiculous proposition. Furthermore, the strong and emphatic nature of her statements — particularly her promise that she would not lead the party to the 2010 election — implicitly established a bond of trust between herself and the electorate. In essence, Gillard's language 'painted her into a credibility corner' (Counihan 2010) where any course of action other than remaining as Rudd's deputy would represent a breach of that bond.

Trust is central to political legitimacy (Ruscio 1996) and Margaret Levi (1998) notes that the major means by which political leaders establish their trustworthiness are proven character, demonstrated consistency and encapsulated interest: 'The first requires a presentation of the self that includes a demonstrated willingness to act for principle and against self-interest. Consistency is an indicative measure of trustworthiness, based on the track record of the actor', while encapsulated interest is the willingness of a political actor 'to honour her agreements or to act according to a certain standard' (Levi 1998: 86). Gillard's rhetoric throughout May 2010 conveyed a strong sense that she was willing to put her party and the public interest ahead of her own self-interest. When she then challenged Rudd for the prime ministership, just weeks after making these strong statements of support, she revealed that she lacked consistency and was not, in fact, willing to honour her past commitments. By breaching the public's trust so flagrantly, Gillard demonstrated that she lacked the key quality of trustworthiness, and so placed a significant question mark over the legitimacy of her leadership. While much has been made of her violation of trust over the introduction of a carbon tax, I argue that this initial breach was more significant because it represented the first major fracture in the public's perception of her character.

In short, Keating's rhetoric in the period preceding his challenge to Hawke firmly positioned him as a prime minister-in-waiting with a strong right to lead. By loudly publicising his vision and energy, along with his status as Hawke's chosen successor, Keating laid a strong foundation for his leadership well before he came to office. By contrast, Gillard not only failed to prepare the ground for her leadership in any useful way, she actively discarded one of the critical tools she would need for a successful transition — trust — by emphatically telling the public one thing and then doing the opposite.

Cometh the hour, cometh the (wo)man

Having positioned themselves differently for the impending leadership transitions, Keating and Gillard also diverged significantly in their rhetoric at the moment of their respective ascensions. A comparison of their speeches as prime minister indicates that Keating symbolically embraced his new role from the first moment, while Gillard was more tentative about staking her claim to the nation's top job. Furthermore, where Keating was unapologetic about challenging Hawke for the leadership, and again drew on the language of generational renewal to explain his actions, Gillard presented herself as a reticent conscript to the role, one spurred into action only because the Rudd government had 'lost its way'.

Speaking to the Canberra press gallery immediately after winning the party room ballot, Keating briefly paid tribute to Hawke before launching into a direct dialogue with the Australian electorate. He began:

> In my first words as Prime Minister-elect to you, the Australian people, I want to make three commitments. The first is I pledge to give everything I've got to the job and the country. The second is to deal honestly with the people, to tell them the truth. In tough times the temptation is always to gild the lily. I'll be resisting that temptation as much as possible. I'll speak honestly with them, realistically, and I'll listen accordingly. The third commitment is that I pledge to fight the battle against unemployment and for economic recovery with all the energy I can muster. (1991b)

In the space of a single paragraph, Keating explicitly claimed the mantle of prime minister and set the tone for his leadership: frank, focused, pulling no punches. By addressing himself directly to 'the Australian people', describing himself as the 'Prime Minister-elect' and making a series of commitments about his dedication and commitment to serve, he subtly mirrored the traditional tropes of an election-night victory speech and so presented himself in the triumphant-yet-humble mould of a newly elected leader. This language dispels from the outset any suggestion that Keating was less than a rightful prime minister.

In driving home his reasons for taking over the reins of leadership, Keating reiterated the themes that had formed the basis of his claim since his 1990 speech to the Press Club:

> This period gives us great opportunities and the '90s hold for Australia very great promise indeed … I believe the Australian people are looking both for hope and direction for the 1990s and this country can be in a very good position in the 1990s, notwithstanding the fact we've got a recession … We can be well set up in the 1990s and I believe I can play a role in that and that's why I believe that I will serve the Labor Party well. (Keating 1991b)

Keating's invocation of 'hope and direction' is a direct reference to his earlier musings on the purpose of leadership and highlights his emphasis on leading from the front; in implied contrast with Hawke's famously consensual, populist leadership style. His repeated invocation of 'the 1990s' further serves to underline his focus on the times ahead and so solidifies the self-perpetuated account of him as a leader for the future, while also drawing a symbolic line under Hawke's leadership, which belonged to the previous decade. In case his audience was in any way unclear about Keating's intention to move beyond Hawke's legacy and forge his own path, the new prime minister went on to state this explicitly:

> Bob and I conducted a government which contained two leaders. And we worked as a good team for a very long period of time … but, time tells … I think that the need for policy shifts, that dexterity I mentioned earlier, and generational change is important. I think it is important for a political party to change itself. (Keating 1991b)

This statement also served a useful purpose in subtly reminding listeners of Keating's other significant claim to the prime ministership: his status as Hawke's chosen successor. While he did not explicitly invoke the Kirribilli agreement or Hawke's past commitments to him, the interlinked references to his partnership with Hawke and 'generational change' implicitly frame the transition in this light.

In all, the overwhelming impression conveyed by Keating's first speech as Prime Minister is that he was firmly in control of the ship of state and had already begun steering it on a new course, which had long been charted in his mind. Keating's rhetoric brooked no challenge to his right to lead and acknowledged no doubt that the moment called for a leader such as him. And so, by appearing as a legitimate prime minister, Keating became one.

By contrast, Gillard's first speech after accepting her party's nomination as prime minister offered a qualified account of her claim to the job and raised significant questions about both her commitment and capacity to lead. The speech appears designed to head off criticism about Rudd's deposition and minimise perceptions that Gillard had acted dishonourably or disloyally, but by directly acknowledging these negatives, Gillard inadvertently gave them weight and credibility.

In contrast with Keating's bold opening, Gillard started her speech by saying:

> It's with the greatest humility, resolve and enthusiasm that I sought the endorsement of my colleagues to be the Labor leader and to be the Prime Minister of this country. I have accepted that endorsement. I am truly honoured to lead this country which I love. (2010e)

She went on to give an extended outline of her guiding beliefs in education, family, hard work and fairness before stating:

> It is these beliefs that have been my compass during the 3.5 years of the most loyal service I could offer to my colleague, Kevin Rudd. I asked my colleagues to make a leadership change because I believed that a good government was losing its way … I love this country and I was not going to sit idly by and watch an incoming opposition cut education, cut health and smash rights at work. My values and my beliefs have driven me to step forward to take this position as Prime Minister. (2010e)

Where the public may have expected to see Gillard trumpet her historic status as Australia's first female prime minister, in fact her opening remarks framed the leadership transition primarily as a changing of personnel within the Labor Party, with the associated change in the nation's leadership presented more as a necessary consequence of this than the purpose of the exercise. Furthermore, her eagerness to share the responsibility for replacing Rudd with the parliamentary caucus, and her reticence to directly describe herself as the prime minister, conveyed the impression that Gillard felt uneasy about the manner of her rise.

Gillard's statement that she had provided 'loyal service' to Rudd but could not 'sit idly by' and watch the government lose its way was clearly intended to create a narrative bridge between her statements of the preceding months and her actions on the evening of the challenge. It invited her audience to believe that she had been genuine in her support for Rudd up to some unspecified tipping point, and asked them to see her as a dutiful, capable foot soldier stepping forward with a heavy heart to take the reins from a floundering commander. In reality, however, her remarks served to emphasise both the brief nature of Rudd's tenure as leader and her prominent role in the government that had 'lost its way'. Gillard acknowledged this latter point a moment later in saying:

> I take my fair share of responsibility for the Rudd Government's record, for our important achievements and errors made. I know the Rudd Government did not do all it said it would do. And at times, it went off track. (2010e)

Although perhaps intended to portray Gillard as humble and realistic about the government's failings, this statement invited unflattering questions about her own fitness for the leadership for, if she was part of the problem, how could she be trusted to lead the search for solutions? And, if she had been there, working alongside Rudd while mistakes were made, why did he have to leave while she got to lead? The remainder of Gillard's speech offered no answer to these questions, leaving them to fester in the minds of the Australian public.

While Gillard's first comments failed to strike a confident or persuasive note, these rhetorical failings were hardly fatal. It could be argued, however, that her next remarks proved to be, because they explicitly linked the legitimacy of her leadership to the upcoming federal election result. Gillard stated:

> I also certainly acknowledge that I have not been elected Prime Minister by the Australian people. And in the coming months I will ask the Governor-General to call for a general election so that the Australian people can exercise their birthright to choose their Prime Minister. Between now and this election, I seek their consideration and support. (2010e)

This is a curious statement from a prime minister-elect, as there is nothing in Australia's system of parliamentary democracy which requires that leaders be elected by 'the people', nor does any mechanism exist for them to actually exercise what Gillard calls 'their birthright' — two facts of which she would have been undoubtedly aware. Her remarks appear calculated to head off public criticism about the secretive and autocratic manner of Rudd's removal by emphasising her commitment to democratic ideals. They are also a direct response to Rudd's assertions about the illegitimacy of her challenge (discussed below). By promoting this inaccurate characterisation of a prime ministerial mandate as deriving from the people, and specifically describing herself as an unelected leader, Gillard in fact implied what many in her audience may have been thinking: that she did not have a rightful claim to the role. Furthermore, by emphasising the importance of elections in conferring such a rightful claim, Gillard implicitly positioned her leadership as contingent upon winning that poll. This was underlined by her commitment — under questioning from the media — not to move into the Lodge until she had been elected in her own right, as she stated: 'I believe it is appropriate for me to stay [in Melbourne] until we have an election and I have fulsomely earned the trust of the Australian people to be prime minister.' (2010e)

In other words, Gillard eschewed the language of parliamentary democracy — which would have provided a ready-made rationale for the challenge and her leadership — in favour of appeals to direct, popular democracy. This may not have posed a lasting problem if she had indeed won the 2010 poll outright, but given the election resulted in Australia's first hung parliament and minority government since the 1940s, this decision arguably created a fundamental and enduring weakness at the core of Gillard's prime ministership. Some have gone so far as to suggest that the low level of support for Labor at the 2010 election can be interpreted as an attempt by the voters of Australia to deny Gillard the win she needed to truly legitimate her leadership (Thampapillai 2010).

As though explicitly linking the legitimacy of her leadership to an electoral mandate was not problematic enough, Gillard also used this first speech to commit herself to solving a number of specific problems that had arisen during the Rudd administration. These ranged across some of the policy areas most closely associated with Rudd's 2007 election pitch for office, and included: 'establish[ing] a community consensus for action' on climate change, negotiating 'a fairer share of our inheritance, the mineral wealth that lies in our grounds', and 'bringing the Budget back in surplus'. Although praising Rudd, Gillard distinguished herself from him as a leader who would prioritise results over rhetoric in these areas, saying: 'Ultimately, Kevin and I disagreed about the direction of the government. I believed we needed to do better' (Gillard 2010e). By singling out these areas of high-profile policy failure, Gillard presumably intended to underline why a change of leadership was necessary and set out her immediate priorities for action in the months ahead. In specifically committing to succeed where Rudd had failed, however, Gillard made her leadership contingent upon 'doing better' than the former prime minister. As Gillard should have realised, the danger of linking her claim to the role to an ability to deliver better policy outcomes was that any perceived failure to do so would implicitly diminish her right to lead. This is arguably what happened throughout 2011 and 2012, and helps to explain why Gillard's policy stumbles almost always led to speculation about the security of her leadership during her term as prime minister (see, for example, Pearson 2011; Taylor 2012).

Comparing Keating's and Gillard's first speeches as prime minister reveals that the two could not be more different in their tone, content, symbolism and subtext. Keating's was clearly a victory speech — one delivered by a man who had long worked to demonstrate his credentials to be prime minister, who believed in the strength of his claim to the role, and who was impatient to begin wielding the power that was rightfully his. Keating's rhetoric left no room for doubt or ambiguity about the fitness of his rise to the nation's highest elected office, and so helped him to appear as a legitimate leader from the first moment of his prime ministership. By contrast, Gillard's speech was part justification, part apology and part bargain. It raised unanswered questions about her right to lead and shackled her fate to a range of events beyond her direct control and, in doing so, fostered an enduring legitimacy deficit which dogged her to the end. It must be assumed that this was the unintended result of poor rhetorical choices and a lack of strategic foresight, rather than a deliberate effort by Gillard, for it seems unlikely that any leader would wilfully hobble their own fortunes as comprehensively as she appears to have done.

The view of the vanquished

Finally, examination of the rhetoric of the two leaders who were deposed by Keating and Gillard indicates how their accounts of these events boosted or diminished the legitimacy of their successors. For the most part, Hawke and Rudd stuck closely to the script expected of former leaders — thanking their colleagues and the nation for the opportunity to serve, highlighting their achievements, and wishing the new leader well (see, for example, ABC 1993; Mills 1993: 288–95; Rudd 2010b). They diverged specifically and significantly, however, in their language describing the party room challenge against them: Hawke professed to respect his colleagues' judgement and the validity of their decision to change leaders, while Rudd denied his party's right to do so by invoking the idea of a popular mandate. Where Hawke's rhetoric supported Keating's perceived right to lead, Rudd's effectively (and presumably deliberately) undercut Gillard's efforts to establish herself as his legitimate replacement.

In the immediate aftermath of his sacking, Hawke declined to comment on the leadership spill and focused instead on cementing his legacy as 'a bloke who loved his country, still does, and loves Australians, and who was not essentially changed by high office' (Mills 1993: 294). He broke his silence in a broadcast television interview some weeks later however, telling the nation that he was 'hurt' by his colleagues' decision to replace him, but that they would not find him criticising them for doing so:

> Interviewer: Was the action in dumping you, fair?
>
> Hawke: Well, the Caucus has always got the right to make the decision about leadership. They have always got that right.
>
> Interviewer: I didn't ask you about right though — fair.
>
> Hawke: Well, whether people exercise — if people have a right, you can hardly say that they shouldn't exercise it. I have thoughts about how it was done ... [but] I don't think right now is the time to open up on that.
>
> Interviewer: Well, was it a just decision?
>
> Hawke: Well, in politics, in the end, it's numbers that count ... it was very tight, but in the end, the numbers were there.
>
> (Hawke 1992)

This is an important statement because Hawke explicitly positioned his deposition in the context of Australian parliamentary convention, and emphasised that the ALP had simply exercised a long-established right. Even when pressed by the interviewer to make a distinction between the act being 'right' and 'fair', Hawke insisted that his party had acted within their powers and emphasised Keating's valid win in the party ballot process.

Hawke's magnanimity is in sharp contrast with Rudd's rhetoric on the evening of Gillard's challenge. Admittedly, Rudd was speaking in the heat of the moment rather than with the benefit of time for reflection, but his strident remarks framed the change of leadership as a direct challenge to democracy itself and a deliberate subversion of the Australian people's will. Speaking live to the nation with all the symbolic splendour of the prime minister's suite behind him, Rudd said:

> I was elected by the people of Australia as Prime Minister of Australia. I was elected to do a job, I intend to continue doing that job ... I was not elected by the factional leaders of Australia, of the Australian Labor Party, to do a job — though they may be seeking to do a job on me, that's a separate matter. The challenge therefore is to honour the mandate given to me by the Australian people. (2010a)

The suggestion that Rudd was elected by 'the people of Australia' or was in possession of a mandate given by them is a falsehood. Given Rudd's famed attention to detail, his use of such misleading rhetoric can only be seen as a deliberate attempt to frame Gillard as a usurper and delegitimise the internal party processes then underway. Rudd's relationship with the Australian electorate had always been his primary source of power — first as Opposition leader, and later as prime minister — so it is perhaps not surprising that he would fall back on this at a moment of crisis (Wilson 2013). But what is surprising is the extent to which his rhetoric appears to have influenced the following discussion of these events. Countless media organisations echoed the spirit of his remarks in describing Gillard's challenge as a 'coup', a 'putsch' and a power grab by the ALP's 'faceless men' (see, for example, Benson 2010; Kenny 2010; Rodgers 2010; Santow 2010; Coorey 2010). As previously discussed, even Gillard herself adopted Rudd's characterisation of the situation, by acknowledging that she lacked an electoral mandate and asking Australians for their forbearance until she could obtain one. Of course, he could not have anticipated that she would tie her fortunes so directly to the idea of an electoral mandate or that this would work out as poorly as it did for her. But it could certainly be argued that Rudd sowed the seeds for these later events — and so contributed to Gillard's legitimacy deficit — by effectively shaping the criteria that would be used to assess her right to lead.

Hawke and Rudd's contributions suggest that the rhetoric of the vanquished can play an important role in influencing perceptions of the victor. By presenting his sacking as a valid exercise of the party's right to choose its leader, Hawke confirmed that Keating had a legitimate claim to the prime ministership. Rudd's rhetoric achieved entirely the opposite effect as, by denying his party's right to choose in the first place, he undermined the legitimacy of their chosen leader — Gillard.

Lessons from (for?) Labor

Sacking a sitting prime minister is a rare and extreme act, and it is tempting to view such acts as isolated incidents without any wider lessons to offer. But this discussion of the Hawke/Keating and Rudd/Gillard transitions suggests that there are indeed important insights to be gained from comparing these events.

If we return to the idea that political legitimacy rests upon the public's perception that the exercise of power is 'desirable, proper, or appropriate within some socially constructed system of norms, values, beliefs and definitions' and that those in power 'deserve to rule', it is clear that the rhetoric of Keating's rise actively promoted such perceptions. By contrast, the rhetoric surrounding Gillard's ascension fostered, at best, a qualified sense of her right to the role and, at worst, outright denial that she possessed any such right. This chapter's core argument is that their differing fortunes as prime minister can be traced — at least in part — to this essential fact.

This highlights two important things about political rhetoric. Firstly, it emphasises the point that rhetoric is part of the foundation upon which political legitimacy is built. Studies of rhetoric often focus on how political leaders wield this as a persuasive tool when governing (see, for example, Masters and 't Hart 2012; Roncarolo 2005; Wood 2007), but the Keating and Gillard cases remind us that rhetoric is also critical for establishing a leader's right to govern in the first place; it is a tool for creating leadership as much as exercising it. If a political leader cannot persuade the public of their essential legitimacy, then they will lack the authority and autonomy to lead — as Gillard arguably experienced throughout her three years in office. Rhetoric builds political legitimacy and, in doing so, can help make or break political leaders.

Secondly, the Keating and Gillard cases emphasise the different outcomes that can be achieved with the calculated use of rhetoric, as compared with rhetoric that is ad hoc or inconsistent. An important factor in the success of Keating's rhetorical approach was his ability to develop a compelling and coherent message, and then deploy this consistently at key moments to build his perceived legitimacy as a replacement prime minister. Similarly, our discussion highlights how Gillard weakened her own perceived legitimacy through a lack of strategic foresight about the possible consequences of her rhetorical choices. Given that political rhetoric often forms part of an ongoing dialogue with the public, it makes sense that perceptions of legitimacy will be boosted when individual speech acts can be integrated into a broader, coherent narrative about the leader and their leadership, or diminished when it cannot. Rhetoric, then, is a tool to be wielded strategically to construct a sound foundation for leadership.

These insights come too late to be of use to former prime minister Julia Gillard, but future leadership aspirants would certainly do well to consider them. For scholars of Australian politics and the wider field of political leadership, these cases emphasise the point that rhetoric constructs political outcomes even as it seeks to explain or embellish them, and is therefore an important focus for ongoing study.

References

Australian Broadcasting Corporation (ABC) 1993. Episodes 4 and 5. *Labor in Power*. DVD. ABC Television News and Current Affairs Documentary Unit, Sydney.

Anderson, D.G. 1988. Power, rhetoric and the state: A theory of presidential legitimacy. *The Review of Politics* 50(2): 198–214.

Beetham, D. 1991. *The legitimation of power*. London: Macmillan.

Benson, S. 2010. Why a coup was on the menu for Gillard. *Daily Telegraph* 25 June: 10.

Carew, E. 1992. *Paul Keating: Prime minister*. Sydney: Allen & Unwin.

Coorey, P. 2009. The Rudd supremacy. *Sydney Morning Herald* 30 March. URL: http://www.brisbanetimes.com.au/national/the-rudd-supremacy-20090330-9g6s.html. Consulted 8 January 2013.

—— 2010. The faceless men who conspired to bring down the Prime Minister. *Sydney Morning Herald* 24 June. URL: http://www.smh.com.au/national/the-faceless-men-who-conspired-to-bring-down-the-prime-minister-20100623-yz8u.html. Consulted 2 February 2013.

Counihan, B. 2010. Gillard gets creative in ducking the leadership question. *Sydney Morning Herald* 18 May. URL: http://www.smh.com.au/federal-politics/political-opinion/gillard-gets-creative-in-ducking-the-leadership-question-20100518-va4d.html. Consulted 10 February 2013.

d'Alpuget, B. 2010. *Hawke: the prime minister*. Carlton: Melbourne University Press.

Edwards, J. 1996. *Keating: The inside story*. Ringwood: Penguin Books Australia.

Gillard, J. 2010a. Interview with Neil Mitchell. Radio 3AW 10 May. URL: http://ministers.deewr.gov.au/gillard/radio-interview-3aw. Consulted 2 August 2013.

—— 2010b. Interview with Fairfax Media 12 May. URL: http://media. nationaltimes.com.au/opinion/national-times/gillard-id-act-with-brad-but-wont-take-the-lead-1444007.html. Consulted 2 August 2013.

—— 2010c. Interview with Chris Smith. Radio 2GB 15 May. URL: http:// ministers.deewr.gov.au/gillard/radio-interview-2gb-afternoonshow. Consulted 2 August 2013.

—— 2010d. Ministerial press conference, Brisbane. 18 May. URL: http://parlinfo.aph.gov.au/parlInfo/search/display/display.w3p;adv =yes;orderBy=customrank;page=0;query=Author%3AGillard%20 Date%3A17%2F05%2F2010%20%3E%3E%2018%2F05%2F2010%20 Dataset%3Apressrel;rec=5;resCount=Default. Consulted 2 August 2013.

—— 2010e. Joint press conference with Deputy Prime Minister Wayne Swan, Parliament House, Canberra. 24 June. URL: http://pmtranscripts.dpmc.gov. au/browse.php?did=17511. Consulted 2 August 2013.

—— 2013. Statement by the former Prime Minister, the Hon. Julia Gillard. 26 June. URL: http://parlinfo.aph.gov.au/parlInfo/search/display/display.w3 p;adv=yes;orderBy=customrank;page=0;query=Author%3AGillard%20 Date%3A25%2F06%2F2013%20%3E%3E%2027%2F06%2F2013%20 Dataset%3Apressrel;rec=4;resCount=Default. Consulted 2 August 2013.

Gordon, M. 1993. *A question of leadership. Paul Keating: Political fighter*. St Lucia: University of Queensland Press.

Hall, L.J. and Donaghue, N. 2012. 'Nice girls don't carry knives': Constructions of ambition in media coverage of Australia's first female prime minister. *British Journal of Social Psychology*: 1–17.

Hawke, B. 1994. *The Hawke memoirs*. Port Melbourne: William Heinemann Ltd.

—— 1992. Interview with Mike Willesee. *A Current Affair* 6 January. URL: http:// parlinfo.aph.gov.au/parlInfo/search/display/display.w3p;adv=yes;orderB y=customrank;page=0;query=Autho rSpeakerReporter%3AHawke%20 Date%3A01%2F01%2F1992%20%3E%3E%2007%2F01%2F1992%20Da taset%3Aemms,radioprm,tvprog;rec=1;resCount=Default. Consulted 31 January 2013.

Hood, C. 2004. *The art of the state. Culture, rhetoric and public management*. 2nd edition. New York: Oxford University Press.

Kane, J. and Patapan, H. 2010. The artless art: Leadership and the limits of democratic rhetoric. *Australian Journal of Political Science* 45(3): 371–89.

Keating, P. 1990. Doing the Placido Domingo. In M. Fullilove ed. *Men and Women of Australia: our greatest modern speeches*. Milsons Point: Random House Australia.

—— 1991a. Interview with Laurie Oakes. *Sunday Program* 2 June. URL: http://parlinfo.aph.gov.au/parlInfo/search/display/display.w3p;adv=yes;orderBy=customrank;page=0;query=AuthorSpeakerReporter%3AKeating%20Date%3A01%2F06%2F1991%20%3E%3E%2003%2F06%2F1991%20Dataset%3Aemms,radioprm,tvprog;rec=8;resCount=Default. Consulted 31 January 2013.

—— 1991b. Press Conference, Parliament House, Canberra. 19 December. URL: http://pmtranscripts.dpmc.gov.au/browse.php?did=8367. Consulted 31 January 2013.

Kenny, M. 2010. A lightning and very Labor coup. *Adelaide Advertiser* 25 June: 2.

Krebs, R.R. and Jackson, P.T. 2007. Twisting tongues and twisting arms: The power of political rhetoric. *European Journal of International Relations* 13(1): 35–66.

Levi, M. 1998. A state of trust. In V.A. Braithwaite and M. Levi eds. *Trust and governance*. New York: Russell Sage Foundation.

Masters, A. and 't Hart, P. 2012. Prime ministerial rhetoric and recession politics: Meaning making in economic crisis management. *Public Administration* 90(3): 759–80.

McKew, M. 2012. *Tales from the political trenches*. Carlton: Melbourne University Press.

Mills, S. 1993. *The Hawke years: The story from the inside*. Ringwood: Viking.

Mitchell, A. and Bassanese, D. 2003. Economic reform: A barrel of thrills and spills. In S. Ryan and T. Bramston eds. *The Hawke government. A critical retrospective*. North Melbourne: Pluto Press.

Nelson, T.E. 2004. Policy goals, public rhetoric and political attitudes. *The Journal of Politics* 66(2): 581–605.

Pearson, C. 2011. Carbon tax calls Gillard's leadership into question. *Australian* 23 April: 10.

Robinson, G. and Lowe, D. 2012. Rudd's presidential politics vs Gillard's Westminster wisdom: Who will win out in the style battle? *The Conversation* 24 February.

Rodgers, E. 2010. Swan denies factions knifed Rudd. *ABC News Online* 25 June. URL: http://www.abc.net.au/news/2010-06-25/swan-denies-factions-knifed-rudd/880824. Consulted 8 February 2013.

Roncarolo, F. 2005. Campaigning and governing: An analysis of Berlusconi's rhetorical leadership. *Modern Italy* 10(1): 75–93.

Rudd, K. 2010a. Leadership challenge announcement speech, Parliament House, Canberra. 23 June. URL: http://www.adelaidenow.com.au/news/transcript-of-prime-minister-rudds-speech/story-e6frea6u-1225883458033. Consulted 2 February 2013.

—— 2010b. Farewell speech, Parliament House, Canberra. 24 June. URL: http://www.theaustralian.com.au/in-depth/full-transcript-of-kevin-rudds-farewell-speech/story-fn5vfgwx-1225883796571. Consulted 2 February 2013.

Ruscio, K.P. 1996. Trust, democracy and public management: A theoretical argument. *Journal of Public Administration Research and Theory* 6(3): 461–77.

Santow, S. 2010. Faceless men install new PM. *The World Today* 24 June.

Stuart, N. 2010. *Rudd's way. November 2007 – June 2010*. Carlton: Scribe.

Suchman, M.C. 1995. Managing legitimacy: Strategic and institutional approaches. *Academy of Management Review* 20(3): 571–610.

Tanner, L. 2012. *Politics with purpose. Occasional observations on public and private life*. Melbourne: Scribe Publications.

Taylor, L. 2012. Policy holds fate of political futures. *Newcastle Herald* 30 June: 3.

Thampapillai, D. 2010. Democratic legitimacy in the Gillard period. *Online Opinion*. URL: http://www.onlineopinion.com.au/view.asp?article=10896. Consulted 6 February 2013.

Tost, L.P. 2010. *The psychology of legitimacy: Implications for organisational leadership and change*. Durham: Duke University.

Tyler, Tom R. 2006. Psychological perspectives on legitimacy and legitimation. *Annual Review of Psychology* 57: 375–400.

Wanna, J. 2007. Political chronicles: Commonwealth of Australia July to December 2006. *Australian Journal of Politics and History* 53(2): 281–88.

Wilson, J. 2013. Kevin Rudd, celebrity and audience democracy in Australia. *Journalism: Theory, Practice & Criticism*. Online first edition 17 June 2013. URL: http://jou.sagepub.com/content/early/2013/06/13/1464884913488724. Consulted 10 July 2013.

Wood, B.D. 2007. *The politics of economic leadership: Causes and consequences of presidential rhetoric*. Princeton: Princeton University Press.

Zarefsky, D. 2004. Presidential rhetoric and the power of definition. *Presidential Studies Quarterly* 34(3): 607–19.

4. Unintended rhetoric: The 'Little children are sacred' report

Barry Hindess

Definition of Rhetoric: 1: the art of speaking or writing effectively

2.a: skill in the effective use of speech

2.b: a type or mode of language or speech; *also* insincere or grandiloquent language

(*Merriam-Webster Dictionary Online*)[1]

Aristotle's familiar conception of rhetoric as 'the faculty of observing in any given case the available means of persuasion', corresponds to the *Merriam-Webster* definitions 1 and 2.a. It suggests that rhetoric is something in which one might be trained and, after training, put to use. Rhetoric, in this understanding, carries with it a sense of intention. One employs rhetoric with the intention of setting a framework for discussion, or of persuading others to do or think something, or not to do so. The *Merriam-Webster* definition 2.b carries no such sense, except in the case of insincerity: rhetoric refers to features of the language that one uses, features that may or may not be intended. My discussion draws on these various usages, suggesting that the employment of political rhetoric may be either intended or unintended and that the latter may well be consequential.

What if the authors of a speech or report deploy means of persuasion that are so effective that, without intending to do so, an outcome is produced that is utterly remote from what they had in mind? In order to explore a small part of this question, I examine the fate of the *'Little children are sacred'* report, which was commissioned by the Northern Territory Government, but taken up and acted upon, in a manner contrary to the express advice of its authors, by the federal government in Canberra.

Australian governments operate on the principle that one should never commission a report unless one can be sure of what it is going to say — although, like many of us, they have been known to make mistakes. In the case of *'Little children are sacred'* both the NT minister who commissioned the report and its authors wanted the report to say that federal and NT governments should get off their butts and do something about sexual abuse in Indigenous communities.

---

1 Consulted 19 November 2013.

The report was exemplary in many respects, making clear and unambiguous recommendations. It noted that, although there had been several earlier government inquiries into child sexual abuse in Australian Indigenous communities, these had not led to significant action by the governments concerned. In its first recommendation, the report insisted that both the federal and NT governments should treat the issue of 'Aboriginal child sexual abuse in the Northern Territory … as [one] of *urgent* national significance' (Anderson and Wild 2007: 22; emphasis added). The word 'urgent' would normally suggest a sense of immediacy, especially when placed alongside the reference to 'little children' in the report's title, but it should be read here in the context of the report's stress on persistent government inaction — it should be read, that is, as asking that *this time* something be done, not necessarily as insisting that it should be done this minute or even sooner. In considering what might be done about the problem it described, the report attempted to frame policy discussion by focusing on the improvement of education, the building of community trust, the provision of family support services and the empowerment of Aboriginal communities, while insisting that action should be organised in consultation with local communities. The report nevertheless offered the federal government an excuse to misread its use of 'urgent' and thus to ignore, as it might have done anyway, the report's point about consultation and to send troops to police Indigenous communities in the Northern Territory.[2] Neither its friends nor its enemies would accuse members of John Howard's ministry of interest in the careful reading of texts, but in this case, the misinterpretation seems more than simply careless.[3]

How could the report's authors and the NT Government have got things so wrong? There is no simple answer to this question, but any satisfactory answer should include a rhetorical variation on the idea of the unintended consequence.

Before developing this point, there are two things to consider: unexpected rhetorical effects of speech or writing and the idea of human progress. First, the rhetorical effects of speech or writing may deviate from their authors' intention for several reasons. The most obvious of these is authorial failure and/or incompetence, as when, for example, Republican Presidential Candidate Mitt Romney tried to convince American voters of his commitment to buying American by telling them that one of his cars was a Cadillac; he thereby

2   Popularly known as the Intervention or, less popularly, as described in its enabling legislation, the Northern Territory National Emergency Response. The NT Intervention is not unique. Similar, but less dramatic, attempts by government agencies to intervene in the affairs of indigenous communities, ostensibly to protect children from sexual abuse, have been documented in the United States. See, for example, Williams 2012.

3   Many commentators (e.g. Altman and Hinkson 2007, 2010; Behrendt n.d.) have noted that the procedures implemented by the Intervention bore little relation to the recommendations of the report. Those who have been exposed to Swift's brilliant satirical pamphlet *A modest proposal* (1729), or have learned to distrust the Coalition parties, will suspect that the government's talk of protecting children was a cover for other, more sinister, motives, for example, as suggested in Stringer 2007.

unwittingly displayed his unusual wealth and suggested, moreover, that he had other cars, not all of them American. A second reason is an accident of timing — an Australian leader tries to sell the case for 'finishing the job' in Afghanistan on a day when backbencher Kevin Rudd[4] makes yet another speech, a tsunami smashes into the east coast of Australia or Secretary of State Hillary Clinton announces America's intention to pull out more of its own troops.

Incompetence and unanticipated events can undermine the best of intentions, but intentions can also be undermined by another kind of accident: the unintended deployment of rhetoric (*Merriam-Webster* 2.b). In the case that concerns us here, the report's authors, perhaps without recognising its continuing potency, made use of a contrast between modern and traditional, whose force derives primarily from a Eurocentric rhetoric of human progress.

The idea of human progress has been employed in European social and political thought, and in Western political thought more generally, for several hundred years, appearing in different forms, many of them derived from a Christian (Augustinian) doctrine of (limited) human perfectibility (Nisbet 1979, 1980).[5] While apparently universalistic, talk of human progress has always been tied to a ranking of societies: while all of humanity is thought to progress, different portions are seen to have done so at different rates and to different degrees. In practice, most societies are likely to be seen as being more advanced today than at any time in their past.

Europeans and, later, Americans have persuaded themselves, along with far too many others, that they have progressed further than non-Europeans, that some Europeans have progressed more than others, and that human societies/peoples can be ranked according to their capacity for, and their actual achievement of, progress. The Indigenous peoples of Australia, along with some pigmy communities in Africa, have usually been ranked at or near the bottom of this order. Their failure to progress was once deemed so significant that their ability to survive in the face of the progress of others was in doubt (McGregor 1990; Stocking 1968: 110).

While this unsavoury complex of ideas may have lost much of its earlier appeal, it remains influential both in the West and in international affairs; for example, in contemporary discourses of development and modernisation — although earlier

---

4   Kevin Rudd was leader of the ALP (from 2006) and prime minister of Australia from 2007 until 2010 when he was deposed by his party in favour of Julia Gillard. He was minister for foreign affairs for a period during Gillard's government and returned to the backbench early in 2012. Throughout Gillard's leadership, Rudd was suspected of plotting to regain the leadership. Anything he did created headlines.
5   Students of political theory and of international relations will be familiar with the comparative, developmental aspects of this idea from Immanuel Kant's 'Idea for a universal history' (Reiss 1970: 41–53). For the religious foundations of Kant's argument see his 'Religion within the bounds of reason alone' (Kant 1996: 39–216).

references to 'underdeveloped' or 'premodern' societies have been displaced in favour of less obviously offensive talk of 'developing' or 'modernising' societies. The rhetoric of progress also underlies the idea of modernity, a term that has been used in diverse ways (Appadurai 1996; Chakrabarty 2000; Bhambra 2007). What concerns me here is its usage as a term of periodisation, serving to characterise the most recent period in European (Western) history, a condition that appears to have spread like a plague across much of the world.

Modernity, in this sense, is thought to come after, and therefore to be more advanced than, the 'medieval', 'renaissance' or 'early modern' periods (Toulmin 1990). Whereas the inhabitants of medieval Europe, and most non-Europeans, were thought by Enlightenment Europeans to have been dominated by tradition (Fasolt 2004), we moderns are often said to inhabit a post-traditional society (Giddens 1990, 1991).

The most important residue of the rhetoric of progress for my argument is the contrast between modern and traditional. In *Keywords*, Raymond Williams notes that while the English term 'tradition' was once, and still is sometimes, associated with 'ceremony, duty and respect', a usage I consider below, it is now 'often used dismissively' to indicate hostility 'to virtually any innovation' (1983: 319–20). The latter usage is perhaps the more influential in the social sciences and more generally in public life.

In their treatment of tradition, the social sciences, with the partial exception of anthropology, have not advanced much beyond Max Weber's venerable discussion of the types of social action (1978: 24–26). Weber identifies two rational types of social action, instrumental and value-rational (that is, action concerned with putting values into practice), and two non-rational types: affective and traditional. He adds that action of the traditional type 'is determined by ingrained habituation' (1978: 25). This dismissive treatment of tradition reflects the tendency of the modern social sciences, and of modern social thought more generally, to treat many non-Western peoples as if, unlike us, they are dominated by tradition and can therefore be viewed as irrational.

Despite its service in the rationalisation of colonial rule, the origins of this unpleasant tendency are to be found, not only in European imperialism and Enlightenment Orientalism (Halbfass 1988: 60), but also in conflicts between Protestants and Catholics in early modern Germany. Among the many issues at stake in these conflicts were the claims of the papacy and the Holy Roman Empire to be eternal. Since their claims to legitimacy were based on continuity over a long period, they also maintained that many decisions made in the past should continue to hold in the present. Against these claims, humanist and

Protestant historians argued that they misrepresented the past and that, in any case, whatever had really happened then should not be allowed to dominate conduct in the present.

One outcome of this 'historians' revolt', Constantin Fasolt (2004) argues, is the radical modern distinction between past and present, which suggests that the former is somehow less 'rational' than the latter, and that there was a time in which people were dominated by the past, allowing themselves to be ruled by custom and tradition in a manner best summarised as irrational. While, in its original form, this crude perception was turned mainly against European Catholics, whose communities were contemptuously described as priest-ridden, it has also surfaced recently in no less dismissive Western accounts of the Islamic world.

'Tradition' and 'traditional' are often used dismissively, yet Williams identifies a second, earlier English usage, associated with 'ceremony, duty and respect'. Just as Dalits in India and members of targeted populations in the West (for example, homosexuals, transgender people, transsexuals; see Bhagavan and Feldhaus 2008; Hacking 2006) have sometimes adopted pejorative categories and treated them as positive identities, indigenous peoples, in Australia and elsewhere, have given a positive spin to the 'traditional' categories to which they have been assigned. Thus, inverting the conventional valorisation of the modern, many Indigenous Australians celebrate a culture that, in their view, has continued for 40,000 years or more while some market selected aspects of that tradition to 'mainstream' Australians and foreign tourists.

While in one familiar usage the divide between traditional and modern reflects poorly on the former, there is countervailing usage in which the latter is devalued; in between, we find cases in which the divide serves as little more than a conventional marker of difference. Yet it is difficult to avoid a sense of an opposition between them.

The postcolonial scholar Homi Bhabha (1994) urges us to unsettle conventional oppositions, but this is easier said than done. One of the most interesting twentieth century attempts to tackle the traditional/modern opposition directly is present in Eric Hobsbawm and Terence Ranger's edited collection *The invention of tradition* (1983), which contains fine essays on the traditions fabricated by imperial authorities in Africa, India and various parts of the British Isles. Yet, Hobsbawm's introduction inadvertently reproduces the opposition in another form. Hobsbawm notes that modern societies have their own traditions, a point that might seem to undermine the usual contrast between modern and traditional, and he describes these traditions as 'invented'; that is, as 'responses to novel situations which take the form of reference to old situations' and continues by noting that 'tradition in this [invented] sense must be distinguished from 'custom', which dominates so-called 'traditional' societies' (1983: 2). While this suggests that there are societies with invented traditions and others that are dominated by 'custom', which does not seem to be invented, Hobsbawm insists that 'there is probably no time or place ... which has not seen the invention of tradition' (1983: 4). Yet, if the invention of tradition is universal, it happens more in some societies than in others: 'Societies since the industrial revolution have naturally been obliged to invent, institute or develop new networks of ... convention or routine more frequently than previous ones' (1983: 3). In place of the opposition between modern and traditional, we now have one between post-industrial revolution societies that are always fabricating new traditions and societies that have yet to experience their own industrial revolution.

We might note that in its appeal to 'the industrial revolution', Hobsbawm's approach, like the older rhetoric of progress, takes Europe as a model for the rest of the world. In contrast, the Argentine–Mexican philosopher Enrique Dussel (1995, 1996) seeks to undermine the traditional/modern opposition indirectly by confronting its second term and, with it, the conventional Eurocentric myth of modernity. Dussel argues that where most accounts of modernity treat it as developing first in Europe and then affecting other regions, it should really be seen as relational, embracing both Europe and regions subjected to European imperialism. Modernity, he maintains, begins with the Spanish invasion of the Americas, starting in 1492, and with Portuguese military/colonial ventures into Africa and Asia at around the same time. Taking modernity in this sense, one would have to say that contemporary Europe and postcolonial societies in other parts of the world were all equally modern.

Dussel's approach offers a powerful alternative to the conventional contrast between modernity and its others, but it has had limited impact on the social sciences in the Americas (but see Mignolo 2003, 2011) and no impact elsewhere. For the moment, and short of substantial intellectual changes in Australian academic and public life, it seems that we are stuck with an opposition between modern and traditional that commonly suggests that people who follow traditional ways are less rational and less morally and intellectually advanced than we moderns, just as Enlightenment Europeans viewed their medieval predecessors as backward and less than fully rational.

I should also note that, while in Australian public life 'modern' and 'traditional' are commonly seen as distinct and opposed, the contrast between them does not always involve a disparaging perception of the latter. At times, traditional ways are regarded as serving to sustain Indigenous communities or, like many endangered species, as things that should be preserved, if only for the sake of tourism, while at others, they are seen as obstacles to be overcome. At still other times, and again like endangered species, they are seen both as something to be preserved and as obstacles to be overcome. Either way, the modern and the traditional are opposed: tradition is thought both to stand in the way of modernisation and to be undermined by contact with the modern — and is seen accordingly by modern observers, and by many who identify with tradition, as in the process of breaking down. In practice, where the traditional/modern opposition is deployed, we are likely to find reports of the weakening of the social fabric or breakdown of Aboriginal communities. Neither 'breakdown' nor 'social fabric', as used in this context, are clear concepts. Social problems appear in Indigenous communities as they do in most others, but, while they add little new information, the terms 'breakdown' and 'social fabric' convey an additional sense of seriousness.

The *'Little children are sacred'* report does its best to avoid suggesting that Aboriginal society is in some way inferior to Australia's larger, mostly white, settler society. It refers, for example to 'Aboriginal culture' and 'European or mainstream society' as 'two branches of [Australian] society' (Anderson and Wild 2007: 12). While not describing one branch as superior or inferior to the other, it nevertheless acknowledges that there is a 'major difference' between them. The report points out specifically that, as earlier commentators had also noted, there was an ongoing 'breakdown of Aboriginal culture'. And again the word 'mainstream' is used to refer to 'European [i.e. settler] society', but without invoking the invidious distinction between those who are 'modern' and others who are not; without directly asserting, in other words, that 'Aboriginal culture', in contrast to 'mainstream' society, is not yet modern.

Unfortunately, in spite of its authors' intentions, there are too many places in the report where the contrast between 'modern' and 'non-modern' creeps in. For example, the report cites approvingly a 1998 coroner's inquest into four suicides among young Aboriginals in the Tiwi Islands that notes 'a weakening of the *traditional* and cultural values in *modern* Australian society' (Anderson and Wild 2007: 13; my emphasis). Here *traditional*, in contrast to *modern*, is presented as a feature of Aboriginal culture. This opposition between traditional and modern reappears several times in the report, usually in such a way as to suggest that they cannot easily coexist, that when they are found together, each is likely to undermine the other.

> *Traditional* marriage practices as they once existed cannot continue in the *modern* world, especially when they conflict with modern international human rights. Practices such as accepting goods in exchange for a 'wife', for example, are not consistent with *modern* international human rights. (Anderson and Wild 2007: 71; my emphasis)

This passage manages to damn traditional ways both for not being modern and for contravening human rights; it suggests that the latter are associated with the modern and that, conversely, denying them is a feature of the pre-modern world.[6] Finally,

> [t]he Inquiry observed that many Aboriginal people are struggling to understand the 'mainstream' modern world and law. They therefore do not know how to change Aboriginal law so that it works positively within the framework of the modern 'mainstream' world. (Anderson and Wild 2007: 179)

Notice how the modern is presented here as a framework to which whatever is not modern has to adapt.

The report illustrates the difficulty facing 'many Aboriginal people' with statements by two Aboriginal elders who were interviewed in the course of the Inquiry:

> 1. 'In the old days we were going in a straight line, now we are turning around and going in different directions.'
>
> 2. 'Whitefella law is very slippery, like a fish.'

It is not clear how these comments distinguish Indigenous Australians from the rest of the Australian population. The first might be read as expressing a sense of the confusing character of contemporary life that will be familiar to many older 'mainstream' Australians, while the second says something similar about contemporary law. Many non-Indigenous people, including the present author and more than a few practicing lawyers, will admit that they have problems making sense of modern 'mainstream' law.

So, where did the report go wrong? For the most part, it remains neutral, offering neither a negative nor positive assessment of what it sees as traditional. The most notable exceptions are the references, noted above, to 'modern "mainstream" world' and '"mainstream" modern world' (Anderson and Wild 2007: 179) and the counter-position, also noted, of *traditional* marriage and '*modern* international human rights' (Anderson and Wild 2007: 71; my emphasis). Nevertheless, even if the authors intended no denigration of tradition, the report's persistent use of the contrast between traditional and modern suggests that tradition, however valuable, must make it more difficult for Indigenous people than it is for other Australians to cope with the (modern) world in which they live — a suggestion that is reinforced by the report's observation that traditional ways are breaking down.

---

6 Rejali (1994) disputes another version of this modernist prejudice.

Yet, once tradition is viewed as an obstacle to modern ways, the report's insistence on consultation becomes a recipe for disaster or, at best, a waste of money and time. Most dictionaries offer a minimalist definition of consultation as the act or process of consulting, but some describe it more expansively. The *Oxford English Dictionary* (1989) offers several definitions, including 'A conference in which the parties consult and deliberate; a meeting for deliberation or discussion.' Where the first definition requires the activity of those doing the consulting — the consulted just have to be there — the *OED*'s reference to deliberation suggests that consultation involves the activity of both the consulting and the consulted. In practice, consultation more often conforms to the first than to the second definition.

The conventional mode of consultation by government is the public meeting, a consultation that, in this context, is all too likely to result in an unproductive slanging match between politicians and their officials on the one side and Indigenous representatives on the other, after which each side goes away convinced that it has been misunderstood by the other: the Indigenous team is perceived as revealing its inability (or refusal) to engage in modern discussion; the other side is regarded as a bunch of patronising bastards whose job is to tell the intended victims what government is planning to do to them.

Yet governments, who like to present themselves as service delivery agencies, are increasingly following the standard business model of consultation by administering a questionnaire, designed on the model of a commercial customer satisfaction survey, in which the questions address issues that concern the service provider and leave little space for the consulted to convey their own concerns.

In both the public meeting and the customer survey, consultation runs the risk of being little more than a longwinded way of insulting the consulted by suggesting that, where they depart from the concerns of the consulting side, their concerns are inconsequential. The main drawback is the possibility that the consulted might catch on to the insult too early in the process. The traditional/ modern demarcation suggests that the consequences of the consulted catching on will be more serious if those consulted are traditional people. Where it is usually safe to assume that moderns will have learned to tolerate, or resign themselves to, the routine indignities of their lives, there is no reason to expect that traditional types will have acquired any such skill. It is easy to understand why the official side, armed by its misunderstanding of the appeal for urgency, might feel that there was little to be gained by risking consultation. Here, we can see how the rhetoric (*Merriam-Webster* 2.b) of the report undermines one of its central recommendations.

This last point raises two questions: first, what did the report's authors think they were doing when they insisted on consultation?; and second, could these problems have been avoided? On the first question, we might also wonder whether (a) the report's authors have ever been on the receiving end of consultation by government; (b) had anticipated a more sensitive mode of consultation, perhaps with themselves acting as specialist advisors; or (c) expected this recommendation to be ignored by government, a move that would enable the authors to deny responsibility for whatever mess the actions of government created.

Arguably, there is no way to insulate a report from the efforts of foolish or unscrupulous politicians to exploit it for their own ends. What the Coalition government did with *'Little children are sacred'* involved a poisonous mix of bad faith and foolishness that was barely tempered by any kind of scruple. Yet, the difficulty faced by the report's authors and other critics of the subsequent intervention was not so much that members of the government misread the report, although they clearly did, but that this misreading was supported by elements of the report itself — by the reference to little children in the title, the word 'urgent' in one of its most important recommendations, and the use of the modern/traditional dichotomy throughout. The first of these may have been unavoidable, given that the report's remit was to look into sexual abuse of children. (Although the term 'little' is certainly redundant, the added reference to the 'sacred' strengthens the sense of urgency, suggesting that action is an urgent and sacred duty).

As for the second element, the word 'urgent' is easily misunderstood and there are other ways in which the report could have made the point about the need for government action.

The third element, the report's reliance on the modern/traditional dichotomy has been the main focus of my discussion.[7] While the conventional usage of this dichotomy leads towards the disparaging of traditional ways, the report's authors may have had something different in mind — perhaps intending it as a simple marker of difference. The report invites trouble, not so much because it disparages one side or the other, but because of the opposition between traditional and modern, and the related suggestion that they cannot easily coexist — each gets in the way of the other.

Undoing this pernicious opposition might be easier said than done, however, pragmatic moves can mitigate the problem. The report's use of 'mainstream' and 'modern', sometimes both together, to identify the, mainly white, settler society

---

7   Of course, this is not the only way in which the report distinguishes between Aboriginals and others in the Australian population. I noted earlier, for example, that the report refers to 'Aboriginal culture' and 'European or mainstream society' as 'two branches of [Australian] society' (Anderson and Wild 2007: 12). Few readers of the report will focus on its rhetorical moves and thus be tempted to reflect on its contrast between (Aboriginal) *culture* and (European) *society*, or its identification of non-Aboriginal Australia as European.

suggests that its authors may have toyed with the possibility of replacing the word 'modern' with 'mainstream'. While they finally kept it, trying to write without the word 'modern' seems to me an excellent idea (Helliwell and Hindess 2013: 70–83). While the use of 'mainstream' instead of 'modern' risks generating problems of its own, at least it would avoid the worst connotations of 'modern'. In any event, 'modern' can often be abandoned, or replaced, without losing anything more substantial than its unsavoury connotations.

References

Altman, J. and Hinkson, M. eds. 2007. *Coercive reconciliation: Stabilise, normalise, exit Aboriginal Australia*. Melbourne: Arena Publications Association.

——— eds. 2010. *Culture crisis. Anthropology and politics in Aboriginal Australia*. Sydney: New South Press.

Anderson, P. and Wild, R. 2007. *Ampe Akelyernemane Meke Mekarle: 'Little children are sacred'*. Report of the Northern Territory Board of Inquiry into the Protection of Aboriginal Children from Sexual Abuse. Darwin: Northern Territory Government.

Appadurai, A. 1996. *Modernity at large: Cultural dimensions of globalization*. Minneapolis: University of Minnesota Press.

Behrendt, L. n.d. A convenient intervention. Article. *Australians All: Justice Security a Fair Go*. URL: http://australiansall.com.au/archive/post/a-convenient-intervention/. Consulted 29 September 2012.

Bhabha, H.K. 1994. *The location of culture*. London: Routledge.

Bhagavan, M. and Feldhaus, A. eds. 2008. *Claiming power from below: Dalits and the subaltern question in India*. New Delhi: Oxford University Press.

Bhambra, G.K. 2007. *Rethinking modernity: Postcolonialism and the sociological imagination*. Basingstoke: Palgrave Macmillan.

Chakrabarty, D. 2000. *Provincialising Europe: Postcolonial thought and historical difference*. Princeton: Princeton University Press.

Dussel, E. 1995. *The invention of the Americas: Eclipse of 'the other' and the myth of modernity*. New York: Continuum.

——— 1996. *The underside of modernity: Apel, Ricoeur, Rorty, Taylor and the philosophy of liberation*. Amherst: Humanity Books.

Fasolt, C. 2004. *The limits of history*. Chicago: University of Chicago Press.

Giddens, A. 1990. *Modernity and self-identity*. Cambridge: Polity.

—— 1990. *The consequences of modernity*. Cambridge: Polity.

Hacking, I. 2006. Making up people. *London Review of Books* 28(16–17): 23–26.

Halbfass, W. 1988. *India and Europe: An essay in understanding*. Albany: State University of New York Press.

Helliwell, C. and Hindess B. 2013. Time and the others. In S. Seth ed. *Postcolonial theory and international relations*. London: Routledge.

Hobsbawm, E. and Ranger, T. eds. 1983. *The invention of tradition*. Cambridge: Cambridge University Press.

Kant, I. 1996. *Religion and rational theology*. A.W. Wood and G. Di Giovanni trans. and eds. Vol. 6. Cambridge Edition of the Works of Immanuel Kant. Cambridge: Cambridge University Press.

McGregor, R. 1990. The doomed race: A scientific axiom of the late nineteenth-century. *The Australian Journal of Politics and History* 39(1): 14–22. URL: http://eprints.jcu.edu.au/10653/1/doomed_race_axiom.pdf.

Mignolo, W. 2003. *The darker side of the Renaissance: Literacy, territoriality, & colonization*. Ann Arbor: University of Michigan Press.

—— 2011. *The darker side of Western modernity: Global futures, decolonial options, Latin America*. Durham, N.C.: Duke University Press.

Nisbet R.A. 1979. The idea of progress. *The Literature of Liberty* 2(1). URL: http://oll.libertyfund.org/index.php?option=com_staticxt&staticfile=show.php%3Ftitle=1290&Itemid=99999999.

—— 1980. *History of the idea of progress*. New York: Transaction.

Reiss H. ed. 1970. *Kant's political writings*. Cambridge: Cambridge University Press.

Rejali, D. 1994. *Torture and modernity*. Boulder: Westview Press.

Stocking, G.W. 1968. *Race, culture, and evolution: Essays in the history of anthropology*. New York: The Free Press.

Stringer, R. 2007. A nightmare of the neocolonial kind: Politics of suffering in Howard's Northern Territory Intervention. *Borderlands e-journal* 6(2). URL: http://www.borderlands.net.au/vol6no2_2007/stringer_intervention.htm.

Swift, J. 1729. *A modest proposal for preventing the children of poor people in Ireland from being a burden to their parents or country, and for making them beneficial to the publick.* e-book, Project Gutenburg, EBook-No 1080. URL http://www.gutenberg.org/ebooks/1080.

Toulmin, S. 1990. *Cosmopolis: The hidden agenda of modernity.* New York: Free Press.

Weber, M. 1978. *Economy and society. An outline of interpretive sociology.* Berkeley: University of California Press.

Williams, R. 1983. *Keywords: A vocabulary of culture and society.* London: Fontana.

Williams, T. 2012. A tribe's epidemic of child sex abuse, minimised for years. *New York Times* 19 September.

5. The gilded cage: Rhetorical path dependency in Australian politics

Dennis Grube

Every writer at the start of a new project is confronted by something that is at once terrifying and liberating — a blank piece of paper. They are given a clean slate on which to shape and build a story full of rich characters and events that respond to each push of the writer's pen. In politics, rhetorical actors seldom enjoy the luxury of a clean piece of paper. Each speech act does not stand alone as a fresh start, but is rather the next in a long line of speeches, media statements and framing narratives that have helped to define a political actor in the public mind over time. Every time a political leader speaks, they do so dragging behind them the collected rhetorical baggage of a lifetime in politics. In the process of accumulating this baggage, they have had to make rhetorical choices at each point that have narrowed the range of rhetorical options open to them for the future. To suddenly depart from established lines of rhetoric that have shaped a politician's image leaves them exposed to looking inauthentic, inconsistent and untrustworthy — an array of attributes that can spell death in contemporary politics.

This chapter examines the idea of path dependency, a well-established concept in the field of policy studies, and applies it to the study of political rhetoric. I argue that political leaders are caught between the desire to utilise fresh and engaging rhetoric in order to better explain a new policy direction and the reality that they can't be seen to be contradicting themselves. They are effectively hemmed in by their own rhetorical choices, leaving them unable to easily start afresh in new rhetorical directions. They are trapped in a gilded rhetorical cage of their own making. To prosecute this argument, I draw on three recent case studies in which Australian political leaders have found themselves restrained by their own previous rhetorical choices, preventing them from effectively explaining changes in policy direction.

Kevin Rudd, on assuming the Labor leadership in 2006, argued consistently that climate change was the 'greatest moral challenge of our time', which required determined leadership in order to address it. The desire to formulate new rhetoric in 2010 to explain why immediate action had to be postponed was thwarted by rhetorical baggage of his own creation. During the 2010 election campaign, Prime Minister Julia Gillard insisted that there would be 'no carbon tax under the government I lead'. When confronted with the reality of a minority parliament and the demands of the Greens for climate action, the prime minister fought a losing rhetorical battle to differentiate the new policy realities from her previous political rhetoric. Tony Abbott, as Opposition leader, presented a consistent rhetorical refrain that the boats of asylum seekers had to be stopped, and turned around on the high seas where it was safe to do so. Upon attaining office as prime minister in September 2013, Abbott faced the task of reshaping his political rhetoric to avoid conflict with the Indonesian Government without looking like he was deviating from his earlier rhetorical position. Before examining each of these three cases in detail, I turn first to the concept of path dependency.

Path dependency and political rhetoric

Path dependency is an idea that emerged from theories of historical institutionalism. In essence, path dependency argues that no actor is capable of escaping easily from her or his own history. 'Path dependency speaks to the common observation that the legacy of the past conditions our future, at the policy level and at the level of institutions' (Gains et al. 2005: 27). Path dependency applies not just to individual actors, but to bureaucratic departments, policy processes and programs.

Whenever a political actor or an institution adopts a particular policy position, processes are put in place to allow that policy to be implemented. A new agency might be set up, staff recruited and headquarters built. Legislation might be passed. Money will be spent rolling out the policy in whichever way is appropriate. These types of sunk costs mean that a complete change in policy direction becomes increasingly difficult. In fact, not only do the costs of change become prohibitive, but there are 'increasing returns' that will flow to those who stay on the path originally selected. As one of the first theorists to explain the applicability of path dependency to questions of political science, Paul Pierson explains it this way:

> Increasing returns dynamics capture two key elements central to most analysts' intuitive sense of path dependence. First, they pinpoint how the costs of switching from one alternative to another will, in certain social contexts, increase markedly over time. Second, and related, they draw attention to issues of timing and sequence, distinguishing formative moments or conjunctures from the periods that reinforce divergent paths. In an increasing returns process, it is not only a question of what happens but also of when it happens. Issues of temporality are at the heart of the analysis. (2000: 251)

Such path dependent effects are seen clearly in policy development processes:

> In terms of policy development, path dependency captures the tendency for a policy step in one direction to encourage the next step to be in a similar direction. Fundamentally, the set up of the policy conditions later choices. A period of instability leads to a policy being defined and once defined the development of policy tends to follow the underlying assumptions, sense of direction and the coalition of interests that accompanied its launch. The key theoretical insight to emerge from the path dependency literature is that increasing returns experienced by the actors involved keeps them along the same path. (Gains et al. 2005: 27)

A recent Australian example illustrates such effects well. Instigated under the Rudd government, the National Broadband Network (NBN) project saw the establishment of a new government-owned corporation — NBN Co — and the spending of billions of dollars to begin the roll out of fibre to the home across Australia. The Coalition, under the leadership of then Opposition leader Abbott, made clear that it did not support the NBN project in its current form. But in laying out its own plan in the lead up to the 2013 election, the Abbott-led Coalition did not have a clean policy slate on which to draw. In theory, they could have promised to rip up every piece of cabling already laid to individual homes in various parts of Australia, abolished NBN Co and begun a new tendering process for an alternative model of high-speed broadband delivery. In practice, the costs of such an option are simply too high in both financial and policy terms. Too much money has been spent, and too many processes established, to simply start again in an entirely new direction. The stated policy of the Coalition government involves some change in direction going forward, but the point of departure from the policy of the previous government is already well down a path that they cannot and will not seek to reverse in its entirety.

I argue here that this type of path dependency is just as applicable to the rhetoric of political leaders as it is to policy outcomes. Political 'talk' is important in part because it helps to shape our views of the person doing the talking. The rhetoric of political leaders contributes to the shaping of the public's perception of them. It helps to frame their political persona. The more often they repeat particular rhetorical choices and stick to a particular formulation, the more it becomes entrenched as part of their public face. This can bring significant rewards for leaders who are able to then live up to that rhetoric by delivering on what they have promised. But equally it can leave them little room for rhetorical readjustment when things change. As leaders are reminded every day, politics is difficult. Public opinion can shift, government finances can change, and what seemed like a wonderfully clear piece of persuasive rhetoric can become, instead, a millstone around a political leader's neck.

The incentives for leaders to adapt and change their rhetoric are, therefore, high because the complexities and nuances of political reality require leaders to have room to move and opportunities to change position. But perversely, the more 'successful' leaders have been in their political rhetoric, the less room for manoeuvre they leave themselves. Political rhetoric has a narrowing effect as leaders are pushed towards clear, unequivocal statements that they can then be held to. The result is that rhetorical refrains become ever more deeply etched in political concrete and the costs for leaders of starting afresh in a new rhetorical direction become prohibitive.

But our political leaders have little choice other than to take some rhetorical risks and state a position. They cannot simply refuse to say anything and commit to nothing and still hope to govern effectively. Having decided on a form of words that they believe will be persuasive in carrying their policy narrative to the wider public, political leaders receive the increasing returns of being seen to be consistent and committed to the path they have identified. But if a political leader changes rhetorical direction, no amount of further consistent rhetoric is sufficient to offset the cost of the initial change. For example, having embraced a price on carbon, Prime Minister Gillard explained its virtues consistently for over two years, but was unable to overcome the weight of the initial rhetorical commitment not to introduce a carbon tax.

As Pierson's analysis of path dependency indicates, at the outset a leader is faced with an array of possible rhetorical formulations for carrying a policy message. But, having once selected a particular formulation, it immediately raises the political cost of then adopting an alternative.

> In an increasing returns process, the probability of further steps along the same path increases with each move down that path. This is because the relative benefits of the current activity compared with other possible options increase over time. To put it a different way, the costs of exit — of switching to some previously plausible alternative — rise. (Pierson 2000: 252)

For example, Ryan Walter's chapter in this book on the language of economic management examines how the Gillard government painted itself into a rhetorical corner by repeatedly promising to deliver a surplus in 2013. It passed up many early opportunities to reshape or reframe the promise and, instead, entrenched it further by repetition and insistent commitment. At each point, the costs of adopting different rhetoric increased, making anything other than strong repetition of the commitment untenable. Of course, as Walter explains, the contingent nature of political reality finally caught up with the rhetoric.

The resultant political pain of the rhetorical shift away from promising the surplus was commensurate with the distance the government had gone down that particular rhetorical path.

So, once adopted at the outset, a particular rhetorical formulation will naturally enough become further entrenched through repetition and further explication. But there is also a small temporal window for clarification, in which a rhetorical misstep can be reversed without the same level of cost that will apply if the original misstep is expanded on and entrenched. For example, in 2010 Abbott was forced in an interview on the *7.30* program to backtrack on a commitment he had made not to increase any taxes under a Coalition government. He committed himself to a policy direction that he had not intended and tried immediately to withdraw the comment:

> I know politicians are going to be judged on everything they say, but sometimes in the heat of discussion you go a little bit further than you would if it was an absolutely calm, considered, prepared, scripted remark. Which is one of the reasons why the statements that need to be taken absolutely as gospel truth are those carefully prepared, scripted remarks. (Australian Broadcasting Corporation (ABC) 2010)

Abbott's 'clarification' about the policy position on tax, whilst attracting criticism and even ridicule for the manner of his clarification, enabled him to stop a particular piece of policy rhetoric from becoming embedded. It cost him some political capital to deviate immediately from a rhetorical formulation, but it also enabled him to stop it from growing into a more path dependent rhetorical formulation that he would then become 'stuck' with.

I turn now to an in-depth discussion of three recent Australian cases that highlight the effects of rhetorical path dependency at work.

Kevin Rudd and climate change

For much of the first decade of the twenty-first century, Australia was experiencing severe drought conditions across multiple states. Amongst concerns over dramatically reduced water flows in the Murray–Darling Basin, failing farms and the drying up of urban water reservoirs, the climate change debate seemed grounded in real, practical and visible environmental consequences. Under Prime Minister John Howard, long considered something of a climate change sceptic, the push for action became irresistible. He flexed the Commonwealth's financial muscle to assert some control over the Murray–Darling Basin and, by 2007, he and his ministers were openly discussing options for a market-based mechanism to put a price on carbon.

Part of the pressure for action was being built by the Australian Labor Party under the leadership of Rudd, who had replaced Kim Beazley in late 2006. Rudd promised that if Labor won government, one of its first acts would be to sign the Kyoto Protocol — the international agreement pledging action to control the rates of carbon entering the atmosphere. In an October 2006 piece in the *The Monthly* magazine, Rudd suggested action on climate change was an ethical duty for people of faith:

> By definition, the planet cannot speak for itself. Nor can the working peoples of the developing world effectively speak for themselves, although they are likely to be the first victims of the environmental degradation brought about by climate change. Nor can those who come after us, although they are likely to be the greatest victims of this inter-generational injustice. It is the fundamental ethical challenge of our age to protect the planet — in the language of the Bible, to be proper stewards of creation. The scientific evidence is now clear, and the time for global, national and local action has well and truly come. (Rudd 2006)

When Labor gained government in November 2007, the Kyoto Protocol was indeed signed as the first official act of the new government.

Rudd continued to build his rhetoric throughout 2008 and 2009, ramping up the need for action. In July 2008, the draft report of the Garnaut Climate Change Review was released. The Prime Minister used the report to again stress the central importance of the issue:

> And that is why the stark warnings contained in Professor Garnaut's report about the cost of inaction should focus our entire national debate on what we do on climate change. The bottom line is this, if we fail to act on climate change we are condemning great river systems like the Murray Darling to an entirely perilous future and the resolve of our Government is to act. It will be tough, it will be difficult, it will be expensive. But we intend to take on this challenge and to do our absolute best in responding to what I think is the great challenge of our generation. (Rudd 2008)

In the lead up to the December 2009 Copenhagen conference to tackle climate change, Rudd continued down his established rhetorical path of advocating the absolute necessity of action and the cowardice of inaction. Internationally, the Copenhagen summit failed to usher in a comprehensive agreement, and domestically Abbott had replaced Malcolm Turnbull as leader of the Liberal Party, bringing with him a sceptical view of the need for Rudd's proposed climate change policy solutions. What had been a bipartisan policy area suddenly became a heavily contested one, tying Rudd ever more publicly into rhetorical support for the importance of acting on climate change.

Having failed multiple times to convince the Greens in the Senate to support an emissions trading scheme incorporating modest emission reduction targets, Rudd was faced with the choice of pursuing a double dissolution election on the issue or delaying action. He chose the latter. At a press conference on 27 April 2010, Rudd announced that the government would delay acting on a carbon pollution reduction scheme because of the Liberal Opposition's intransigence and the indecisiveness of the rest of the world. He was immediately challenged with multiple questions from journalists, citing his earlier rhetorical narrative on the central importance of climate change:

> Journalist: A little while back you said that climate change is the greatest moral, economic and social challenge of our time. With this now being delayed, do you still believe that to be the case?

> PM: Climate change remains a fundamental economic and environmental and moral challenge for all Australians, and for all peoples of the world. That just doesn't go away for the simple reason that it's not in the headlines. Therefore, the practical question is this. Our current actions delivered through until the end of the current Kyoto commitment period which finishes at the end of 2012 — the critical question then is what actions postdate 2012, and the decision that we've taken as a Government is that that provides the best opportunity to judge the actions by the rest of the international community before taking our decision about the implementation of a Carbon Pollution Reduction Scheme from that time on. (Rudd 2010)

The news media highlighted the policy shift with gusto. Paul Kelly, editor-at-large for the *Australian* wrote: 'As retreats go, they come no bigger than Kevin Rudd's delaying of his once cherished emissions trading scheme — one of the most spectacular backdowns by a prime minister in decades' (2010). Lenore Taylor wrote in the *Sydney Morning Herald* that:

> When the Coalition began insisting on a wait-and-see position, Rudd said it was 'absolute political cowardice … an absolute failure of leadership'. It would be a 'failure of logic', because if every nation said it could not do anything until everyone else did, no one would ever do anything. Now he's adopted the same position himself. He was right the first time. (2010)

In the weeks and months that followed, Rudd was not able to successfully reframe his climate change policy in a way that could again be rhetorically persuasive. He had simply proceeded too far down the rhetorical path of the need for Australian leadership on the great moral challenge of the age to be able to adopt a new message. His message had become a path-dependent prisoner of its own initial success in framing the climate change problem and the need for action.

Julia Gillard and the carbon 'tax' or 'price'

Gillard became prime minister on 24 June 2010, assuming the position following an extraordinary 24 hours in which the Labor caucus committed to a dramatic leadership change. As the new prime minister, Gillard faced allegations in the media that she had been one of the key ministers who had helped to block Rudd's initial desire to push through an emissions trading scheme (Hartcher 2010). On 27 June 2010, she was interviewed on Channel 9 by Laurie Oakes, who quizzed her on the topic:

> Oakes: Now, you've now been pinged, along with Wayne Swan, as responsible for the shelving of the emissions trading system, the decision that more than anything else shredded Kevin Rudd's credibility. Do you accept responsibility for that?
>
> PM: I accept my fair share of …
>
> Oakes: … Which sounds like the lion's share from the reports we've had of the discussion.
>
> PM: Well, I accept my fair share of the responsibility for all of the decisions that happened when Kevin Rudd was prime minister. I accept my fair share for the good things and the bad things.
>
> Oakes: But you did argue that the ETS should be dumped because it was hurting Labor politically. Is that true?
>
> PM: Laurie, [I] was concerned that if you are going to do something as big to your economy as put a price on carbon, with the economic transformation that implies, with changing the way in which we live, you need a lasting and deep community consensus to do it and I don't believe we have that lasting and deep community consensus now. Now I believe we should have a price on carbon and I will be prepared to argue for a price on carbon, to lead so that we get to that lasting and deep community consensus, but we're not there yet … . (Gillard 2010a)

The Prime Minister's stated view on the need to delay the pricing of carbon until community consensus could be reached was widely picked up and reported in the print media — further entrenching the rhetorical path chosen and increasing the political cost of any later change. The *Australian* reported the interview under the headline 'Gillard says she led push for delay on ETS' (Maiden 2010) and the *Australian Financial Review* (*AFR*) under the headline 'Seeking "community consensus" ahead of an ETS' (2010).

After implementing swift policy solutions on the issues of asylum seeker arrivals and the mining tax — issues on which Rudd was perceived as having underperformed — Gillard called a federal election for 21 August 2010. During the campaign, when pressed further on the carbon pricing issue during a television interview on Channel 10, the Prime Minister ruled out implementing a carbon tax:

> There will be no carbon tax under the government I lead. What we will do is tackle the challenge of climate change. We have invested record amounts in solar and renewable technologies. I want to build the transmission lines that will bring back clean green energy into the national average is the grid. I also want to make sure that we have no more dirty coal-fired power stations and make sure we tried [sic] greener cars and word [sic] from greener buildings. I will deliver those things and the[n] lead a national debate to reach a consensus about putting a cap on carbon pollution. (Gillard 2010b)

Once again, the print media picked up and amplified the core message that there would be no carbon tax under a Gillard government. Headlines such as 'Gillard rules out imposing carbon tax' (*Sydney Morning Herald* 2010) emphasised the seemingly definitive nature of the Prime Minister's rhetoric on the matter. It is now a matter of historical record that the Australian election of 2010 produced the first hung parliament since World War II. Gillard and Abbott each spent the subsequent days attempting to woo the support of key independents in order to form government. In Gillard's case, this included signing an agreement with the Greens to lock in the support of the new Greens MP for Melbourne, Adam Bandt, in the lower house. One aspect of the deal was the formation of a multi-party committee to examine options for action on climate change that could be presented to cabinet.

In February 2011, Gillard announced that the government would seek to introduce a carbon price to tackle climate change. She held a press conference on 24 February 2011, flanked by the members of the multi-party committee:

> Today, accompanied by the members of the Multi-Party Climate Change Committee and we're here together today because we're releasing a paper which describes a proposed carbon mechanism.
>
> Now this proposed mechanism for pricing carbon is agreed by the Australian Government and by the Australian Greens. Mr Windsor and Mr Oakeshott, who have joined us and who are members of the Multi-

Party Climate Change Committee, have agreed that this proposal should be released to be considered by the community and to demonstrate that progress is being made ... I do want to take a few moments to explain why I am so determined to price carbon. (Gillard 2011)

In answering questions from journalists, Gillard framed the policy change as being a necessary reflection of the parliament that the Australian people had voted for:

Journalist: Thank you very much, Prime Minister. Is this announcement today a breach of faith with the electorate, given that immediately prior to the election you ruled out a carbon price?

PM: This is the parliament the Australian people voted for. You're seeing it on display in front of you. This is the parliament Australians voted for, and we have to get on with the job of pricing carbon. (Gillard 2011)

The Opposition seized on the announcement as a broken promise and the battle of the rhetorical frames between seeing the 'carbon price' as an important national reform and seeing the 'carbon tax' as a broken promise was played out through the media in the days, weeks, months and years that followed. Gillard had effectively been caught in the net of her own clear rhetorical formulations about what she would and would not do. Her rhetoric was so clear and consistent that it did what it was intended to do, which was entrench her position in the public mind. Each repetition of it took her further along a rhetorical path as she enjoyed the increasing political returns that come with enunciating a clear position on an issue. Equally, however, it raised the stakes of any subsequent change in rhetoric having a major impact on perceptions of her authenticity and trustworthiness. The political pain Gillard experienced when she announced the government's intention to price carbon was the direct mirror image of the political gain she had enjoyed from entrenching a particular rhetorical position.

Reflecting on her prime ministership in September 2013, Gillard, writing for the *Guardian* newspaper online, acknowledged that the policy shift had exacted a heavy political toll as she lost the rhetorical battle:

I erred by not contesting the label 'tax' for the fixed price period of the emissions trading scheme I introduced. I feared the media would end up playing constant silly word games with me, trying to get me to say the word 'tax'. I wanted to be on the substance of the policy, not playing 'gotcha'. But I made the wrong choice and, politically, it hurt me terribly. (2013)

Tony Abbott and stopping the boats

The issue of what to do with asylum seekers who attempt to reach Australia by boat has played a dominant role in Australian political debate for over a decade. In the 1970s and 1980s, a bipartisan consensus operated to avoid pitched partisan disagreements over the arrival of 'boat people' fleeing Asia's trouble spots and, in particular, the conflict in Vietnam. The consensus was challenged and broken in 2001, when Howard was successful in reframing the issue of asylum seekers from a humanitarian problem to a border security problem. Just before the beginning of the 2001 election campaign, allegations surfaced that asylum seekers had thrown their children overboard to make sure that their boats would be picked up and taken to Christmas Island by Australian authorities. This allegation was later proven to be false. Howard vowed during the campaign that he would 'stop the boats.' In his formal election launch speech, he struck upon the powerful rhetorical appeal that: 'we will decide who comes to this country and the circumstances in which they come' (2001). Re-elected with an increased majority, Howard put in place a policy which came to be known as the 'Pacific Solution' to excise Australia's offshore islands from its migration zone, and for asylum seekers to be processed offshore.

It was against this background that Abbott, as Opposition leader from 2009–2013, vowed that he would once again 'stop the boats' if he was elected as prime minister. Following their election win in 2007, the Rudd government had dismantled the Pacific Solution suite of policies, while conflicts in Afghanistan, Sri Lanka and Iraq fed into a renewed wave of asylum seekers attempting to reach Australia by boat. Abbott argued that only a Coalition government could effectively stop the boats because only a Coalition government believed in it (see Wroe and Hall 2013). The phrase 'stop the boats' was underpinned by a set of specific policy proposals, including turning boats around where it was 'safe to do so'.

Abbott's rhetoric was tested by comments from various experts suggesting that turning boats around would be unworkable. Abbott's constant recommitment to this goal entrenched it further in a path dependent fashion. It generated suitably decisive sounding headlines such as '"I'll turn back every boat", says Tony Abbott' (Kelly 2012) and 'No turning back on Abbott navy stance' (Peake 2012). When criticised, Abbott simply reinforced the point. For example, the *Australian* on 7 July 2012 carried criticisms of the policy from former chief of defence, Admiral Chris Barrie:

> Mr Abbott said Admiral Barrie, who executed the policy under the Howard government, had been misrepresented and the navy could tow back asylum boats once again. 'Under the Coalition government, there will always be the option of turning boats around where it is safe to do

so,' Mr Abbott said. 'The turn-back-the-boats option is what we need if we are going to discourage reckless behaviour by people-smugglers and their clients,' he said. (Wilson and Vasek 2012)

Abbott, Foreign Affairs Shadow Minister Julie Bishop and Immigration Shadow Minister Scott Morrison were questioned intensively by journalists as to whether the policy would need to take greater account of the concerns of the country from which many of the boats set sail — namely Indonesia. They maintained strongly that Australia did not need the permission of another country to protect its own borders (e.g. Hall 2013).

The suite of policies to help 'stop the boats' were entrenched further during the 2013 election campaign, with press releases promising to:

> Implement a $20 million program with the International Organisation for Migration to engage and enlist Indonesian villages to support people smuggling disruption, including a capped boat buy-back scheme that provides an incentive for owners of dangerous vessels to sell them to government officials, not people smugglers. (Abbott 2013a)

The Coalition parties decisively won the 2013 election, and Abbott vowed that Operation Sovereign Borders would begin the moment the government was formally sworn in. Immediately following the election, the impact of the Coalition's rhetoric on Australia's relationship with Indonesia was drawn into sharper relief. Abbott's rhetoric began to soften in response, with less focus on Australia's right to protect its borders and more on the benefits that would flow to Indonesia, with whom Abbott pledged to work closely and cooperatively. An interview on the Channel 7 program *Sunrise*, immediately following the election win, provides a flavour:

> David Koch: Mr Abbott, your message to the Indonesians? Coverage of your election was a bit mixed in the media there, and saying the boat policy is just unrealistic.
>
> Tony Abbott: It's in Indonesia's long term best interests for the flow of people to Australia to stop because the vast majority of them come via Indonesia. Many of them stay for many months in Indonesia. While they are in Indonesia, they can be a problem for the Indonesian authorities. I accept that this is a smaller issue for Indonesia than it is for Australia. Indonesia is a vast archipelago with many developmental, economic and social issues. Nevertheless it is going to be good for Indonesia as well as good for Australia that these boats are stopped. (Abbott 2013b)

In New York, Foreign Minister Bishop met with her Indonesian counterpart during a gathering of the United Nations General Assembly and continued with the softened rhetoric. Bishop described the meeting as 'positive and very productive'. She emphasised the depth of Australia's respect for Indonesia:

> There can be some misunderstanding as to what our policy is and it is certainly not to in any way show disrespect for Indonesian sovereignty and for anyone to think that that was our policy that would be a mistake. Our policy respects Indonesia's sovereignty, respects Indonesia's territorial borders, just as Indonesia respects ours. (Connolly 2013)

Indonesian Foreign Minister, Marty Natalegawa, took a different view of proceedings and emphasised that he had passed on a message 'loud and clear' that 'Indonesia cannot accept any Australian policy that would, in nature, violate Indonesia's sovereignty' (Connolly 2013).

The battle for rhetorical consistency came to a head in early October 2013 when Abbott met with Indonesian President Susilo Bambang Yudhoyono in Jakarta. When asked at a post-meeting press conference about his policy for stopping the boats, Abbott's rhetoric focused squarely on the need to work in partnership with Indonesia in every way. He refused to repeat his rhetoric on turning boats around, buying boats in Indonesia or paying Indonesians to provide Australia with information on people smugglers. He fell back on the broader rhetorical point that: 'In the end that is all that really counts — have we stopped the boats?' (Abbott 2013c). Journalists pushed for clearer answers, but Abbott stayed with his higher level rhetoric focused on stopping the boats:

> Question: But you are not answering the question will you still turn the boats back to Indonesia?

> Prime Minister: Again my object here is to stop the boats. It is to stop the boats and in order to ensure that the boats are stopped I want to have the best possible relationship with Indonesia. We have a great relationship what we are looking to develop is even stronger cooperation on this particular matter in the future than we have always had in the past. (Abbott 2013c)

By being seen to maintain consistency with the broad 'stop the boats' rhetoric, Abbott was able to jettison the sub-parts of that rhetoric without suffering high levels of political pain.

But the tricky balance needed to maintain a unified message whilst delivering different rhetoric to different audiences was highlighted when Morrison, as Immigration Minister, held a press conference in Canberra on 4 October. In an attempt to reassure the domestic Australian audience about the rhetorical consistency of the government's position, Morrison insisted that all aspects of the 'stop the boats' policy suite were still available and could be used. 'Despite the wishful thinking and projection by some that I saw in some media reports, there is no change to the Government's policy on border protection. Our resolve, our policies, our commitments to the task remain as strong and are indeed stronger than ever before' (2013). Whilst the press picked up on the rhetorical inconsistency between the message to the two audiences, Abbott's trip was seen as having successfully calmed an issue of dispute between Australia and Indonesia. For example, the softening of rhetoric led to headlines such as 'PM's boats compromise offers a way to ditch tow-back policy' (Bachelard and Wroe 2013).

The importance of rhetorical choices

The three case studies demonstrate that rhetorical choices matter. They can have enormous consequences for the future political fortunes of political leaders. Particular rhetorical formulations that are successful in entrenching a policy position become ever harder to undo as repetition and recommitment pushes a political actor firmly down a particular path. Each rhetorical act helps to shape not just a policy, but also the public persona of the leader. Any subsequent deviation from a rhetorical path is then seen not just as a change of policy, but as some form of 'betrayal' of a leader's entrenched rhetorical position. Such a betrayal moves the effects of rhetorical path dependency away from simply questions of policy consistency into deeper questions of trustworthiness and authenticity. A change in policy language in one area does not simply result in localised policy pain, but a wider loss of trust in the prime minister and the government they lead.

The fates of both Rudd and Gillard in entrenching a particular policy line, and then attempting a U-turn off that rhetorical path, show just how much rhetorical choices can shape overarching perceptions of a government. Accusations of betraying the electorate and their own principles were so damaging because the change in rhetorical direction reshaped the public persona of both prime ministers in negative ways. Abbott has thus far avoided a similar fate, despite the clear changes in rhetorical emphasis about turning boats back to Indonesia or buying boats in Indonesia. Abbott declined to recommit to either policy despite several invitations to do so during his press conference on the outcomes of his Indonesian visit. It remains to be seen whether this will create similar problems of trust and authenticity in the longer term. In the short term at least, Abbott has been able to maintain the wider rhetorical frame of 'stopping the boats', and shifts in second-tier rhetoric on ways to achieve that broader goal have therefore been less damaging. If Abbott had instead announced in

Indonesia that changing conditions meant 'stopping the boats' would need to be postponed for three years, the deeper damage to perceptions of his authenticity would have been immense.

So, are political leaders forever stuck with the rhetorical formulations they generate? Can rhetorical path dependency ever be wound back, allowing the clean page to be reset so that a political leader can start again? Tentatively, there do seem to be several options. One means of punctuating this rhetorical path dependence is through an institutionalised action of overriding democratic legitimacy. For example, Howard overcame the stigma of diverting from his promise to 'never ever' again consider a goods and services tax (GST) by taking the policy to an election and being able to claim a democratic mandate for its introduction. In essence, the renewed democratic legitimacy provided by an election was able to wipe clean Howard's rhetorical slate so that he could effectively argue for an alternative policy outcome.

The effects of rhetorical path dependency also appear to be at their strongest only for political leaders rather than backbench members or even ministers. Like the leeway given to teenagers who may stray as they establish the behavioural norms of adult life, politicians are given a chance over time to develop their defining rhetorical refrains and can be forgiven for early inconsistencies. For example, prior to becoming leader of the Liberal Party, Abbott was on the record in support of a market-based mechanism to combat climate change (see Farr 2011). His campaign as Opposition leader against Labor's carbon price/tax and the emissions trading scheme not only contradicted his earlier narrative, but has defined his leadership. Whilst the shift against earlier rhetorical formulations was easily forgiven, as leader it would now be inconceivable for him to argue in favour of a carbon tax without suffering significant political costs. Similarly, as Treasurer in 1985, Paul Keating was an advocate for a consumption tax only to later, as prime minister, win an election by destroying Opposition leader John Hewson's proposal for a consumption tax. It was his rhetoric as leader against a GST that defined his position in a path dependent way. It would then have become inconceivable for him to change again to advocating for a GST without suffering a prohibitive amount of political pain.

Of course, holding an election in order to wipe clean a rhetorical slate is self-evidently not a tool that can be used easily or often. It is full of electoral risk, with Howard himself only just returning to power in 1998 in pursuit of his policy to introduce the GST. Should our political leaders, therefore, simply choose their political rhetoric more carefully, weighing every word lest they make an error or commit to a rhetorical formulation that they will come to regret? There are at least two strong reasons why such an approach would provide little benefit. Firstly, political leaders who weigh their words too carefully risk sounding inauthentic — an ironic outcome considering that speaking rashly and then changing your rhetoric down the track has the same result. John Kane and Haig Patapan's (2010) reflections on the 'artless art' of modern rhetoric demonstrate how difficult it is to be both careful and authentic at the same time. Secondly, rhetorical statements that are open and low-risk are unlikely to mount a persuasive case and can leave a leader looking vacuous and unwilling to stand for anything.

As the wide body of literature on the interplay of politics and the media attests, the media plays an important role in framing and entrenching particular rhetorical moments into the wider public imagination (see Weaver 2007, Greenfield and Williams 2003). What the media chooses to focus on can magnify or diminish its impact on the minds of the electorate. Plenty of rhetorical gaffes are made and only mentioned in passing, ensuring that they do not become the basis for an entrenched, path-dependent rhetorical statement. But in many cases, the media are simply responding to what political leaders themselves have sought to emphasise. It was Rudd, not the media, who consistently labelled climate change as a great moral challenge and, in reporting on the subsequent policy about face, the media were simply reflecting on the rhetoric of Rudd's own creation. Similarly with the cases of Gillard and Abbott — each leader emphasised again and again the rhetorical formulation that they wanted to frame their policies within. The fact that the style and content of media reporting, and the desire for 'gotcha' moments, can amplify a rhetorical shift does not diminish the fact that it is political leaders who choose a particular rhetorical path in the first place.

The challenge for political leaders is to be authentic and clear in their rhetorical choices, and accept that this involves a degree of risk that they may be derailed by the difficulties of politics or the complexity of an issue. Representative parliamentary democracy is, after all, a system based on a battle of ideas and competing policies, which cannot hope to be carried out through vague, nondescript rhetorical choices. But equally, leaders must understand the real power that lies in the rhetorical choices they make and the political costs that come from veering from one rhetorical path to another.

References

Abbott, T. 2013a. A regional deterrence framework to combat people smuggling. *Liberal Party of Australia*. 23 August. URL: http://www.liberal.org.au/latest-news/2013/08/23/tony-abbott-regional-deterrence-framework-combat-people-smuggling. Consulted 4 October 2013.

—— 2013b. Interview with David Koch and Samantha Armytage. *Sunrise*. *Liberal Party of Australia*. 10 September. URL: http://www.liberal.org.au/latest-news/2013/09/10/tony-abbott-interview-david-koch-and-samantha-armytage-sunrise. Consulted 4 October 2013.

—— 2013c. Joint press conference with Minister Julie Bishop, Jakarta. *Prime Minister of Australia*. 1 October. URL: http://www.pm.gov.au/media/2013-10-01/joint-press-conference-minister-julie-bishop-jakarta. Consulted 17 October 2013.

Australian Broadcasting Corporation (ABC) 2010. Abbott under fire for 'gospel truth' gaffe. *ABC News* 18 May. URL http://www.abc.net.au/news/2010-05-18/abbott-under-fire-for-gospel-truth-gaffe/830636. Consulted 14 October 2013.

Australian Financial Review (*AFR*). 2010. Seeking 'community consensus' ahead of an ETS. 28 June. URL: http://www.afr.com/p/national/seeking_community_consensus_ahead_DoPyom16hbN8c6by6fsaaJ. Consulted 25 September 2013.

Bachelard, M. and Wroe, D. 2013. PM's boats compromise offers a way to ditch tow-back policy.*Sydney Morning Herald* 2 October. URL: http://www.smh.com.au/federal-politics/political-news/pms-boats-compromise-offers-a-way-to-ditch-towback-policy-20131001-2uqs1.html. Consulted 4 October 2013.

Connolly, E. 2013. Indonesia voices concerns about Coalition's boats policy 'loud and clear'. *Canberra Times* 25 September. URL: http://www.canberratimes.com.au/federal-politics/political-news/indonesia-voices-concerns-about-coalitions-boats-policy-loud-and-clear-20130925-2ucuz.html?skin=text-only. Consulted 11 October 2013.

Farr, M. 2011. Opposition leader Tony Abbott changes line, says he never supported ETS. *Daily Telegraph* 20 July. URL: http://www.dailytelegraph.com.au/news/national/opposition-leader-tony-abbott-changes-line-says-he-never-supported-ets/story-e6freuzr-1226098237952. Consulted 17 October 2013.

Gains, F., John, P.C. and Stoker, G. 2005. Path dependency and the reform of English local government. *Public Administration* 83(1): 25–45.

Gillard, J. 2010a. Transcript of interview with Laurie Oakes, *Weekend today* 27 June. URL: http://parlinfo.aph.gov.au/parlInfo/search/display/display.w3p;adv=yes;orderBy=customrank;page=1;query=Gillard%20%22Climate%20change%22%20Date%3A26%2F06%2F2010%20%3E%3E%2027%2F06%2F2010%20Dataset%3Apressrel,pressclp,emms,radioprm,tvprog,broadcastOther;rec=14;resCount=Default. Consulted 25 September 2013.

—— 2010b. Transcript of interview on *Ten News*. 16 August. URL: http:// parlinfo.aph.gov.au/parlInfo/search/display/display.w3p;adv=yes;orderB y=customrank;page=0;query=Ten%20Date%3A16%2F08%2F2010%20 %3E%3E%2017%2F08%2F2010%20Dataset%3Aemms,radioprm,tvprog, broadcastOther;rec=1;resCount=Default. Consulted 11 October 2013.

—— 2011. Transcript of joint press conference, Canberra. 24 February. URL: http://parlinfo.aph.gov.au/parlInfo/search/display/display.w3p;adv=yes;orde rBy=customrank;page=0;query=Gillard%20%22carbon%20price%22%20 Date%3A20%2F02%2F2011%20%3E%3E%2028%2F02%2F2011%20 Dataset%3Apressrel;rec=12;resCount=Default. Consulted 25 September 2013.

—— 2013. Julia Gillard writes on power, purpose and Labor's future. *Guardian* 14 September. URL: http://www.theguardian.com/world/2013/sep/13/julia-gillard-labor-purpose-future. Consulted 25 September 2013.

Greenfield, C. and Williams, P. 2003. Limiting politics: Howardism, media rhetoric and national cultural commemorations. *Australian Journal of Political Science* 38(2): 279–97.

Hall, B. 2013. Coalition defies Indonesia with boat tow-back policy. *Sydney Morning Herald* 8 July. URL: http://www.smh.com.au/federal-politics/ federal-election-2013/coalition-defies-indonesia-with-boat-towback-policy-20130707-2pkb2.html. Consulted 4 October 2013.

Hartcher, P. 2010. How Abbott found an unexpected ally over climate change in the Gang of Four. *Sydney Morning Herald* 26 June. URL: http://www. smh.com.au/federal-politics/political-opinion/how-abbott-found-an-unexpected-ally-over-climate-change-in-the-gang-of-four-20100625-z9r6. html. Consulted 25 July 2013.

Howard, J. 2001. John Howard's 2001 election campaign policy launch speech. 28 October. *Immigration Museum*. URL: http://museumvictoria.com.au/ immigrationmuseum/discoverycentre/identity/videos/politics-videos/john-howards-2001-election-campaign-policy-launch-speech/. Consulted 16 October 2013.

Kane, J. and Patapan, H. 2010. The artless art: Leadership and the limits of democratic rhetoric. *The Australian Journal of Political Science* 45(3): 371–89.

Kelly, P. 2010. Rudd's dangerous climate retreat. *Australian* 28 April. URL: http://www.theaustralian.com.au/opinion/rudds-dangerous-climate-retreat/ story-e6frg6zo-1225859076778. Consulted 24 September 2013.

—— 2012. I'll turn back every boat, says Tony Abbott. *Australian* 21 January. URL: http://www.theaustralian.com.au/national-affairs/ill-turn-back-every-boat-says-tony-abbott/story-fn59niix-1226249863706#. Consulted 4 October 2013.

Maiden, S. 2010. Gillard says she led push for delay on ETS. *Australian* 28 June. URL: http://www.theaustralian.com.au/news/gillard-says-she-led-push-for-delay-on-ets/story-e6frg6n6-1225884955922. Consulted 25 September 2013.

Morrison, S. 2013. Minister for Immigration and Border Protection and Acting Commander of Operation Sovereign Borders Joint Agency Task Force address press conference on Operation Sovereign Borders. *Australian Customs and Border Protection Service*. 4 October. URL: http://www.customs.gov.au/site/131004transcript_operation-sovereign-borders.asp. Consulted 17 October 2013.

Peake, R. 2012. No turning back on Abbott navy stance. *Canberra Times* 12 July. URL: http://www.canberratimes.com.au/national/no-turning-back-on-abbott-navy-stance-20120711-21wld.html. Consulted 4 October 2013.

Pierson, P. 2000. Increasing returns, path dependence, and the study of politics. *American Political Science Review* 94(2): 251–67.

Rudd, K. 2006. Faith in politics. *The Monthly* October 2006. URL: http://www.themonthly.com.au/issue/2006/october/1330040298/kevin-rudd/faith-politics. Consulted 11 October 2013.

—— 2008. Joint press conference with Minister Penny Wong and Premier Mike Rann, Lower Lakes, Murray Darling, South Australia. *Prime Minister of Australia*. 5 July. URL: http://pandora.nla.gov.au/pan/79983/20081112-0133/www.pm.gov.au/media/Interview/2008/interview_0348.html. Consulted 24 September 2013.

—— 2010. Transcript of doorstop. Nepean Hospital, Penrith. *Prime Minister of Australia*. 27 April. URL: http://pandora.nla.gov.au/pan/79983/20100624-1429/www.pm.gov.au/node/6708.html. Consulted 24 September 2013.

Sydney Morning Herald 2010. Gillard rules out imposing carbon tax. 17 August. URL: http://m.smh.com.au/federal-election/climate/gillard-rules-out-imposing-carbon-tax-20100816-1270b.html. Consulted 25 September 2013.

Taylor, L. 2010. Decision to put climate action on hold smacks of political cowardice.*Sydney Morning Herald* 28 April. URL: http://www.smh.com.au/federal-politics/political-opinion/decision-to-put-climate-action-on-hold-smacks-of-political-cowardice-20100427-tq1h.html. Consulted 17 October 2013.

Weaver, D. 2007. Thoughts on agenda setting, framing, and priming. *Journal of Communication* 57(1): 142–47.

Wilson, L. and Vasek, L. 2012. I will still turn boats around, Tony Abbott says. *Australian* 7 July. URL: http://www.theaustralian.com.au/national-affairs/i-will-still-turn-boats-around-tony-abbott-says/story-fn59niix-1226419434930#. Consulted 4 October 2013.

Wroe, D. and Hall, B. 2013. Say we vote to turn back those boats. What next? *Sydney Morning Herald* 13 July. URL: http://www.smh.com.au/federal-politics/federal-election-2013/say-we-vote-to-turn-back-those-boats-what-next-20130712-2pvkg.html. Consulted 17 October 2013.

Part II: Standards of rhetoric

6. Looking backwards to the future: The evolving tradition of ideal political rhetoric in Australia

Mark Rolfe

In 2007 Robert Manne extolled the television series *The West Wing* as a model for what leaders and political rhetoric should be in contrast to 'what … democratic politics is not' under John Howard, 'one of the most unscrupulous but effective politicians in our history'. The program is 'so attractive (and perhaps ultimately fictitious)' because 'despite their willingness to play the game according to its inescapable rules, no corrosion of character has taken place in any of the players'. There was real grand debate between Senator Arnie Vinick, played by Alan Alda, and Congressman Matt Santos, played by Jimmy Smits. 'Both candidates are granted rhetorical victories', wrote Manne, 'The debate has been spirited, occasionally angry, but sharp and clean. The candidates' handshake at its conclusion is a moment of genuine political epiphany'. For Manne, everyone was elevated rather than degraded by the experience (2007: 12–13).

Manne is not alone with such fervent political desire for the elevation of the quality of politics and of political language. There has been a habitual tendency in Australia to think that the current state of political discourse is appalling and to envisage what it should be like, drawing frequently on an imagined past when political leaders and their rhetoric were better. 'Soaring political oratory' existed 'back then' for the journalist Annabel Crabb. She doesn't tell us when, but we know it was eventually killed by the sound bite, the 24-hour news cycle and social media (Crabb 2013). A similarly mysterious 'back then' lurks in a book by Lindsay Tanner, an ex-Labor politician who vented his spleen at social media, trivia and celebrity promoting the constant media cycle and degrading politics (Tanner 2012).

The problem with such analyses is that nostalgia does not withstand closer historical investigation. Ultimately, we arrive at the quip that 'nostalgia ain't what it used to be'. But that still leaves the question of why people resort to these historical longings. To wit, I argue that creative imaginings of past leaders and their rhetorics have been essential standards for judging current leaders and their language principally because there is no abstract universal point for judging this discourse.

This argument has a necessarily historical dimension that needs exploration. Depictions of 'back then' or the 'good old days', when leaders and their language were better, have been part of representative democracies since the early nineteenth century, even 'back then' in those supposed better days. This is not only the case in Australia, but also in those countries to which Australians looked — Britain and America. They have a common myth about the political past and for generations they have shared discussions about great leaders of the past, although it must be said that America led the way as the first representative democracy.

Such idealisations of political leadership and political rhetoric have been intrinsic to an evolving tradition of myth-making about admired political leaders, which is then used in partisan politics to judge the current crop of politicians and candidates. General themes of great leadership are deployed in contextualised circumstances. Competitors for office must try to measure up to these exacting standards, while simultaneously warding off the disrepute associated with the stereotype of the despised politician and pushing it in the direction of opponents. The rhetoric of anti-politics is a powerful accompaniment.

This tradition necessarily involves complex manoeuvres of *ethos* by politicians with popular audiences. Politicians battle each other in partisan games around *ethos*, willing to foster the stereotypical disrepute in others while not exciting suspicions of their own *ethos*. In part these games are played with idealised notions of rhetoric and of great leaders, which are counter posed to exaggerated notions of unruly or deceitful language and stereotyped politicians. This myth-making happens in tandem with a popular revulsion for stereotypical politicians and their disreputable vocation and with popular demands for political candidates who live up to the mythical *ethos*.

Myth, tradition and rhetoric

My argument does not depend on a notion of myth as falsity. Rather, political myth-making is 'a normal feature of political life … linked to the existence of competing sets of ideological beliefs about what society is and how it ought to be' (Flood 2002: 11–12). It is a species of rhetoric engaged in the deliberative genre that appeals to the collective memory of historical events; for example, the foundation of Rome, the Magna Carta, the French Revolution, the American Revolution or, in the case of this chapter, American presidents. Such memories are not nuanced accounts, but neither are they fabrications. They *do* have a semblance of fact and truth to them, but at the same time, they *are* guilty of simplification and anachronism. To be fair, though, such sins can also be committed by scholars who impose their priorities on the past and make familiar much that is alien. For example, political theorists have a provisional and ambivalent relationship with history 'as a quarry' for their enterprise (Condren

1997: 45). Clearly, the need for scholarly sensitivity to historical context points us to the more common human dilemma of hermeneutic interpretation that troubles the public and academics alike.

For both Flood (2002) and Tudor (1972: 132), myth is a narrative that serves ideological functions, specifically in competitions over 'what society is and how it should be'. Consequently, it connects the treasured beliefs and figures of a social group in a sequence of events in what purports to be a true account. It must therefore be 'sufficiently faithful to the interpretation of facts, sufficiently faithful to the relationship between facts, and sufficiently faithful to their meaning and significance' to ensure that it cannot be discredited as mere fantasy, irrationality or distortion (Flood 2002: 9).

Political myth has validity to a social group, says Flood, which is why it is a rhetorical resource for different groups to deploy in contests. Any rhetor of that social group must take myths seriously if they want to be taken seriously. In that respect, we can see a link between political myth and what is called in rhetoric *endoxa*. That is, a rhetor must resort to the common knowledge and beliefs of a group as the basis of unexpressed presumptions and conclusions in arguments (Tardini 2005) that have a tentative plausibility for an audience (Walton 2007: 12–13). *Endoxa* form the basis of informal reasoning in persuasion and explain why political myths are reproduced through a social group: as widely shared *endoxa*, they are powerful resources for arguments. Of course, this also means they are used in political contests within that community.

Given the reasonable grounds for a social group to indulge in a political myth over time, this reproduction connects directly to the concept of rhetorical tradition. In his exploration of American democratic discourse Russell Hanson defined rhetorical tradition as 'an historically extended, socially embodied argument' over the meanings of essential and widely admired ideas (1985: 23–24). Over generations, Americans have debated the meaning of democracy because it is a prized and widely shared belief, otherwise people would not fight for it. Despite being a valued belief, however, this does not mean that democracy is a simple concept. On the contrary, democracy is widely accepted as a complicated entity (Saward 2003; Sartori 1987). It is no wonder there is no single model of democracy that has stamped political societies across the world, but a plethora of adaptations that arise according to circumstances and of tinkering resulting from persistent debate.

In fact, says Hanson, the historically extended argument exists because democracy is a contested concept open to continual debate and dispute (1985: 23–24). Numerous scholars agree that there are three areas that complicate any arrival at consensus in argument over the term. That is, contest arises over the definition of democracy, over the application of the definition to events, and over the social attitudes it displays (Connolly 1983). Argument between debaters may occur over the criteria that make up the definition of democracy. Even if by some minor miracle agreement can be gained between them over definition, disagreement may still ensue over the application of that definition. Furthermore, debaters will use the term with a social attitude or evaluation that provokes dissension. The nature of democracy lends itself to continuous conflict and, so, it is always being constituted and reconstituted through persistent argument as each generation of citizens seeks to make democracy meaningful to themselves.

By implication, one may add that such continual rhetorical construction is not unique to America, but is inherent to all meaningful representative democracies, including Australia. Moreover, these societies are continually feeding each other with insights, arguments and discontents because of their common interest in debating the meaning of democracy. This is most obvious in the fact that Manne drew on an American television show to make a local point. But he is not the first Australian to do this. One can trace our habit of looking to America to the 1820s. After all, America was the first representative democracy, for its white males if not for others, and it created examples for others to contemplate, discuss, borrow and adapt. It is therefore necessary to turn to America to see how their imaginings of leadership and language began and functioned.

The West Wing and *ethos*

Clearly, Manne loved *The West Wing*, and one can assume that, like so many devotees, he idolised President Josiah 'Jed' Bartlet. Although the writers of the show were liberals with a contempt for George W. Bush always in the back of their minds, Bartlet's impeccable ancestry and convictions displayed their devotion to core American principles beyond partisanship. For a start, they cast him as a descendant of one of the signers of the Declaration of Independence.

This lineage is connected to ideals of public service to others: to ideals rather than to selfish materialist pursuits. We know that Bartlet followed the contemplative life through the priesthood and academia, yet he also pursued the active life of politics where he applied his knowledge of economics for the benefit of the people. He was still the sometimes-formidable professor with a predilection for historical, literary and biblical allusions, thus further hinting at the Platonic ideal of the philosopher–king, which hovers in the background. He was faithful to his wife, family and religion, which is very much in line with the popular expectations of an American political candidate. Tragically, but also typically in line with the stories of presidential martyrdom, he suffered multiple sclerosis for his people — which echoes Franklin D. Roosevelt's polio — a disease that will be given no quarter until he has laid down the mantle of office in accordance with his oath to others.

Thus, in his fictional biography, Bartlet satisfied the threefold categories that make up *ethos*, the rhetorical term for credibility with an audience. No matter how much we think rhetoric should be based on logic, audiences will not listen if they don't respect the orator. In fact, according to Aristotle, the prime proof (*pisteis*) for all audiences is the credibility and reputation of the speaker. They need to be persuaded of the practical wisdom (*phronesis*), benevolence to others (*eunoia*), and excellent moral character (*arête*) of the orator (Rolfe 2008). Bartlet proves himself in all three areas, which is why we find him so easily admirable and why we expect to find these attributes in all political candidates who wish to woo voters.

For many people, a focus in politics on the person is wrong; a shallow concern with image rather than a serious focus on issues, on personalities when it should be on policies. Such nostrums are regularly repeated at every election, says Trevor Parry-Giles citing another scholar, yet it is a 'treacherous piety' since:

> *Human beings* make up a government, not 'measures' or 'issues'. The quality of a government is thus a function of the quality of Leadership, not of the policies advocated by that government. (2010: 39)

Whether a person is suitable for the top political job in the land is not a trivial matter. We can justifiably expect that a president or prime minister should display self-mastery and good judgement (unlike, for example Labor leader Mark Latham when seeking office in 2004) and have the right sort of education and experience to make sensible decisions. Finally, we should rightly expect that a leader has the prudence (*phronesis*) to calculate ends and means with regard to both particular situations and general principles so as to leave the community better off. This requires levels of implementation, effectiveness and achievement that acquire legitimacy with a community. It was over such specifics, for example, that both Kevin Rudd and Julia Gillard had problems, with consequent damage to their *ethos* and difficulties with voters listening to them during their terms as prime minister. For these reasons of *ethos*, it is understandable that fantasy and mythical presidents have a place in political debates about the quality of leadership. However abbreviated they may seem from a scholarly point of view, as *endoxa* they provide some standards to discuss current political leaders and hopefuls.

Imagined presidents and the American jeremiad

Paradoxically, it is the fantasising about Bartlet's *ethos* that has deep American antecedents and proves it is not unwarranted. Drawing on Benedict Anderson's notion of imagined communities, Jeff Smith observed in his assessment of American presidents that 'If nations themselves are imaginative constructions, their leadership is even more so. Rulership of any kind is an essentially metaphorical act, a community's projection of authority onto an individual in much the same way that love is metaphorically projected through a red rose' (2009: 7). And, we may add, if political leadership is imagined then so is political rhetoric.

The intellectual material for imagining American presidents existed long before George Washington became president; after all 'the presidency had to be imagined before it could be created' (Smith 2009: 7). Much of this can be traced to England during the time of Robert Walpole's premiership and developments of parties, partisanship and the early Westminster model (Smith 2009; Bailyn 1968). His Robinocracy, as it was called, was accused of gross corruption of public monies and deplorable lies. But for the most part, these sallies came from his Tory opposition. As well, they counter posed such negatives to idealisations of a unifying patriot king beyond politics. It is an early lesson in the same rhetorical ploy advanced by Manne some 300 years later. Portrayals of ideal leadership have a partisan context, but at the same time have an anti-political thrust to them. This unusual rhetorical combination easily travelled the Atlantic to the American colonies where it became standard fodder for politics.

None of this background detracts from the fact that Washington was widely admired during his lifetime, so much so that he eased the anxieties of many attendees at the convention of 1787 about the new presidency that they were creating. Nevertheless, his personality could not resolve the vagaries of the new office and its tensions with the legislatures within a system of checks and balances designed to force separation *and* cooperation. Power was not only shared between president and congress but also with states and an overseeing Supreme Court. Yet distrust of political power, fed by intellectual inheritance and revolutionary experience, was tempered for the attendees by realisation of the weakness of the executive they created in the first confederation of 1781. As a result they bolstered the position of president. Still, their novel political creation was a recipe for continuing dispute over the role and extent of this single national political institution in the land. This immediately manifested in battles between Federalists and Anti-Federalists, as they were called, the centralisers and anti-centralisers of political power.

Of course, the vagaries and complexities were only temporarily alleviated by Washington's reputation while he was alive. He became a modern day Cincinnatus;

even his army officers called themselves 'Society of the Cincinnati', a reference to the humble Roman aristocrat and consul who became a legend of selfless civic virtue for saving the republic in its time of need and for returning to the farm plough rather than holding to power. He appealed to Americans wary of those who liked power too much. Given all this, Washington's death ensured that a larger than life mystique soon enveloped the man as a standard for leadership. He became the epitome of perfect political leadership for a perfect republic. By the new century each side was fighting for the mantle of the great man.

This tendency merged with another American twist to European ideas. John Dunn has written that 'that democracy entered the ideological history of the modern world reluctantly and facing backwards' with one eye on Athenian democracy (2006: 39). But one may also say that Americans were also looking backwards to the beginning of their republic. From around 1800 political partisans bewailed opponents for corruption of the 'New Jerusalem' so distinct from corrupt aristocratic Europe. Here was the rhetoric of the American jeremiad, a narrative that harks back to the mixed religious and political ideals of America as a 'shining city on the hill' girded by a covenant with God. In line with the distant Puritan forebears, the American Founding Fathers were deemed to be renewing the covenant of their country as both a religious and secular perfection (Bercovitch 1978: Chpt 1).

Thus, the combined legacies of American jeremiad and Washington mystique decreed a tremendous narrative for future citizens to cherish, but a tremendous challenge for future politicians to meet. There were bound to be disappointments, especially when with time, retrospection and partisan competition politicians were judged against an evolving 'invented tradition' of a few mythologised presidents (Kazin 1998: 21). Washington obviously set the tradition, but he was gradually joined by Thomas Jefferson and Andrew Jackson and then, many decades later, by Abraham Lincoln and Franklin D. Roosevelt. All were subject to partisan abuse during their lifetimes, but were eventually elevated after death to a non-partisan pantheon of great leaders of the republic. They became yardsticks to measure others and mourn a perceived loss to politics; the political mythology of the nation was continued through personification. It was an easy recipe for any capable political orator to cultivate disappointment in an opponent and promote a favourite alternative. It also meant that political nostalgia for past leaders was embedded from the beginning.

Public opinion and rhetoric

Such rhetoric became political fodder after major political developments. The extension of the white male franchise in the 1820s changed politics from an exclusive gentlemen's game to an inclusive participatory culture. Public opinion was now a force to be reckoned with and the following decades amplified this force with the evolution of the 'penny press', transport and communication (Schudson 1978). For the rest of the century, says Andrew Robertson, there was thematic recurrence in American discourse because of the profound need to persuade the masses (2005: vii). From such origins populism became an essential part of political life in the United States and a 'persistent yet mutable style of political rhetoric' that continues to the present (Kazin 1998: Chpt 1). The American jeremiad had a new lease of life in party politics for the masses, a rhetoric constantly positing the betrayal of the special mission of that nation and the Founding Fathers and demanding a return to the original values through the ejection of certain politicians and the election of others. Disappointment with the present was ever present.

Rhetoric became more hortatory in order to rouse the emotions and values of the populace and more admonitory in order to rouse partisanship and warn of the failures resulting from wrong political choice at election time. In addition, this popular style required familiarity with the people and demanded bluntness that valued truth over politeness. The old gentlemanly decorum of dignified reserve and distance by which one had shown respect for others was now replaced by a new decorum that demanded one be friendly and familiar in order to show respect (Cmiel 1990: Chpt 2). The requirements of *ethos* changed accordingly.

This was the beginning in public political debate of 'plain speaking' and of personal invective by those considered outside gentlemanly circles. Jackson built his anti-authoritarian political *ethos* assaulting 'aristocrats' and using the new 'stump speaking' (Eastman 2009: 184). This was indicative of a larger change in *ethos* as a 'man of the people'. For example, in the chase for popular attention, in 1824 Jackson began a tradition of presidential campaign biographies that have followed the same narrative contours to the present, emphasising the rise of an ordinary man of the same ilk as the voters. Repeatedly, the men were depicted as devotees of Cincinnatus, just like Washington (Brown 1960: 83–89). Many politicians acquired a familiar or folk decorum in order to fulfil the ethical expectations of their audiences. The word slang, which was once a synonym for vulgar in the previous century, was now associated with an informal style of language that signalled class associations.

The middling style of rhetoric had arrived in America, much to the consternation of gentlemen who thought it cheapened politics and broke traditional cultural boundaries. It appalled the likes of Henry Clay, the representative of Kentucky in both chambers of congress and thrice presidential candidate, who was revered as a link to the revolutionary era. To such refined critics, middling style mixed high and low, the erudite and the folksy, such that lapses in style were considered lapses in character. But we can also see how such views lined up with the politics of democracy. Clay was a bitter enemy of Jackson.

Australia and battles over rhetoric

As America underwent these political struggles as the sole and, later, leading example of white male representative democracy, so these developments were communicated to Australia and the world in what may be called the intricacies of Americanisation. This process did not entail the story of an aggressive Other imposing its culture upon a vulnerable Australia. The transmission was rather more complicated, selective and adaptive and worked at several levels; much passed unnoticed while controversy settled on some of the more noticeable or superficial elements (Rolfe 1997). Adding to the complexity was the tendency to cast America as both a promise and a threat:

> From early days the United States has had a curious and very entertaining career in Australia as a kind of storehouse of ideas to be raided, a powerfully justifying precedent to be invoked or a dreadful example with which to shame the thoughtless. (C. Hartley Grattan cited in Rolfe 1997)

Although comparisons of an imagined Australia with an imagined America were made before 1788, it became common to think in the Antipodes and the British Colonial Office that the two countries were treading similar paths. For decades until colonial self-government in the 1850s, such comparisons emerged as ominous warnings or progressive hopes that disputes between Britain and her colonies would lead to war, independence and republicanism following the American precedent.

Writers often saw Australia as 'a new America', another America, 'the Future America', a 'humble imitation of the United States', 'the United States of Australia', the 'America of the South'. Or, as English Liberal politician Sir Charles Dilke remarked in 1867, 'In Australia, it is often said, we have a second America in its infancy' (McLachlan 1977: 367). Australia was often cast as a younger sibling, treading somewhere behind its elder 'Brother Jonathan'. As a result and from earliest days, Australians were abreast of even minor developments in America. For example, Australians could read the political wisdom in Benjamin Franklin's autobiography while expounding upon 'John Bull' (Britain), Brother Jonathan and some local political matter (Anonymous 1829a: 3). So it is not surprising that the work of Alexis de Tocqueville elicited early interest here and influenced the British Colonial Office when granting measures of government in 1842 and 1850 (Patapan 2003: 6).

The identity of Australia in the nineteenth century was explicitly relational, with America and Britain serving as contrasting points of reference. Few sought actual revolution and republic; most only aimed at prising political reform from the Colonial Office or local authorities while staying firmly within the imperial fold. Warnings and wishes were issued in the context of local politics, such as the development of representative institutions, disputes over land distribution, and protests against restoring transportation of convicts in the late 1840s.

The explorer, barrister, landowner and politician William Charles Wentworth was typical of many people in his time with his regard for both Britain and America. In 1819 he imagined Australia's own War of Independence being fought in the Blue Mountains. In 1824 he and Robert Wardell started the *Australian* newspaper and agitated for a free press, trial by jury and a local house of assembly. Decades later Wentworth approvingly cited de Tocqueville when debating the 1853 New South Wales Constitution Bill. He also attracted derision for his idea of a local aristocracy for the upper house and for being a conservative old fogy.

But the idea was evident in 1825 when he and Wardell reproduced sections of a letter in which the author discussed development 'of the highest importance, viz. the formation of a wealthy and high-minded Aristocracy'. This was happening in America and would happen in Australia where things were 'not yet ripe for Representative Government' (Anonymous 1825: 2). Here was debate about representative institutions, quality of leadership and British constitutionalism, which for many embodied the Aristotelian mixed constitution of monarchy, aristocracy and democracy.

Typically, Wentworth and Wardell reproduced in 1831 a section from Thomas Paine's *Rights of man* discussing the 'grafting [of] Representation upon Democracy' in America. They included the magnificent praise: 'What Athens was in miniature, America will be in magnitude. The one was the wonder of the ancient world; the other is becoming the admiration, the model of the present.' Representative government, they continued, 'exists not by fraud and mystery, it deals not in cant and sophistry; but inspires a language that, passing from heart to heart, is felt and understood' (Anonymous 1831: 4).

Here was an idealisation of democratic discourse that resembles the imaginings elsewhere in this chapter and purports a true congruence with the people over other forms of political society that spread insincerity. The section includes Paine's discussion of the qualities of an American president, where 'more power is delegated … than to any other individual member of Congress', and declares 'that no man in his sober senses will compare the character of any of the kings of Europe, with that of General George Washington'.

Such discussions are a much earlier demonstration of the point made by Gregory Melleuish that politics after the granting of responsible government to New South Wales in 1856 was not so much understood 'in terms of institutional design but focused rather on quality of leaders'. Certainly, citizens looked to British civilisation, British constitutionalism and British traditions because they believed themselves to be British and worthy of such an inheritance. And all this formed a political culture that emphasised 'the quality of the men elected into Parliament and political office rather than the way the political structure operated' (Melleuish 2013: 1, 6).

In addition to Britain, though, Australians looked throughout the century to America for measures of quality. In 1827 the editor of the 'conservative' *Sydney Gazette* praised the appointment of George Druitt — major, settler and landowner and a man with political enemies — as a 'modern Cincinnatus [who] has proved an ornament and beneficial appendage to his fellow-Colonists'. He has 'manifested the uprightness, correctness, and honour of a Gentleman, and his estate displays the state of a true English farmer' (Anonymous 1827: 2). Such common references to Cincinnatus easily and often extended to favourable mention of Washington. The *Sydney Monitor*, started in 1826 and considered more in the 'liberal' camp, reproduced in 1832 from *Tait Magazine* of Edinburgh an article with the caption that it was 'a great deal too true'. It examined the virtues of chancellor Lord Brougham and decided 'we are looking for the patriotism of a Regulus, the self-denial of a Scipio Africanus, and the magnanimity of a Cincinnatus, or a Washington'. We see an early demonstration of the gap drawn between ancient examples of leadership and contemporary leaders: 'It only leads us to regret, that in the present day, your Broughams, Greys, and Radnors, seldom equal the expectations of mankind, and fall short of the ancient heathen Patriots (Anonymous 1832: 2). In 1860, one letter wrote, 'without supposing that we have among us a Cincinnatus or a Washington', on the vexed issue of finding the fit parliamentarians who were not '"restless demagogues" and "unfit men"' (Citizen 1860: 5). In 1887 Wybert Reeve, an actor and author famous in his time, gave a public lecture on heroes of 'incorruptible truth and devotion to a great cause'. Amongst their number he included Cincinnatus as well as Washington 'with his integrity of character, and a sense of justice so great that no influence could swerve it from the proper course' (Anonymous 1887: 6).

As we saw earlier, qualities of American leaders were a part of American populism, a rhetoric and decorum that found ready recipients in early Australia. It was always possible for the emancipists to refract local struggles through the populist lens and to see the exclusives working in similar cabals and conspiracies to those operated by American aristocrats. In particular, Jackson's vitriolic attacks on the Bank of the United States in 1832 made him a popular hero fighting a body that made 'the rich richer and the potent more powerful' (Greenstein

2009: Chpt 8, location 18). Hence the liberal *Morning Chronicle* derided the *Sydney Morning Herald* and its advocacy of the 'Pure Merino gentlemen' and their 'Pure Merino Bank' or Bank of Australia (Anonymous 1845a: 2). As it had on many occasions, the *Chronicle* invoked Old Hickory, as Jackson was known, against money interests and so did Reverend Dr John Lang with his audiences. Adelaide readers received extracts from 'the democratic paper', the *Daily Boston Times*, celebrating the victory of James K. Polk, who was christened 'the Young Hickory' for carrying the legacy of his predecessor over Henry Clay (Anonymous 1845b: 3). The same raging rhetoric against financial conspiracies arose with the Labour Party in the 1890s (Love 1984), at the same time that the Populist Party made famous inroads on American politics. The rhetoric lived on for decades.

A democratic rhetorical style and *ethos* accompanied this populist politics as it did in America. Again, Wentworth was an exponent since he was the point man 'for an assortment of bond and free, indigent and wealthy, needy men and hangers-on, knock-abouts and ne'er-do-wells'. The *Australian* was their 'scandalous, vitriolic rag that exhibited no respect for legitimate authority, according to the exclusives' (Cochrane 2006: 17). Their man was notorious for 'virulent abuse', 'scandalous and vituperative imputations' and 'the filth of the missiles hurled from his mud-cart' (Cochrane 2006: 3).

From its earliest days politics in Australia was rowdy, raucous and replete with hortatory admonitory rhetoric that divided people according to the politics of the time. In other words, it was similar to America and we see similar assessments about *ethos* made with judgements of rhetorical decorum. In 1829 Governor Ralph Darling found an implacable opponent in the irascible Wentworth who sought his recall and impeachment and who had support in his quest from many newspapers. Darling thought the 'style and matter' of Wentworth's language was 'the best criterion of his character and motives'. In other words, he was 'a vulgar, ill-bred fellow, utterly unconscious of the Common Civilities due from one gentleman to another' (Cochrane 2006: 514). Darling had support from the *Sydney Gazette*, which was on the side of the established order, and damned Wentworth as a 'factious partisan' and pompously advised him to 'cultivate the arts of fair, upright, gentlemanly controversy, treating with candour, if not with civility, those whose opinions may happen to clash with his own, and shunning, as he would shun a grey snake, the vulgar epithets and phraseology of the pot-house, and the abusive slang of the milling-ring' (Anonymous 1829b: 2).

Clearly, in a similar fashion to America, views of rhetorical style aligned with political stance on populist causes. The *Sydney Morning Herald* of that time has been labelled conservative and in that vein it reproduced from the English *Fisher's Colonial Magazine* a review of a book of Clay's life and speeches. Clay was an appropriate choice for those who preferred the literary and gentlemanly style of rhetoric over the boisterous democratic style of Jackson, since the *Herald* feared democracy and the working class. Consequently, the reviewer favourably compared the Tory Edmund Burke, 'the unequalled Hibernian Cicero' to 'the classical and ornate' style of Clay (Anonymous 1845c: 4). For the editor of the *Hobart Courier* in 1852 the quality of rhetoric was connected to the quality of leadership of the 'great future for these our southern confederate republics'. He was mourning the death of Clay, a man 'gifted with great power of persuasion', with an antipodean sentiment:

> To us, in these Australasian colonies, the younger children of the Anglo-Norman family, not without note or instructiveness do such men as Henry Clay pass from the theatre of action … In that fast-coming time none could utter a more benevolent wish for the welfare of Australasia than that a man or men like Henry Clay should be raised up to lead and to counsel these youthful communities (Anonymous 1852: 2).

Sixty years after the death of Clay, a Melbourne newspaper could still refer to him as 'a genius' of oratory who acquired fame through hard work (Anonymous 1912: 3). Given that to date Australia followed the American battles over democracy and rhetoric, we were bound to also follow the next phase in the construction of rhetorical and presidential traditions, which included someone so often admired these days for oratorical greatness.

Lincoln and the middling style

Lincoln was subject during his presidency to the sort of abuse that is regularly dished out these days at politicians and it was directed as much at his middling-style rhetoric as at his character. The two were linked in many minds. Democratic and Republican politicians alike called him the 'original gorilla', which was an attack on his *ethos* in connection to the lack of refinement displayed by his language. After a meeting at the White House, even a sympathetic Republican was confused by his style and called him 'a barbarian, Scythian, yahoo or gorilla' because of his linguistic lapses (Cmiel 1990: 119).

Lincoln was in the middle of the battles over rhetorical style connected to character. He was a 'slang-wanging, stump speaker' (Williams 2001: 140) to one critic. One reporter heard the Gettysburg Address and reported: 'The cheek of every American must tingle with shame as he reads the silly, flat dish-watery utterances of the man who must be pointed out to foreigners as the President of the United States' (Spiegel 2002: 246). A February 1864 editorial in the influential *New York Herald* exclaimed: 'The idea that such a man as he should be President of such a country as this is a very ridiculous joke … His inaugural address was a joke' (Dallek 2001: xiii). A paper in his home state called him 'The craftiest and most dishonest politician that ever disgraced an office in America'

(Boller 1996: 127). Not only was Lincoln criticised for his style, but also subject to the stereotype of politicians that has been common to Australia since the beginning and to Britain since the Robinocracy.

The accompanying point to be made here is that it has always been an advantage for politicians to trade on the disrepute of politicians because the public has readily believed the worst of them. Tony Abbott has found eager audiences for such attacks when he railed successfully against a politicians' republic in 1998 and, more recently, accused Julia Gillard of being a liar. Abbott is only the latest in generations of politicians that have successfully accused opponents of lies. In particular, political neophytes across Anglosphere countries have had striking success with this ad hominem through parading their own lack of experience in the political game against the disrepute of the political establishment. So one finds this connection in rhetorical topos between such disparate political forces as the first Labor members of the NSW parliament in 1891, Pauline Hanson in 1996, the Australian Democrats in the 1970s and Jefferson Smith, the main character in the famous 1938 Hollywood movie *Mr Smith Goes to Washington* (Rolfe 2008). Perhaps the most successful and famous recent example, however, was Barack Obama's 2008 advancement of his political innocence against the dirty politics of Washington in combination with appeals to the great Lincoln and the jeremiad.

It was ever thus with American populism, which has always encouraged the ideal and the anti-political at the same time. Even though Lincoln was accused of dishonesty, he was not above exploiting the stereotype of politician to bolster his own *ethos*. In 1837 he told the Illinois legislature 'Mr Chairman, this movement is exclusively the work of politicians, a set of men who have interests aside from the people and who, to say most of them, are, taken as a mass, at least one long step removed from honest men. I say this with greater freedom because being a politician myself, none can regard it as personal' (Spiegel 2002: 2).

Death did not immediately vault Lincoln into the pantheon of democratic heroes whose rhetoric is treasured. It took decades. His gradual metamorphosis, however, demonstrates the larger point about the evolving tradition of standards of leadership and rhetoric, in America and elsewhere. Until the turn of the century Lincoln was the partisan preserve of the Republicans to be wielded against Democrats. The battle extended to his rhetoric as well. Edward McPherson was a Republican congressman and, later, a keeper of the Lincoln flame, so to speak, as an officer of the Gettysburg Battlefield Memorial Association. As American and Australian readers found (Anonymous 1887), McPherson claimed 'it is strange that the genuine literary abilities of the man were so long and persistently ignored by literary people'. This was not so strange given the partisan divide over the middling style. Lincoln, he said:

knew that cultivated men, even after his debates with Douglas, and after his first inaugural, were of opinion that he was utterly without other literary powers than those of a good stump speaker. He was believed to be a man of strong character, but wholly without literary polish, and it was generally believed that such a polish as his greatest speeches, such as that delivered in Cooper Institute in the winter revealed, was the work of some cultivated friends or some skilful secretaries. (Anonymous 1888: 7)

In nineteenth century England, Lincoln was abhorred by the Tories and aristocrats who associated him with the 'mob rule' of democracy. Alternately, Lincoln was a hero to liberals and labourites until World War II because they considered him a champion of the ordinary people (Smith 2011: 125–27). In this category of political celebration he was joined by such admired Liberal heroes as John Bright, Giuseppe Garibaldi and, of course, William Gladstone. This was, says Smith, 'radical political celebrity culture' that helped to perpetuate Liberalism as a radical tradition well into the next century. Winston Churchill was engulfed by it. Importantly, it was a British Liberalism that had learnt much from America as a test of the 'democratic principles of progress and liberty', which they fervently supported (Gerlach 2001: 5). Most of all there was Gladstone, nicknamed 'The People's William' for his recognition of public opinion and admired for his oratory.

Deification of Lincoln

It was only in the early twentieth century that Lincoln was transmuted 'from flawed politician [into] secular deity' (Zarefsky 1986: 363) to be fought over by all sides of American politics. By then he had joined the 'invented tradition' of mythologised presidents along with Washington, Jefferson and Jackson to be used and abused for partisan purposes. A further result of secular deification was that his rhetoric became a model to follow not an idiosyncrasy to scorn. He was no longer the crafty dissembler nor the awful purveyor of the middling style. Instead his rhetoric was elevated from its context. Politicians from Walter Mondale in 1984 to Newt Gingrich and the Texas Tea Party in 2011 (Camia 2011) have called for the emulation of the Lincoln–Douglas debates of 1858, with the intent of boosting their own *ethos* with a public that is widely suspicious of politicians and political rhetoric. The debates are, however, 'vastly more admired than read' (Zarefsky 1986: 162) and their reputation 'far outweighs their value' (Holzer 2012).

Lincoln's political metamorphosis in the early twentieth century was not only an American phenomenon but also British and Australian. The cult of Lincoln rose aloft a sentiment of Anglo-Saxon community that redescribed the man as the embodiment of English values. The mission of American exceptionalism and the role of British imperial defender of liberty merged in the racial ideology of Anglo-Saxonism. This was most needed during World War I when the struggle was seen as a fight against a Prussian militarism, just as the Civil War was a fight against slavery. In Edwards' words 'Lincoln's image was "internationalized" during the war' (2013: 30) under the auspices of Anglo-Saxon racialism.

Naturally, in Britain the Welsh Prime Minister David Lloyd George invoked Lincoln just as easily as did his Welsh counterpart Prime Minister William Hughes in Australia, who was often hailed from 1916 onwards as another Lincoln. This approbation was given by the *New York Herald* (Anonymous 1916a: 5), but closer to home even the premier of South Australia was willing to say:

> At present Mr. Hughes was in a similar position to that which faced Abraham Lincoln, when the great American President had to resort to compulsion against his wishes and sentiments. Lincoln was assailed, and Mr. Hughes was being assailed … He took his stand beside Mr. Hughes. If any penalty was to be meted out to the Prime Minister, all honour to him for daring to do what was right in the face of opposition which he did not think was fair. (Anonymous 1916b: 5)

With this wartime context in mind, a biographer insisted on ranking Hughes with the great Lincoln (Anonymous 1916c: 4). Such repeated associations had obvious ethical purpose against opponents during the conscription debates, presenting them as on the wrong side of the fight for democracy. This was the case of Liberal leader Joseph Cook in building the case for a referendum by pointing to Lincoln's conscription during the civil war (Anonymous 1916d: 5). Lincoln was also a continuation of Hughes's fascination with symbols of radical Liberal sympathies for the working class. On train trips to Melbourne for parliament he often practised oratory by listening to recordings of Gladstone's speeches. Obviously he was a model of oratory for the young Hughes.

The cult of Lincoln continued after the war. British and Australian newspapers called Prime Minister Stanley Baldwin a second Lincoln or a miniature Lincoln. In 1929, new prime minister James Scullin was 'Another log cabin to White House story', according to one journalist, in the tradition of Lincoln, as were his predecessors John Christian Watson, Andrew Fisher and Billy Hughes. Scullin did not stack up against Alfred Deakin, who had of course the reputation as 'Australia's greatest orator'. This journalist seems put off by Scullin's more hortatory style.

> At times he emphasises the 'soap box'-type of oratory, which, while aggressive, is not always appreciated by those unaccustomed to the stresses of inflammatory speech. (Anonymous 1927: 22)

By then, the dead Deakin's style was being favourably compared to that of the even longer dead Gladstone (Jose 1933: 19). Yet we can still see how the middling style had become commonplace in the twentieth century. On the one hand Prime Minister Robert Menzies displayed the erudite side with his insertion of poetry into his speeches, most infamously his 1963 speech to the Queen, although by then the change in *endoxa* had rendered this aspect of the decorum obsolete. On the other hand, during his state election campaign in 1929, Menzies told an audience in Malvern: 'What we want in politics today is plain speech about plain subjects for plain people' (Anonymous 1929: 7–8). As we know, Menzies was an admirer of Baldwin, the second Lincoln, who cultivated the plain folksy style and *ethos* disclaiming any oratorical pretensions. So it was only a short rhetorical leap to Howard in 1988, who projected the *ethos* of the plain thinking man with Future Directions, but without any of the literary aspects expected of middling style. In 1929 Menzies also highlighted his reformist and Young Turk *ethos* and, in the process, protested against the dissembling often associated with politics. Thus, to another audience, he deployed the stereotype of politicians to state 'the political occupation is regarded as one which a really intelligent and decent person does not bother about' (Martin 1993: 66, 72–73).

Come World War II, Lincoln was again enlisted to the Allied and Anglo-Saxon cause on behalf of democracy and against militarism. Lincoln's words and visage appeared in speeches, statues, radio plays and especially in films such as *Young Mr Lincoln* and *Words for Battle*, both of which were widely distributed in Australia. The latter was a documentary offering a 'potted history of the idea of liberty in English history' (Smith 2010: 503). Again the cause of Anglo-Saxonism connected England, America and Australia in war, but with a difference. Now Churchill's words had joined those of Abe, Milton, Browning, Blake and Kipling. He had joined the rhetorical tradition with the man he greatly admired in his own *History of the English-speaking peoples*.

This chapter has discussed rhetorical standards in terms of history, tradition and myths that have been part and parcel of continuing debates in three political societies going back to the early 1700s. The ultimate point to be made about these standards is that they cannot be considered as impeccably distinct from the rhetoric they judge. They are part of the continuing political contests and discussions that are the essence of representative democracy. In other words, they have arisen endogenously from social practices, rather than being imposed on people from above. This is the stance of John Dryzek (2002: 1), Iris Marion Young (2003: 7, 47, 65, 154) and Chantal Mouffe (2000: 5–6) who are critical of Jurgen Habermas's projection of ideal political discourse. Against charges of not existing in the world, the ideal has been defended as something to aim for and as a regulative 'fiction', a 'presupposition', such that 'we act counterfactually as though the ideal speech situation … were not merely fictitious but real' (2001:

102). But this chapter has demonstrated that Habermas is following many others who have projected similar regulative fictions and used them persuasively in political combat. Such abstractions have always been appealing but cannot be considered as floating somewhere beyond the political realm. They are part and parcel of political conflict.

References

Anonymous 1825. New South Wales — Extract of a letter inserted in *Morning Chronicle*. *Australian* 3 March.

Anonymous 1827. Shipping intelligence. *Sydney Gazette and New South Wales Advertiser* 25 June.

Anonymous 1829a. Franklins prophecy: To the editor of the *Sydney Gazette*. *Sydney Gazette and New South Wales Advertiser* 9 July.

Anonymous 1829b. Advance Australia. *Sydney Gazette and New South Wales Advertiser* 24 December.

Anonymous 1831. The value of a representative government. *Australian* 29 July.

Anonymous 1832. Beer or Wine?: To the editor of the *Sydney Herald*. *The Sydney Monitor* 15 September.

Anonymous 1845a. The Bank of Australia, or 'Pure Merino' Bank. *Morning Chronicle* (Sydney) 8 February.

Anonymous 1845b. American news. *South Australian* 15 April.

Anonymous 1845c. Review. *Sydney Morning Herald* 27 May.

Anonymous 1852. Henry Clay. *Courier* (Hobart) 10 November.

Anonymous. 1887. Abraham Lincoln and his Gettysburg Oration. *Maitland Mercury & Hunter River General Advertiser* 25 June.

Anonymous 1887. Heroes: A Lecture By Mr. Wybert Reeve. *South Australian Register* 25 October.

Anonymous. 1888. Written On His knee: How Lincoln Composed His Celebrated Gettysburg Oration. *Logansport Journal* 27 June. p 2.

Anonymous 1912. Genius and hard work. *North Melbourne Courier and West Melbourne Advertiser* 22 November.

Anonymous 1916a. Appreciation of Mr. Hughes: 'Australia's Abraham Lincoln', *Morning Bulletin* (Rockhampton) 20 July.

Anonymous 1916b. Campaign in progress. *Register* (Adelaide) 18 September.

Anonymous 1916c. Reviews. *Register* (Adelaide) 29 July.

Anonymous 1916d. The question of the hour. *Register* (Adelaide) 14 September.

Anonymous 1927. Recent publications: A great Australian statesman. *Advertiser* (Adelaide) 3 December.

Anonymous 1929. Public questions. 'Plain speech' advocated. *Argus* (Melbourne) 14 November.

Bailyn, B. 1968. *The origins of American politics*. New York: Vintage Books.

Bercovitch, S. 1978. *The American jeremiad*. Madison, W.I.: University of Wisconsin Press.

Boller, P. 1996. *Presidential anecdotes*. New York: Oxford University Press.

Brown, W.B. 1960. *The people's choice: The presidential image in the campaign biography*. Baton Rouge: Louisiana State University Press.

Camia, C. 2011. Cain, Gingrich set for Lincoln–Douglas debate. USA Today 26 October. URL: http://content.usatoday.com/communities/onpolitics/post/2011/10/lincoln-douglas-debate-newt-gingrich-herman-cain-/1. Consulted 13 May 2012.

Citizen, 1860. Payment of members of parliament. *South Australian Weekly Chronicle* February.

Cmiel, K. 1990. *Democratic eloquence: The fight over popular speech in nineteenth-century America*. New York: William Morrow & Co.

Cochrane, P. 2006. *Colonial ambition: Foundations of Australian democracy*. Melbourne: Melbourne University Press.

Connolly, W. 1983. *The terms of political discourse*. Oxford: Martin Robertson.

Condren, C. 1997. Political theory and the problem of anachronism. *Political theory: Tradition and diversity*. Cambridge: Cambridge University Press.

Crabb, A. 2013. Has the news cycle killed soaring political oratory? *The Drum* 27 May. URL: http://www.abc.net.au/news/2013-05-27/crabb-political-speech/4714004. Consulted 1 August 2013.

Dallek, R. 2001. *Hail to the chief: The making and unmaking of American presidents*. Hyperion Books.

Dunn, J. 2006. *Setting the people free: The story of democracy*. London: Atlantic Books.

Dryzek, J. 2000. *Deliberative democracy and beyond: Liberals, critics, contestations*. Oxford: Oxford University Press.

Eastman, C. 2009. A *nation of speechifiers: Making an American public after the revolution*. Chicago: University of Chicago Press.

Edwards, S. 2013. 'From here Lincoln came': Anglo-Saxonism, the special relationship, and the anglicisation of Abraham Lincoln, c. 1860–1970. *Journal of Transatlantic Studies* 11(1): 22–46.

Flood, C. 2002. *Political Myth*. New York: Routledge.

Gerlach, M. 2001. *British liberalism and the United States: Political and social thought in the late Victorian age*. Basingstoke: Palgrave MacMillan.

Greenstein, F. 2009. *Inventing the job of President: Leadership style from George Washington to Andrew Jackson*. Princeton: Princeton University Press.

Habermas, J. 2001. *On the pragmatics of social interaction: Preliminary studies in the theory of communicative action*. Trans. B. Fultner. Cambridge, Mass.: The MIT Press.

Hanson, R. 1985. *The democratic imagination in America: Conversations with our past*. Princeton: Princeton University Press.

Holzer, H. 2012. The Lincoln–Douglas debates weren't as great as Gingrich thinks. *Washington Post* 28 January 2012. URL: http://www.washingtonpost.com/opinions/the-lincoln-douglas-debates-werent-as-great-as-gingrich-thinks/2012/01/25/gIQABwX1VQ_story.html. Consulted 10 August 2013.

Jose, A. 1933. Some famous men: What Alfred Deakin did for Australia. *Brisbane Courier* 4 February.

Kazin, M. 1998. *The populist persuasion: An American history*. Ithaca, N.Y.: Cornell University Press.

Love, P. 1984. *Labour and the money power: Australian labour populism 1890–1950*. Carlton: Melbourne University Press.

Manne, R. 2007. The nation reviewed. *The Monthly* April.

Martin, A. 1993. *Robert Menzies: A life*. Vol. 1. Carlton: Melbourne University Press.

McLachlan, N. 1977. The future America: Some Bicentennial reflections. *Historical Studies* 17 (April): 361–83.

Melleuish, G. 2013. Personal politics and being British: Political rhetoric, democracy and their consequences in colonial New South Wales. *Australian Journal of Politics & History* 59(1): 1–14.

Mouffe, C. 2000. Deliberative democracy or agonistic pluralism. Vienna: Institute for Advanced Studies. URL: http://www.ihs.ac.at/publications/pol/pw_72.pdf. Consulted 22 August 2013.

Parry-Giles, T. 2010. Resisting a 'treacherous piety': Issues, images, and public policy deliberation in presidential campaigns. *Rhetoric & Public Affairs* 13(1): 37–63.

Patapan, H. 2003. Melancholy and amnesia: Tocqueville's influence on Australian democratic theory. *Australian Journal of Politics & History* 49(1): 1–16.

Robertson, A. 2005. *The language of democracy: Political rhetoric in the United States and Britain, 1790–1900*. Charlottesville, V.A.: University of Virginia Press.

Rolfe, M. 1997. The promise and threat of America in Australian politics. *Australian Journal of Political Science* 32(2): 187–204.

—— 2008. New wine into old bottles: Ethical appeals and democratic discourse. *Australian Journal of Political Science* 43(3): 513–29.

Sartori, G. 1987. *The theory of democracy revisited*. Chatham: Chatham House Publishers.

Saward, M. 2003. *Democracy*. Cambridge: Polity.

Schudson, M. 1978. *Discovering the news: A social history of American newspapers*. Basic Books.

Smith, A. 2010. The 'cult' of Abraham Lincoln and the strange survival of liberal England in the era of the World Wars. *Twentieth Century British History* 21(4): 486–509.

—— 2011. Lincoln in the English imagination. In R. Cawardine and J. Sexton eds. *The Global Lincoln*. New York: Oxford University Press.

Smith, J. 2009. *Presidents we imagine*. Madison, W.I.: University of Wisconsin Press.

Spiegel, A. 2002. *A. Lincoln Esquire: A shrewd, sophisticated lawyer in his time*. Macon: Mercer University Press.

Tanner, L. 2012. *Sideshow: Dumbing down democracy*. Carlton: Scribe Publications.

Tardini S. 2005. Endoxa and communities: Grounding enthymematic arguments. *Studies in Communication Sciences*. Argumentation in dialogic interaction. Special issue: June.

Tudor, H. 1972. *Political Myth*. London: MacMillan.

Walton, D. 2007. *Media argumentation: Dialectic, persuasion and rhetoric*. New York: Cambridge University Press.

Williams, F. 2001. Abraham Lincoln — Our ever present contemporary. In J. McPherson ed. *We cannot escape history: Lincoln and the last best hope of Earth*. Urbana: University of Illinois Press.

Young, I.M. 2003. *Inclusion and Democracy*. Oxford Scholarship Online.

Zarefsky, D. 1986. The Lincoln–Douglas debates revisited: The evolution of public argument. *Quarterly Journal of Speech* 72: 162–84.

7. Whistling the dog

Barry Hindess

To rule out possible misunderstanding, I should say that I come to bury the idea of dog whistling, not to praise it. The term 'dog-whistle politics' was widely used in the 1990s and early 2000s by commentators on the Left in Australia to describe, and often to deplore, what were seen as rhetorical attempts by the Prime Minister John Howard and his supporters to appeal to anti-immigrant sentiments within the electorate, but to do so in such a way as to avoid incurring the charge of racism. It was alleged that, while the propositional content of Howard's speeches was often uncontentious, many of these speeches were designed to appeal to sections of the electorate who would respond positively to the sentiments they perceived him to be expressing. This was 'dog whistling', a matter of putting out a message that would not be noticed by many, but would be picked up by its intended audience.

I hoped that by mid-2013 the term would be of mainly historical interest, but this was too optimistic. The term resurfaced several times in the course of the year. For example, Senator Doug Cameron and Minister Peter Garrett were both reported as accusing Scott Morrison of dog whistling when he called for police and neighbours to be notified whenever refugees were released into the community (Hall 2013). A few days later, Christine Milne, leader of the Greens, accused the Prime Minister of dog whistling and Tony Abbott, without using the term 'dog whistling', accused her of 'demonising' foreign workers when she said, of 457 visas, that foreign workers should not be put at the front of the jobs queue at the expense of Australian workers. Prime Minister Julia Gillard's response to these accusations is also worth noting:

> I believe in putting Australian jobs first. Others can use whatever label they choose for that. (Ireland 2013)

I will return to this exchange.

Josh Fear's useful discussion (2007) of the dog whistle in Australian politics illustrates the concept with an American example, George W. Bush's use of 'arcane — but seemingly everyday — turns of phrase derived from biblical texts in order to signal his allegiance to America's religious right' (Lincoln 2004: 5). Bush's acceptance speech at the 2004 Republican National Convention referred to 'hills to climb' and to seeing 'the valley below', an allusion to the Israelites' flight from Egypt.

As another American example, during the 2004 campaign Bush and Dick Cheney frequently used the phrase 'He can run but he can't hide', referring to both Osama bin Laden and the Democratic presidential candidate, John Kerry. As I recall from watching broadcast coverage of that election in the Democratic bastion of Baltimore, American audiences usually greeted this statement with wild applause. At first, this reaction made no sense to me. I assumed that the phrase involved some biblical allusion with which I was happily unfamiliar, only to discover later that the phrase had been made famous by Joe Louis, a long-time world heavyweight boxing champion who, while black, was a hero of the American white working class. In repeating the 'He can run ...' phrase, Bush and Cheney were saying both that we are going to hammer him (bin Laden or Kerry) and 'I'm with you guys [i.e. white blue-collar workers]'.

In its Australian usage, 'dog whistling' is a pejorative term that relies on the image of the dog whistle, which was used in sheep herding and was also known as the 'silent' or 'Galton's' whistle, designed, apparently, by Francis Galton in 1876 to resonate at a frequency, 20,000 hertz or more, which would be inaudible to human ears but audible to the more sensitive hearing of dogs. Where humans would be generally unaffected by the sound, except for the odd headache, suitably trained or habituated dogs would receive both a sound and an instruction — telling them, for example, to stop where they were or to round up the sheep that had just broken away from the main flock — and could be trusted to respond accordingly. Dog whistlers knew what they were doing while the dogs reacted without thinking. The same term was also used, perhaps less pejoratively, in the United States and United Kingdom, where it has been labelled as Australian in origin.[1]

My first task in this paper is to explain what dog whistling has to do with rhetoric. At first sight this seems easy enough. Perhaps the most straightforward account of dog whistle politics is presented in Bob Goodin's *Innovating democracy*, which refers to:

> the fundamental perversity of dog-whistle politics, whereby political parties send coded messages that will be heard one way by their core supporters and another way altogether by others. (2008: 7)

---

1 For the United Kingdom, see Bagehot (2005) who suggests that the practice was introduced to British politics by Lynton Crosby, the Tories' 'Australian' campaign director. Crosby developed his trade while working as federal director of the Australian Liberal Party under Howard's leadership. Crosby's responsibility for introducing the term, in a non-pejorative sense, has been suggested by J.F.O. McAllister (2005). For the United States, see William Safire (2005), who describes the dog-whistle issue as having been 'brought about — possibly from Down Under — by the rise of dog-whistle politics'. Safire refers here to Peter Manning (2004) who quotes Mike Steketee of the *Australian* as suggesting that the term may be American in origin. A few years later Safire (2008: 190) quoted Richard Morin, director of polling for the *Washington Post* as writing in 1998 — well before the term was alleged to have been imported from Australia — that 'researchers use the term "Dog Whistle Effect" to refer to puzzling features of questionnaire responses: 'Respondents hear something in the question that researchers do not'.

Later in the same book he describes dog-whistle politics as 'a new and particularly pernicious campaign technique', adding that it:

> Is a way of sending a message to certain potential supporters in such a way as to make it inaudible to others whom it might alienate. The classic case, perhaps, is the 'Are you thinking what we're thinking?' campaign mounted by the Tories in the 2005 British General Election by Lynton Crosby who had perfected the technique in highly successful campaigns to re-elect John Howard in Australia. (2008: 224)[2]

This campaign involved one or more large political billboards located in a prominent roadside position each displaying the words 'vote Conservative'. As Martin Kettle (2005) explains, the first billboard in a sequence poses the question: 'Are you thinking what we're thinking?' A moment later, one sees a second billboard that explains: 'It's not racist to impose limits on immigration.' This last phrase, which also appeared in speeches by the party leader and in the Tory manifesto (Freeland 2005), might seem to be a statement of the obvious since, as Fear points out, all states practise some kind of immigration control (2007: 1). Yet, to its target audience, it said that you are not necessarily a racist if you oppose immigration from Africa and Asia — or, paraphrasing slightly, 'It's not seriously racist to have racist views about things that really bug you — like immigration' (Fear 2007: 1). This message can be read as a deliberate counter to the moderately effective anti-racism campaigns waged by the Left — that is, by elements within the Labour Party and the unions and by various non-Labour activist groups — campaigns that left many people nervous about expressing their (incorrect) views in public. Those in the 'Are you thinking ...' campaign's target audience knew perfectly well that they'd better not be racist. The point of the campaign was not to dispute norms promoted by anti-racism campaigns but to tell the intended audience they need not worry about them. The message of the second billboard was thus 'Labour condemns your racist views on immigration while we, in the Conservative party, understand your feelings about Asian and African immigrants. You can trust us.'

Yet, if we follow the definition offered by the *Oxford English Dictionary* (1989) and see rhetoric as 'The art of using language effectively so as to persuade or influence others', then we should regard dog whistling as a sophisticated kind of rhetoric, one that aims to win support from parts of an audience while also influencing, or at least, not alienating, the rest. Goodin (2008: 7) calls dog whistling perverse because it undermines democratic deliberation — try deliberating with someone who says one thing to you and, at the same time, says something different to others in the discussion — and later in the book he describes it as 'particularly pernicious' (2008: 224). He also said in an earlier

---

2   See Ashcroft (2010) for a sceptical Conservative assessment of this campaign.

paper that it destroyed any sense of a democratic mandate since, if dog whistling is employed successfully, it is difficult to be sure what policies or party platform the electorate has supported (Goodin and Saward 2005). In itself, this last may not be such a bad thing.

Similar points might be made about the use of conventional rhetorical techniques. The political point of rhetoric may simply be to batter one's opponent — or to respond to their battering. In such cases, discerning listeners will know, or at least suspect, that the content of a speech should not be taken too seriously. This may be why Howard was taken by surprise in 1996 when the talk-back presenter John Laws, in his radio program (21 August), pressed him on the difference between 'core promises which are kept and then those other not so important promises, the ones we really didn't mean kind of promises'.[3] Thus, recent Liberal promises to 'turn the boats around' or to 'get rid of the deficit' may not mean what they say — although some clearly fear that they do. Either way, any rhetorical speech may be accused of undermining both the practice of deliberation and the idea of a mandate. It can also give hostages to fortune, as we have seen during much of 2013 in what sounded suspiciously like a Labor promise to deliver a surplus in the current financial year.

Leaving this last complication aside, the issue of dog-whistle politics is less tidy than my earlier brief discussion suggests. First, for all the clarity of the introductory account in Goodin's book (2008: 7), it hardly captures the complexity of the term's Australian, or even American, usage, or indeed of Goodin's usage later in the same book, which declares dog-whistle politics to be 'particularly pernicious' (2008: 224). Second, there are serious problems with the idea of 'coded messages that will be heard one way by their core supporters and another way altogether by others'. I address these issues in turn on my way to the conclusion that the concept of dog-whistle politics is hardly worth the napkin it was probably first scribbled on. Those who level the accusation of dog whistling against conservative politicians certainly point to serious concerns about contemporary politics, but in an exemplary display of intellectual reflexivity, they offer what could itself be described as a clear case of dog whistling.

Exploring Australian usage

Apart from its unfortunate consequences for democratic deliberation and for claims of an electoral mandate, it might seem that the rhetorical trick of sending coded messages that mean different things to different audiences is relatively

---

3 Quoted at http://howardfacts.com/download/now/broken_promises_election_07.pdf, consulted 2 December 2013.

harmless. Following this view, dog whistling is neither good nor bad, in itself, and one's assessment of the practice, as being, for example, 'particularly pernicious' (Goodin 2008: 224), would depend on the content of the coded messages that were broadcast in the public domain.

Consider just a few examples of coded messages that are not normally described as dog whistling. I begin with the widespread use of the word 'independent' in Australian public life to suggest to the public that the 'independent' whatever — Independent Commission Against Corruption (ICAC), economic modelling, environmental impact assessment, and so on — will not be affected by special interests, while those who matter will know perfectly well that economic modelling rarely bites the hand that pays it and that ICAC is funded by the NSW Government. This is dog whistling as endearingly non-partisan. Or again, consider Robert Menzies's well-known 'Forgotten people' speech delivered on 22 May 1942. This speech is usually read as an appeal to and celebration of the Australian middle class — his 'forgotten people' — but, at one point, Menzies insists on the importance of:

> a fierce independence of spirit. This is the only real freedom, and it has as
> its corollary a brave acceptance of unclouded individual responsibility.
> The moment a man seeks moral and intellectual refuge in the emotions
> of a crowd, he ceases to be a human being and becomes a cipher.

There is room for debate about how to interpret these examples, the Australian usage of 'independent', or of 'non-partisan' for that matter, and Menzies's speech (Brett 2007). Was the speech a case of dog whistling? Did Menzies intend to suggest that labour movement activists were seeking 'refuge in the emotions of a crowd' and thus were no longer human, or was he simply carried away by his own rhetoric? Perhaps the activists were dupes of a foreign power, as Menzies's government effectively claimed in its campaign to ban the Communist Party of Australia (CPA).[4]

So, I move on to less contentious cases. The first is Jesus' response, reported in Matthew 22:21, to Pharisees who had tried to trick him into saying that Jews should not pay taxes to the Roman authorities. 'One of them [i.e. a Pharisee] showed him a Roman coin, and he asked them whose name and inscription were on it. They answered, "Caesar's", and he responded: "Render therefore unto Caesar the things which are Caesar's; and unto God the things that are God's".' Here, Jesus says one thing to the Pharisees, and to any Roman spies who might be listening, and something else, perhaps not entirely clear, to others who heard

---

4   Without stating it directly, the Australian Communist Party Dissolution Bill 1950 (Cth) presented the CPA as a threat to the defence of Australia, a view that the High Court rejected in its 1951 ruling that the Bill was unconstitutional.

this exchange. Some of the Pharisees, one suspects, would have been smart enough to see what he was up to. Jesus has been accused of many things, but there are no reports of anyone at the time or later accusing him of dog whistling.

My second example is the infamous speech to the Roman people that Shakespeare attributes to Mark Anthony. Shortly after Caesar's death, Anthony begins:

> Friends, Romans, Countrymen Lend me Your Ears. I come to bury Caesar not to praise him.

Thus far into the speech, the crowd has no clear idea of what is coming next while the conspirators relax, thinking, wrongly, that Anthony is not going to make any trouble.[5] Here, too, the accusation of dog whistling has not to my knowledge been raised.

A final example comes from the realm of political theory. Readers of Leo Strauss will know that, without using the term 'dog whistle', he describes past political theorists as saying one thing to most of their contemporaries and something else, a coded message, to their informed and intelligent readers. Strauss does not condemn this practice but generally treats it as thoroughly sensible.

To these cases, we might add a final generic example, pointing out that a fundamental task of diplomacy has always been to find a form of words that would allow different parties in a dispute to believe that they had gained more than they expected.

Thus far, it seems that there is nothing new about the use of coded messages and that, in many cases, it might not be such a bad thing. Dog whistling, we might say, is problematic in roughly the way that guns are problematic: 'dog whistling does not kill people; people kill people.' Tempting as this line of argument might seem, it is important to recognise that in Australia dog whistling has generally been condemned — as it has, but rather less so, in the United Kingdom and United States — as both promoting and appealing to racist sentiments, much as Goodin condemns it towards the end of his 2008 discussion.

As Fear's invaluable discussion brings out, a central feature of the Australian understanding, which his own paper clearly reflects, is that the dog whistle is an appeal to prejudice:

---

5   The problem with using the Mark Anthony example here is that it is fictional. Shakespeare's theatrical version of Anthony's speech to the Roman people shortly after Caesar's assassination seems tame in comparison to the tactics said to have been urged on Marcus Cicero by his brother Quintus (Cicero 2012). There are reasons to doubt whether Quintus wrote this letter (Wills 2012) but the fact that it was circulated in Rome in the form of a letter from Quintus to his brother suggests something about the tone of Roman electoral politics, just as the decision of Princeton University Press to publish the pamphlet without noting the doubts about its authenticity suggests something unpleasant about academic publishing in contemporary America.

many members of the community still harbour resentments based on race, religion or sexuality. And these people vote. (2007: 2)

Note the disapproving tone of the last phrase. 'And *these people* vote'. As if to reinforce its point, Fear suggests, further, that:

our politicians don't want to alienate members of their constituency who might be put off by blatantly prejudiced remarks. It is important that they communicate in ways that both resonate with the target audience (such as people who harbour suspicions about certain minority groups) and are inaudible to voters who hold more progressive views. Dog whistling is therefore the tactic of choice for a politician who wants to have it both ways. (2007: 2)

A little earlier (2007: 1), he describes dog whistling as 'appealing to our baser instincts'. My initial account of dog whistling, which followed Goodin (2008: 7), should therefore be amended. Accordingly, dog whistling is a practice:

whereby political parties send coded messages that will be heard one way by their core supporters and another way altogether by others.

We have seen that Goodin himself uses the example of the Tory 'Are you thinking …' campaign to amend his account, saying that dog whistling is:

a way of sending a message to certain potential supporters in such a way as to make it inaudible to others whom it might alienate. (2008: 224)

This is much closer to capturing the Australian usage. We need only add the note of disapproval, perhaps by inserting the word 'prejudicial' immediately before 'message'. Dog whistling thus becomes a way of sending a prejudicial 'message to certain potential supporters in such a way as to make it inaudible to others whom it might alienate'. Fear emphasises this worry about alienating potential supporters by insisting that the 'key feature' of dog whistling 'is *plausible deniability*: the dog whistler can say "I didn't mean that, I meant this instead".' (2007: 5)

There are several issues to be noted here. One is simply that most of the discussion of dog whistling focuses on electoral competition, whereas the examples I listed earlier in this section, with the exception of Menzies's speech and his radio talks on the same theme, were not. Talk of 'independent umpires' and the like is solidly bipartisan. The key point to notice is that most of those who talk, or write, about dog whistling treat it as unfair, as a kind of cheating. Not only does it appeal to our baser motives, but there is something base about making such an appeal. I will return to a second issue — the reflexivity of the charge of dog whistling — later in this paper.

A third issue is the question of what Max Weber calls 'value-freedom'. Weber's view (1989), which is now widely shared among social scientists, if not by those who pay for their services, is that, while our values or political commitments may well influence our choice of what topics to investigate, they have no place in the conduct of our investigation. Yet, in the case of the concept of 'dog-whistle politics', we find that the investigator's — in this case, Fear's — disapproval enters into the definition of the object of study. Goodin avoids this problem, clearly signalling his disapproval — for example, with his 'particularly pernicious' (2008: 224) — but not letting it interfere with his own conceptualisation of the phenomenon. The difficulty here is that this abstinence leaves him with no real distinction between the general phenomena of coded messaging, as in the examples listed above, and dog whistling in particular, leaving us to suspect that dog whistling should be seen not so much as a novel form of rhetoric, but rather, to borrow an image from Thomas Hobbes' *Leviathan* (1996: 130), as a familiar form misliked.

Fourth, we might question the use of the term 'deniability' in this context. On the one hand, deniability — an ability to deny accusations of impropriety — would seem to be an attribute of those who might have something to deny, not of what they might have said. Either way, 'deniability' seems a useful enough term in the genre of practical advice to cynical politicians, but out of place as a term of serious political analysis. On the other hand, what precisely might the accused dog whistler say by way of denial?

Coded messages

Goodin describes dog whistling as a practice:

> whereby political parties send coded messages that will be heard one way by their core supporters and another way altogether by others. (2008: 7)

Fear, too, divides the dog whistler's audience into those who are receptive to the prejudicial message and the rest, who fail to 'perceive (or deliberately ignore) the layered or multiple meanings':

> the target audience for a dog whistle can be any group to whom politicians want to send a message without alerting others, or at least without alarming them. (2007: 2)

It seems, then, that the electorate consists of three groups:

1. those who receive and are attracted by the dog whistler's coded message

2. those who are not sufficiently perceptive to pick up this message, and who might be offended if they did

3. the rest who pick up both the overt and the coded message, but do not care enough about the latter's prejudicial import for it to affect their political allegiances.

There is nothing in the literature to suggest that some in the first group might pick up both messages and be offended by the dog whistler's duplicity. As with two, the assumption seems to be not only that members of this group are prejudiced but also that they are not very smart. (Perhaps they failed to pay attention in their social studies classes at school.)

However one reads the charge of dog whistling, the implied description of those who respond to its call is distinctly unflattering. The image of left-wing elites who look down on the tastes and lifestyles of ordinary Australians, as Fear notes (2007: 22–25, 38–42), has long been a staple of right-wing political rhetoric, both in the United States and Australia (Sawer and Hindess 2004). This staple has been reliable because its underlying point remains hard to deny. The charge of dog whistling seems perfectly designed to reinforce this image of Left elitism.

My point here is that making the charge of dog whistling carries within itself an element of dog whistling and, in this respect, the concept is admirably reflexive. I suggest that what is conveyed in Australia when the charge of dog whistling is levelled against members of the Coalition — and even, at times, against a Labor prime minister — is, first, an overt message that those charged are playing dirty. Secondly, a coded message is conveyed to those on the Left who can see the justice in this charge, a message that reinforces an existing sense of superiority over those who are taken in by the Coalition's, or prime minister's, dirty play. The coded message is simply that we constitute an observant, morally superior elite.

This is dog whistling without the unsavoury racism. It seems to me relatively harmless, at least in the short term. In the longer term it simply offers the Right further ammunition to use against the Left.

Conclusion

With regard to the issue of deniability, there are two basic points to be made. First, as already noted, if 'deniability' has any clear meaning, it is best seen as an attribute, not of anything that might or might not have been said, but rather of some person or organisation who might be accused of having said it. As Howard realised, all that was required for a public figure or political party to possess this attribute was the ability to issue the denial with a straight face, along with a reasonably compliant media that would not call him on it. Having lived through the Howard era in Australia, I suspect that many journalists (but not too many of their editors) found this compliance difficult to stomach.

As for what is required in the content of the denial, the answer was made clear by the second billboard of the British 'Are you thinking ...' campaign and, for that matter, in Gillard's response to the charge of dog whistling and xenophobia: simply repeat the offense on a highly visible billboard or with sufficient assurance. All that has to be denied is the suggestion that members of the target group have base motivations.

References

Ashcroft, M.A. 2010. *Minority verdict: The Conservative Party, the voters and the 2010 election.* London: Biteback.

Bagehot 2005. High pitch, low politics: Dog-whistle politics can only take you so far. *Economist* 23 March.

Brett, J. 2007. *Robert Menzies' forgotten people.* Carlton: Melbourne University Press.

Cicero, Quintus Tullius 2012. *How to win an election. An ancient guide for modern politicians.* Princeton: Princeton University Press.

Fear, J. 2007. *Under the radar. Dog-whistle politics in Australia.* Discussion paper 96. Canberra: The Australia Institute.

Freeland, J. 2005. Beware the nasty nudge and wink. *Guardian* 12 April.

Goodin, R.E. 2008. *Innovating democracy: Democratic theory and practice after the deliberative turn.* Oxford: Oxford University Press.

—— and Saward, M. 2005. Dog whistles and democratic mandates. *The Political Quarterly* 76(4): 471–76.

Hall, B. 2013. Refugees much less likely to commit crime. *Sydney Morning Herald* 1 March.

Hobbes, T. 1996 (1651). *Leviathan.* Cambridge: Cambridge University Press.

Ireland, J. 2013. Visa stand not xenophobic: Gillard. *Sydney Morning Herald* 7 March.

Kettle, M. 2005. The Conservative manifesto is a thing of punchlines, not programmes. *Guardian* 8 March.

Lincoln, B. 2004. *Words matter: How Bush speaks in religious code. Boston Globe* 12 September.

McAllister, J.F.O. 2005. Whistling in the dark? *Time Magazine* 3 April.

Manning, P. 2004. *Dog whistle politics and journalism.* Sydney: The Australian Centre for Independent Journalism, UTS.

Menzies, R. 1942. The forgotten people. *Liberals.Net.* 22 May. URL http://www. liberals.net/theforgottenpeople.htm. Consulted 9 March 2013.

Safire, W. 2005. Dog-whistle. *New York Times* 24 April.

—— 2008. *Safire's political dictionary.* New York: Oxford University Press.

Sawer, M. and Hindess, B. 2004. *Us and them: Elites and anti-elitism in Australia.* Perth: API Network.

Weber, M. 1989. *Science as a vocation.* P. Lassman, V. Irving et al. eds. London, Unwin Hyman.

Wills, Gary 2012. Review of Cicero (2012), *New York Times* 27 July 27.

8. Debating the Speaker

John Uhr

Rhetoric refers to the political language used by Australian politicians to lead and shape public opinion. Successful rhetoric is influential rhetoric: words that form a following. Effective rhetoric can be true or false or some mixture in between. Democratic theories about political rhetoric tend to avoid strict stipulations about truthfulness or falsity, referring more to the process of facilitating fair debate among competing political players, rather than the content of that debate. Democratic political rhetoric faces norms of due process about the public scrutiny and accountability of political debaters. I frame a form of accountability for Australian political rhetoric, providing one instance of how greater public knowledge and accountability of parliamentary rhetoric can improve public understanding of Australian parliamentary politics.

Rhetoric reveals leadership strategies that are used in the public argument among those competing for public support. Ryan Walter and I are examining patterns of Australian political rhetoric during the last Parliament under the minority government of Julia Gillard and Kevin Rudd (2010–13). Our theme is that the minority government formed after the 2010 election and led for the most part by Gillard (before Rudd's return to the prime ministership in July 2013) revealed in unusual ways many important features of Australian political rhetoric. The minority government was an unusual type of national government, with parliamentary politics shifted from the conventional binary mode of two-party competition between government and Opposition to a multiparty competition across all parliamentary players in both houses of the national Parliament.

Parliamentary rhetoric is the most carefully scripted and staged form of political rhetoric. The institutional setting of Parliament establishes the public stage and routines of stagecraft that are open to elected members. Usually the stage of the House of Representatives over-represents the government of the day and under-represents non-government parties. The period of the Gillard/Rudd minority government changed this dramatic routine by bringing forward a clearer public display of many of the antagonistic forces at work in Australian political rhetoric. Our initial interest is to make the best research use we can of the unconventional display of political completion fostered by the period of minority government, when so many political parties and interests sought the public stage to legitimate their current role in the governance process and to broaden public support for their preferred role after the 2013 election.

The Speakership

This chapter examines Australian political rhetoric relating to the role of the Speaker of the House of Representatives during the period of the Gillard minority government. The intention is not to highlight Speakers as great political speakers, but to show how debates over the role of the Speaker clarify important themes in Australian political rhetoric (Snedden 1980; Healy 1998). This chapter reports things said by the three Speakers from 2010–13; but the main story is about what they and others have said about the office and role of the Speakership as part of a central debate about one of the few constitutional offices ordering Australian parliamentary politics. The type of institutional order that Speakers bring to Australian politics depends substantially on the powers and responsibilities Parliament delegates to them, historically and currently (House of Representative (HR) 2012: 187). In most parliaments, the Speakership is not the subject of sustained debate. On this theme, the value of the Gillard minority government is that it generated sustained political debate over the Speakership in a rare rhetorical contest over the political norms expected of the constitutional leader of the House of Representatives.

The topic here is political rhetoric *about* Speakers and not the political rhetoric *of* Speakers, which would include not only what is said, but how it is said, including the role of gowns and wigs favoured by traditionalists and opposed by Labor (Bolton 1968, 155; HR 2012: 162). What leading Australian members of the House of Representatives can do on the parliamentary stage depends substantially on the licence or punishment given to them by the Speaker (Inglis 1996). Yet Speakers themselves do not really belong to the same political set as party leaders: Speakers speak differently precisely because their political office differs, in ways that are shaped by the sparse provisions in the Australian constitution. Speakers manage the deliberative process according to rules authorised by the House. The constitution denies Speakers (and only Speakers) a deliberative vote, which is a prominent way of separating Speakers from other members of the House. To a considerable extent, Speakers seldom speak as political deliberators about the merits and content of public policy. But, to an even greater extent, Speakers speak about the merits of the process of parliamentary deliberation over which they preside. The constitution says little about the larger purposes of this presiding officer, or indeed of the Senate's presiding officer, and this gives great power to the House to specify the delegated powers exercised by Speakers as presiding officers.

The Gillard/Rudd minority government had three Speakers over its three-year term: Victorian Australian Labor Party (ALP) member Harry Jenkins; Queensland former Liberal and former National party member Peter Slipper; and Victorian ALP member Anna Burke. What is remarkable is that the ALP government appointed a non-ALP member, Slipper, as its second Speaker, in an unusual attempt to reduce the voting strength of the official Opposition and to increase the voting strength of the governing minority party. Slipper later resigned from the Speakership when facing two criminal charges: one over mismanagement brought by one of his official staff, which Slipper later won; and one over misconduct brought by the Australian Federal Police, which is still awaiting hearing. Most Australian national governments retain one person as Speaker for each parliament or period of government. A few have had more than one, but very few have had three. The Gillard/Rudd minority government made the choice to have more than one in an attempt to manage its minority position; it later made the choice to have more than two when the controversy over Slipper's alleged misconduct brought the original choice into question.

The Speaker is one of the few national political offices defined in the Australian constitution, which has nothing to say in its original version about political parties, the prime minister or the leader of the Opposition. Constitutional amendments in 1977 introduced the first acknowledgement of the place of political parties in order to regulate state choice over replacement senators. My focus here is on the limited role of the Speaker as a constitutional source of debate and disagreement in Australian political rhetoric. The Speaker is not as powerful a political office as many of those other House of Representatives' offices not mentioned in the constitution, such as the prime minister, or leader of the Opposition, or even leader of government in the House. But the Speaker's role is powerful enough to have become the subject of protracted political wrangling during the period of the Gillard/Rudd minority government, as government and Opposition used many rhetorical strategies to promote or oppose the use and abuse of the role. This debate over who can and should be Speaker provides us with a case study of Australian political rhetoric, with a gallery of portraits depicting how different political players and interests define the constitutional characteristics of this basic public office.

The conclusion to be drawn from this is more about parliament than the Speaker. Parliament, or at least the House of Representatives, sets the standards for this core constitutional office (Snedden 1980). My interest is in debate over the Speakership as evidence of a group portrait of political opinion over parliamentary process. The Speaker is the core of the system of self-regulation established by the constitution. Other parts of the regulatory arrangements can come and go, but the Speaker (or a Speaker at least) remains. What elected members say about the Speaker reflects what they think not just about the independence of that public office, but about the independence of Parliament itself, including the independence of Parliament from more powerful forms of a Speaker, which might be consistent with the constitution, but would require sustained parliamentary support. The constitution does little more than identify the office as the first to be filled by a newly elected Parliament, implying that the Speaker is central to the larger operation of the House of Representatives. This permissive quality allows each House to support, modify, or restrict whatever practical functions might be expected of successive Speakers.

The debate during the Gillard/Rudd minority governments reveals something important about Australian parliamentary expectations of a Speaker. The Speaker judges the parliamentary conduct of members; thus the Speaker acts like a judge or, more properly, like a presiding officer responsible for due process of the chamber. As presiding officer, the Speaker's presence stems from their supposed 'independence' from a political (especially governing) party. That 'independence', however, does not confer a substantial *positive role* to determine positive standards of orderly conduct or to regulate what is expected of members. No Speaker has such a degree of independence that they can ignore party interest and introduce what many in the community might like: rules for non-partisan standards of orderly conduct. The Speaker's independence cuts the other way, with important discretionary judgement against disorderly conduct. The 'independence' does confer a substantial *negative role* to curb disorder and to punish members for their disorder. The extensive debate provides us with detailed evidence that a core role of the Speaker is, according to the standing orders, to 'maintain order' in Parliament by punishing disorderly conduct. The standing orders go some way to stipulating required order, but the role still requires important discretionary judgement by Speakers to rule against disorderly conduct, regardless of any political party interest (HR 2012, 174–76).

The constitution

One simple way of indicating the relative power of the office of Speaker is through the Remuneration Tribunal, which places the two presiding officers as the highest paid parliamentary office holders. They receive less salary than the leader of the Opposition but substantially more than any other holder of a non-government office. Their salary is slightly above that of cabinet ministers, equating to that of the leader of the House (or Senate) who manages government business (Remuneration Tribunal 2012, 2013).

A less simple indication is in the constitution, which provides for the office of the Speaker. Of interest is the fact that the constitution provides for the president of the Senate earlier than the Speaker, and differently from the Speaker: the president, like the Speaker, is elected by the House; unlike the Speaker, however, the president has a vote on 'questions arising in the Senate', but no casting vote (as this would break the equal representation of the states). Tied Senate votes are held to be negative (ss17, 22). The constitution provides for the Speaker as the only office required for formal proceedings of the House of Representatives. Before any other business, the House chooses ('elects', according to the heading in the constitution) one of its members to be Speaker and may remove a Speaker by 'a vote of the House' (s35). The Speaker does not have a vote on 'questions arising in the House', but instead has, following British practice, a 'casting vote' to break tied votes in the House (s40) (HR 2012: 163).

The constitution does not clarify what principles Speakers would or should apply when making casting votes. This issue is important for it goes to one of the few distinctive powers of Speakers (Murray 2002). Casting votes only arise when votes in the chamber are equal, implying that a governing party cannot enforce its own vote except with the assistance of the Speaker. In this case, several options might apply (HR 2012: 182–86). One would be always to vote with the governing party; but this would also imply that Speakers were taking close note of the partisan nature of the dispute and regarding the party in government as the primary party to support. Such an option does not tally with the norms of impartiality noted below. Another option is that the constitution anticipates no restrictions on the principles Speakers may apply. This option would allow Speakers great freedom to apply whatever principles they consider appropriate. But a third option is that the constitution leaves determination of the classification of relevant principles to the House. This third option places Speakers under the rule of the House, applying only those sorts of principles considered appropriate by the House. This is a difficult situation to envisage, given that casting votes only arise when opinion is equally divided between government and opposition, such that there is no House view or consensus to follow.

What is the formal constitutional duty of the two presiding officers? The precise content of these duties are left to the conventions of Parliament. John Quick and Robert Garran include two relevant quotations about British conventions: one from James Bryce about official integrity and the requirement for political impartiality (Bryce 1889: vol. 1, 134–35); and one from Erskine May about operational duties through the maintenance of order and due process (Quick and Garran 1976: 479–80). Quick and Garran explain what they think the duties of the president of the Senate are, but do not provide similar commentary on the duties of the Speaker (Quick and Garran 1976: 441). The Senate's presiding officer is defined in part by reference to the other house: for example, the president is to protect against invasions of 'the privileges of the Senate'. While the Speaker is given no specific role, the general duties of 'the presiding officers of legislative bodies' cover both presiding officers and include duties of maintenance, enforcement, appointment and supervision — all suggesting that the presiding officer exercises procedural but not substantive authority. They regulate, but they do not rule, as can be seen from their core duties: 'to maintain order and decorum; to enforce the rules of debate; ... to appoint tellers to take a division; to supervise the officers of the House' (Quick and Garran 1976: 441).

The minority government

The 2010 election is now famous for producing minority government after a messy process of post-election negotiation. Also famous in this period of negotiation are three episodes relating to debates over the 'independence' of the Speaker. The rhetoric of 'independence' dominates these episodes, as Australian shorthand for the traditional Westminster system of Speakership, which has never matched Australian practice (Bolton 1968; Andrew 2002).

Non-government speaker

The first episode relates to the Gillard government's intent in securing non-government interest in the office of the Speaker, perhaps inspired by the ALP's success at state and territory level to persuade non-government members to take on this important role (Murray 2002). Former member for Lyne Rob Oakeshott was targeted as a potential Speaker (Milne 2010). He famously declined to pursue this interest once he learned from the likely leader of the Opposition, Abbott, that the Labor plan for proposed pairing of Speaker and deputy Speaker was unconstitutional, according to advice very critical of Oakeshott prepared by shadow Attorney-General Senator George Brandis (2010a, b). A number of Liberal members, mostly towards the end of their parliamentary careers, were also rumoured to be interested. This openness to non-government models of a Speaker for a minority ALP government gave rise to wider discussion about reforms to the parliamentary office to make it consistent with the 'independent' model required of a reformed parliament.

The primary theme here is the contrast between the model being promoted and the practices of past parliaments, when many governments tolerated only modest independence in their Speakers. Typically, past discussion about 'independent' Speakers came from non-government and especially Opposition interests. What was new in 2010 was that discussion now included the governing ALP party precisely because it thought it could benefit from 'independence': curtailing the voting power of the non-government ranks by appointing a non-government member as Speaker. The relevance is that members of the newly elected Parliament sensed that whoever was Speaker would be expected to act against the inherited ways of past Speakers and past Parliaments, or at least past governments of the day, who tended to see the Speakership as an important government office.

Independent Speaker

Episode two relates to the remarkable *Agreement for a better Parliament: parliamentary reform* of September 2010, which reflects the widespread views of the newly elected Parliament on institutional reform (ABP 2010). The document recognises the need for the Speaker 'to rule with a firm hand' under the 'cultural change' of enhanced participation being promoted. The 'independent Speaker' is listed as item two on the 22 items of proposed parliamentary reform. The Speaker's stated power is to 'rigorously enforce' the standing orders: and a new standing order relating to the direct relevance of answers to oral questions is later identified as requiring a 'strong stance' from the Speaker, eventually with support from government and opposition (ABP 2010: para 4.5). Independence explicitly means 'independent of Government'. Both the government-derived Speaker and Opposition-derived deputy Speaker will 'abstain from attending their respective party rooms' and also 'when in the Chair' they will be 'paired for all divisions', as will other members of the Speaker's panel when acting in the chair. This is the 'independence' plan opposed by the Opposition as unconstitutional because it potentially breaches the Speaker's duty to use the casting vote to resolve tied votes.

Paired Speaker

Episode three includes the formal reference from the Attorney-General to the Solicitor-General for an opinion about the 'independence' of the Speaker, delivered on 22 September (Gageler 2010). The Opposition had raised public doubts about pairing requirements for the Speaker, later using the Solicitor-General's advice as proof of its own case against the proposed pairing scheme (Brandis 2010a, b; Elder 2013: 3–4). Solicitor-General Stephen Gageler's 19-page report to Attorney-General Robert McClelland generally agrees with this opinion, although the main theme of this advice is whether there is 'any necessary constitutional impediment' to the pairing arrangement. The Solicitor-General answered that there was no 'necessary' constitutional impediment, so long as 'two provisos' were met: first, the Speaker's casting vote could not be deprived and the Speaker could not be given a normal deliberative vote; second, the pairing arrangement with the non-government deputy Speaker 'could only be voluntary' (Gageler 2010).

Brandis drew attention to the 'deliberately elliptical' language and argument from the Solicitor-General, which at times was 'striking in its circularity' (Brandis 2010b: 7, 9). The narrow logic of the Solicitor-General's advice was that the constitution did not prevent the government scheme. But the wider logic implied that the government had no power to compel any non-government member to any pairing arrangement, and indeed that Speakers should not act in ways that might interfere with another member's deliberative vote (Brandis 2010b: see, for example, paras 41–42). The Solicitor-General's advice reviewed the Agreement's details on the independence of the Speaker, noting that House members might not exercise their deliberative vote under limited circumstances (for example, conflict of interest, breach of privilege inquiry), while also noting that there can be no parliamentary enforcement of 'pairing' as a form of non-voting, which might, quoting the *House of Representatives Practice*, 'operate as a matter of moral or political obligation' (Brandis 2010b: paras 32, 40). So long as the Speaker did not use a pairing arrangement to exercise influence over deliberative votes by other members, the government scheme was not unconstitutional: or 'not necessarily unconstitutional', according to Brandis (2010c: 827).

Whether it was 'constitutionally proper', or fully or properly constitutional, was another issue, not asked of the Solicitor-General by the government (Brandis 2010b: para 5). Debate over the deeper meaning of the Solicitor-General's opinion arose in the House of Representatives at the election of Jenkins as Speaker, with Anthony Albanese defending government strategy by reference to the opinion and Christopher Pyne citing the more explicit criticism from Brandis as evidence against the government.

Three tales of departure

How then can we compare the rhetorical frameworks generated by these three Speakers? One useful approach is to compare the rhetorics associated with their *decline* from office: these transitions have provoked significant political commentary on the parliamentary roles of presiding officers. The warm praise of welcome found at the time of each Speaker's election reflects the high point of good intentions that every Parliament needs to experience; but the cold dismay found at the time of departure from office reflects more fundamental misgivings about the many roles managed by the House when selecting or replacing its Speaker.

The three tales of departure differ and reflect three competing models of what the House expects of Speakers. Jenkins's resignation upset two norms: that of a party loyalist taking the high office and that of retaining in office a Speaker with the technical skills to do the job well. Slipper's resignation upset the risky innovation of offering the office to a non-government member, but it reinforced the unwritten rule that admirable personal character is a basic requirement of this high public office. Burke's departure reasserts the norm of the rights of a party in government to award the office to one of its own members and it will dampen tendencies that occupants, like Jenkins and Burke, might have to steer the Speakership towards stronger forms of impartiality.

Jenkins resigned with little public expectation that his time was up. He has spoken very little about that political decision, except to convey the impression that he was searching for greater opportunities to play active policy roles in the governing party. He went on to become chair of an important parliamentary committee on human rights, before retiring from Parliament at the 2013 election. Jenkins was widely admired for his technical skills as a manager of parliamentary deliberation; but he was also a frustrated custodian of the civilities that were frequently abused, often during question time, by many House members. Voters can see why such a champion of impartiality might have had enough; but many non-government members feared that his resignation was a forced event, initiated by the government to yet again try to find a non-government member to take the Speaker's job.

There is plenty of evidence to explain why the Gillard minority government could be persuaded that such a move would strengthen their voting power while weakening that of the Opposition, as it did. The timing of such a move can be explained by the growing threats of criminal charges against a government backbencher and the readiness of an Opposition member to take the risk in the final years before retirement. What does the Jenkins' resignation tell us about Australian political rhetoric? I think it tells us that the presiding office is a government gift, to be arranged and rearranged by the government of the day: carefully during times of majority government, and somewhat slyly during times of minority government. The fact that someone so technically gifted and admired came and went at times to suit the serving governments helps clarify the real burdens placed on even the best of Speakers.

Slipper departed in two stages: first by stepping aside from the office while criminal charges were being brought against him; and, later, by resigning after his narrow win over the Opposition's motion to vote him out of office. Slipper, a self-described colourful figure, surprised many with his firm but fair presiding qualities as Speaker, taking on an active role as the 'dressed-for-office' representative of the House, ready to parade to the chamber in attempt to return dignity to parliamentary business. Slipper's departure is marked by the contrast between his elevated public and official style and the questionable personal style of a member not only facing criminal charges for mistreating employees and misusing travel privileges, but also for displaying offensive personal conduct in the email and telephone communications that were circulated during the court process.

Slipper's departure was as political as it was personal in that Opposition activists discredited him as personally unfit to hold high public office. That the Federal Court in turn discredited many of Slipper's most influential critics did little to save him, who had by then already returned to the isolation of the independent back bench. What does the Slipper tale of departure tells us? It reinforces the need for evidence of personal integrity in positions of public integrity and that, again, governments have accountability obligations when they appoint undeserving persons to high parliamentary office. The Opposition knew that the Gillard government was playing with fire in appointing Slipper, one of their former members, as Speaker. The government attempted to share the blame by making the Opposition, even the Leader of the Opposition, accountable for not regulating Slipper as one of their poor performers. The government lost and the Opposition won. Although critics of Slipper acknowledge his valuable deftness as a fair umpire of parliamentary debate, they also lament his unacceptable off-chamber misconduct, which destroyed his constituency (Craven 2012; Marr 2013).

Burke's departure was delayed and was not officially resolved until the newly elected House of Representatives officially elected a new Speaker on its first day of sittings in November 2013. This standard Australian story of departure tells us something important about the ground rules of impartiality in Australian parliamentary politics. Incoming governments do not retain Speakers from their political opponents. Burke experienced the partisan rivalry of the final year or so of the minority government and her parliamentary comments on the decline in parliamentary civility are matched by her increasing criticism of disorderly conduct. Burke acted as well as any other good Speaker in managing parliamentary deliberation and her departure will reflect the greater power of party government, with a preference for one of its own as the House's impartial presiding officer.

Burke illustrates the best available in the standard model of House Speakers: coming late to the office after serving long in the Speaker's panel of junior officers, managing the mess left from earlier misadventures in the Speakership, and finally accepting the convention that the newly elected House will confer the honour of the Speakership on one of the new governing party's favoured members.

Three debates over the Speaker

The following sketches give a richer picture of the rhetorical tone generated by the rise and fall of each of the three Speakers. My interest is not to document their own particular rhetorical signatures but to use their anxiety in office to highlight wider institutional perspectives on parliamentary politics. What follows are three brief accounts of the prevailing tone of parliamentary argument sparked by each Speaker.

Speaker Jenkins

Jenkins (a son of a former Speaker), having served close to 12 years as deputy Speaker during the Howard governments, took office at the time of the Rudd government in 2008 and remained in place after the 2010 replacement of Rudd by Gillard (Elder 2013: 5–6). Jenkins was uncontested in this election and his first term in office is remarkable for the cross-party support provided by the Opposition. Displaying important party-political independence, he avoided ALP meetings about political and parliamentary tactics, although he maintained his association with party meetings about broader policy issues. This traditional experience of the Speakership changed after the 2010 election, mainly because the 'new paradigm' for the new parliament placed a heavy burden on the Speaker to act as the champion of procedural reform. Public rhetoric had not changed, but the internal complexity of multi-party negotiation certainly had (Wright 2013).

Another important factor in this change was the Opposition sense that the minority government could fall at any moment; this expectation placed additional burdens on the Speaker as a potential casualty of any such fall. No Commonwealth Speaker had functioned under such challenging circumstances of minority government since the early 1940s (Bolton 1968: 159–60; HR 2012: 166). Each sitting day provided fresh examples of the awkward balancing act required of Speakers when managing the parliamentary stage, especially during critical episodes, such as question time. The Opposition tended to interrupt question time with motions to suspend standing orders to bring on want of confidence motions against the government, thereby stretching ordinary goodwill between government and Opposition and establishing uncertainty for the House cross-benchers.

These circumstances would test even the most placid of Speakers. Jenkins, who emerged from the Rudd government experience with a reputation for impartiality, was sorely tried under the minority system, when so many House interests looked to the Speaker to promote a sense of order consistent with their own interests. Given that the minority system had not been tried for so many years, the House was divided with competing priorities and with steadily increasing friction between the two major political parties. Oddly, Speakers like Jenkins, with established reputations for unusual impartiality, find these circumstances more testing than more partial servants of the government of the day. Government and Opposition pursued increasingly different models of a presiding officer, with the government wanting greater decisiveness and the Opposition wanting greater responsiveness. A fundamental disagreement between government and Opposition emerged over Opposition attempts to test their powers as sponsors of an expenditure bill, which caused Jenkins to think seriously about returning to the government backbench.

Jenkins, who was again elected after the 2010 election, with Slipper nominated as deputy Speaker by the government and elected, resigned on 24 November 2011 to make way for the Gillard government's nomination of Slipper as Speaker. Jenkins was publicly supported by the Opposition at his 2010 election to the

Speakership, accepting the new paradigm of a reformed parliament announced by Gillard, who argued that the House and not the Speaker comprised the institutional culture required for the Agreement suite of reforms. The three leading speakers at the 2010 election of Jenkins were the Prime Minister as nominator, Leader of the Opposition as seconder, and Oakeshott as a prominent supporter of the new paradigm. Jenkins declared that as part of the new paradigm he would no longer attend ALP caucus meetings.

Slipper was nominated by the government as something of a 'tough cop' model of presiding officer, with the support of the Leader of the Opposition to 'my friend' in his new office. What is important here is that Slipper's election prompted the deputy Speaker into important statements about the new paradigm. In his first statement, Slipper declared that, unlike some of the non-government members of the House, he had not provided any authority to the government of his support for supply or for confidence, and that he had maintained his deliberative vote.

Three significant events took place in 2011, culminating in the resignation of Jenkins. First, on 31 May 2011, in a heated question time, the Speaker gave many warnings to the House about disorderly conduct. At one point, the Speaker formally named one member as deserving a 24-hour suspension, which was moved by Albanese, the Leader of the House. The motion to support the Speaker was lost by one vote: 72 to 71. The Speaker announced that he would 'consider my position' at this first defeat of a motion to implement his ruling. The Leader of the Opposition quickly moved a motion of support for the Speaker, which was seconded by the Prime Minister, who noted somewhat sharply that the House should always support the Speaker. Oakeshott spoke briefly to explain his opposition to the initial motion on the basis of his general support for free expression of all members. The second motion was not opposed.

On 2 June 2011, Jenkins ruled against a bill introduced by Bishop. The general issue was whether a non-government expenditure bill could override the so-called 'financial initiative' conventions traditionally accepted by the House. The core convention was that the constitution required that all expenditure bills be accompanied by support from the Governor-General consistent with explicit constitutional provisions. Jenkins articulated the House's traditional conventions when ruling against the bill. The Opposition challenged the Speaker with a formal dissent motion, arguing that the House and not the Speaker is the formal authority on such matters (HR 2012: 189–92). The parliamentary debate was again heated, with references to writing by the Clerk over how best to manage this vexed issue. Albanese argued in defence of the Speaker's interpretation of the procedure, and Attorney-General McClelland defended the larger constitutional interpretation of the House's opposition to non-government expenditure bills. The Greens member and the two rural independents from

New South Wales all called for a new process for expenditure procedures under minority governments. By the end of the debate, the Opposition motion of dissent was lost 72 to 68 votes.

On 24 November 2011, Jenkins announced his resignation: 'placidly with my humour intact'. The positive account of his departure reported that he wanted to return to the ALP to promote good policy measures. The more strategic account mentioned the voting gain won by the government in stealing an Opposition member for the Speakership. The political rhetoric about Jenkins' departure was that he had been pushed out of office to secure the strategic advantage of greater voting strength. In this case, his departure reflects two interesting models of a Speaker. The first is colourless impartiality, which Jenkins discovered prevented an elected member from getting on with the business of promoting good policy. The second is the deeper impartiality found when an Opposition member, like Slipper, resigns from his party and accepts the nonpartisan office of presiding officer. The defect of Slipper's version of this second model is that such impartiality comes at a high price: Opposition interests will do what they can to smear the new Speaker's reputation; and the wider public will not take kindly to misconduct, even when it has no obvious political or, at least, partisan bearing.

The Leader of the Opposition declared that 'something very unusual' was happening and made clear his strong support for the former Speaker. The Prime Minister noted that the deputy Speaker was now acting Speaker, soon to be elected Speaker, with seriously damaging consequences for the Opposition's voting strength. The switch from Jenkins to Slipper effectively gave the government an increase of two ordinary votes. This change was thought necessary as the government numbers might fall at any time through resignation or, just as likely, criminal findings against a member who was at that time facing charges for earlier misconduct as a union official.

Speaker Slipper

Later on 24 November 2011, Slipper was nominated by the government as an independent member who had resigned from the Opposition party (HR 2012: 166) and was elected Speaker, with Burke from the ALP elected deputy Speaker. He took leave in May 2012 and was replaced by newly elected Burke in October 2012 (Elder 2013: 7–9).

Despite accusations from the Opposition about his inappropriate sexual misconduct and accusations from others about his pre-Speaker breaches of terms and conditions as an elected member, Slipper did not fall because of any proven illegality. Nor was he caught in a procedural battle similar to Jenkins. He fell because his controversial personal qualities emerged as unsuitable for high public office and it was his personal conduct away from the chamber that eroded his credibility in his official conduct in the chamber.

Slipper's nomination as Speaker provoked outrage from the Opposition, which tried valiantly to nominate any government member for the post. Burke was the first of many government members to decline an offer from Pyne. At one point, the independent Tony Windsor nominated the nominator, Pyne, simply in order to shut him up! The Prime Minister praised Jenkins as 'a great Speaker' before welcoming Slipper's 'fierce sense of balance and appropriateness'. Abbott conceded Slipper's 'technical skills' but wondered hard and long about Jenkins's resignation. As ever, Oakeshott got it right by welcoming the first independent Speaker in the new paradigm; and Slipper later described himself as 'an independent Speaker in the Westminster tradition' (*House Hansard* 24 November 2011: 13797).

In February 2012 Slipper made two sets of major announcements about his role. On 7 February, he clarified his role in applying the casting vote required of Speakers to break a tied House vote; and he clarified his implementation of an increased number of Opposition supplementary questions during question time. On 8 February, Slipper announced his application of a Speaker's Procession, adapted from the Canadian House of Commons, and further explained his plans for increased number of non-aligned supplementary questions in question time (*House of Representatives Practice* 172). But, by May 2012, Slipper's hold on the Speakership was weakening. Documents produced in the Federal Court by the prosecution made public Slipper's correspondence in which the language used about male and female sexuality had offensive implications. The later judgement by the Court punished the former political staffer James Ashby team for abusing the court process to ventilate politically explosive documents that did much to discredit Slipper (Farr 2013).

On 9 October, question time was interrupted by an Opposition motion of censure against Slipper, calling on the House to use its constitutional powers under s35 to remove Slipper from the Speakership. The motion was lost by one vote: 70 to 69. Abbott led the attack on Slipper, mentioning his 'misogyny'. This speech provoked the Prime Minister's now famous 'misogyny' speech, in which the accusation was switched from Slipper to the Opposition leader. Other government speeches addressed the imminent Federal Court case against Slipper, calling on the House to avoid premature or rash judgement before the Federal Court had completed its hearing.

Later that day, Slipper resigned, prompting the Opposition leader to declare that Slipper did indeed have good judgement. Slipper's resignation statement made a brave case in defence of his time as Speaker, noting three potential benefits: his stately march to open each new sitting day, his use of supplementary questions, and his often admired strict discipline on disorderly conduct. Still later on that day, Burke was elected the third Speaker in the tenure of the Gillard minority government. Burke's election came soon after the funeral for the first female Speaker Joan Child. Strong support for Burke came from the Opposition and non-government members. The Opposition eventually won its own election contest when Coalition member Mr Bruce Scott was elected as deputy Speaker.

Speaker Burke

Burke's term saw the role of Speaker return from controversy to more conventional modes (Elder 2013: 9–10). The experience of the previous year had upset the standard pathway, however, and released the Speakership from the high degree of respect afforded former Speakers. Burke's time was marked by disruption, as members experimented with new ways (e.g. Twitter) of bringing pressure on opponents; and as visitors brought unwelcome protest into Parliament House. The period was complicated by the fall of Gillard, along with many of her cabinet colleagues, and the return of Rudd as prime minister, leading to the ALP government's loss of office at the 7 September 2013 national election, and the election of a majority Coalition government. Burke's experience of disruption even reached into the election period when she made clear her opposition to Prime Minister Rudd's new direction in asylum seeker protection (Benson 2013).

Burke presided at the time of the judgement by the Federal Court in the case of *Ashby v. Commonwealth of Australia (No 4)* [2012] FCA 1411 (12 December) (Craven 2012; Marr 2013). The careful 55-page judgement by Justice Rares dismissed Ashby's complaints against Slipper as a political exercise amounting to 'an abuse of the process of the Court', threatening its reputation. Of most importance here is Rares's relative silence about the merits or otherwise of Slipper as an employer, and the emphasis on the political use and abuse of court processes in attempting to secure benefits to the Opposition in the House of Representatives. The judgement is an account of a classic political witch-hunt managed by Ashby to discredit Slipper and, so, to damage the Gillard government as his last protector. The case was 'manifestly unfair to Mr Slipper'. The judgement identifies the 'predominant purpose' of the official complaint against Slipper as political rather than legal, resulting in 'irrelevant and scandalous' action in the federal court to discredit Slipper. The management of Ashby's case receives critical examination as a political exercise misusing the legal process for partisan purposes. The court noted that the Commonwealth's case against Slipper's alleged 'Cabcharge' misconduct was a separate issue awaiting determination.

Burke also made a contribution to the debate between Jenkins and the Opposition. She released a set of 'Update Notes' from the Clerk's office to help members consider the full range of issues relating to 'the financial initiative' (Burke 2013a). This set of papers stand out as the approved procedure for House management of expenditure bills, including those initiated or amended by non-government members. These 'notes' say little about the Speaker, but they say much about the House's established conventions on expenditure bills, which Speakers might well be considered to promote. The issues go to the heart of power relations in a minority government by supporting the Clerk's norm that 'only the government may initiate or move to increase appropriations or taxes' (Clerk's Office 2013: 1). The 'rules' might be clear but the 'application' will require careful judgement by all members of the House and especially the Speaker.

Conclusion

A number of conclusions arise from this chapter, which has been about the *listening* powers of the Speaker in the role of presiding officer; Speakers are careful listeners. The most obvious rhetoric of Speakers reflects procedural defects not permitted under the House's standing orders. The 'speaking' roles are largely about procedural orders, especially degrees of punishment given to disorderly members of the House, generally during question time. Few students of political rhetoric would begin to study parliamentary rhetoric through close study of Speakers — because Speakers are not good examples of speakers or orators in the ways expected of party leaders.

The name of the office reflects British tradition regarding the reporting or speaking role of the chief representative of the legislative branch: the one authorised to speak officially about the lower house to other branches of government. This title preceded the later rise of chief ministers, who have assumed vastly greater speaking power, although primarily in relation to the political executive rather than the legislature itself. With the rise of other types of representatives of the legislature, the roles of Speakers have adapted to other forms of institutional management: speaking less but managing more. The best example arising from the three Speakers examined in this chapter is the exemplary British model identified by Rudd when welcoming the first election of Jenkins as Speaker. The newly elected Prime Minister argued in favour of a late-nineteenth century British Speaker who spoke from the chair as little as possible, but with great power and influence.

The House Speaker holds a constitutional and not simply a parliamentary office. The constitution notes that the Speaker does not have a deliberative vote, which explains something important about the role of this office. The absence of a deliberative vote is important in the procedure of a deliberative assembly: it suggests that the deliberative assembly does not look to the Speaker to use its casting vote to make a deliberative judgement about the merits of issues caught up in tied votes. A deliberative judgement would be a judgement about the weight and merits of the issue in question. This suggests that the Speaker has non-deliberative themes in mind when making casting votes. One non-deliberative judgement would be a judgement on process, such as the integrity or impartiality of the deliberative process. The casting vote is the only parliamentary vote exercised by the Speaker and this implies that the House has to give close thought to the principles appropriate to casting votes, which might well concern the sort of deliberative processes requiring the attention of Speakers and their procedural advisers. This implication arises from the heartfelt anxiety of debates over the Speakership in the House between 2010–13.

A third conclusion, rising from the dust of the debates over the same period, is that the House elects the Speaker and can dismiss the Speaker. In this period, the House elected three Speakers and caused the standing aside and later the resignation of one Speaker. Again, this relationship derives from the constitution. The implication is that Speakers are servants of the House carrying out duties that are recognised by the House, but which it is not capable of performing: such as the presiding functions seen most obviously during question time. The conclusion is that the election is a delegation but not a source of power, because it can be revoked at any time. The constitution does not set down criteria for election or dismissal. This does not imply that there are no reasons required for either election or dismissal; it simply implies that the House can determine these as it sees fit, taking account of its own accountability to the voters in each electorate. The larger conclusion here is that elected Speakers are protectors of the House's deliberative processes, which is not quite the same as providers of deliberative answers for the House.

A fourth conclusion also derives from the constitution. Section 50 provides for 'rules and orders', but it does not mention the presiding officers as either ruler-makers or order-makers. Each House may make rules and orders relating to its 'powers, privileges and immunities'; and about the 'order and conduct of its proceedings'. The implication is that the House may authorise rules and orders, and may require Speakers to manage many of the rules and orders, but the constitution does not establish the Speaker as the source of rules or orders. Speakers might well advise the House on preferred rules and orders, and might well manage the House's own preferred rules and orders, but Speakers are not delegated with rule-making powers because the House itself has that important constitutional function. Speakers are functionaries, reflecting the House as its representative, presiding over the many deliberative processes required of this deliberative assembly.

References

Andrew, N. 2002. The Australian federal Speakership. Unpublished speech delivered at University of Adelaide, 17–18 August.

ABP 2010. *Agreement for a better Parliament: Parliamentary reform*. Canberra, 7 September.

Benson, S. 2013. Speaker buckets Rudd on refugees. *Telegraph* 6 August: 7.

Bolton, G. 1968. The choice of the Speaker in Australian Parliaments. In C.A. Hughes ed. *Readings in Australian government*. University of Queensland Press, 155–62.

Brandis. G. 2010a. Re: S.40 of the Commonwealth Constitution. 20 September.

—— 2010b. Critique of the opinion of the Commonwealth Solicitor-General. 23 September.

—— 2010c. *Australian Senate*, 26 October: 827–29.

Bryce, J. 1889. *The American Commonwealth*. London: Macmillan.

Burke, A. 2013a. Law making powers of the Houses. *House Hansard*, 14 May, 34.

—— 2013b. 'The organisation of private Members' business'. Regional Presiding Officers Conference. Canberra, July.

Clerk's Office 2013. The law making powers of the Houses: Three aspects of the financial initiative. Canberra: House of Representatives 13 May.

Craven, P. 2012. The end of the (Slipper) affair. *The Drum Opinion* 18 December.

Elder, D. 2013. The role of the Speaker in minority government. Unpublished paper. Canberra.

Farr, M. 2013. Revealed: What Peter Slipper's sexist text messages actually said. *Australian* 9 October.

Gageler, S. 2010. *In the matter of the Office of Speaker of the House of Representatives*. SG no. 37 of 2010. Canberra: Solicitor-General of Australia.

Healy, M. 1998. *The independence of the Speaker*. Canberra: Parliamentary Library.

HR 2008. *The Speaker of the House of Representatives*. 2nd edition. Canberra.

—— 2012. The Speaker, Deputy Speakers and officers. Chpt 6 in *House of Representatives practice*. 6th edition. Canberra.

—— 2013. Infosheet 3 — The Speaker. Canberra.

Inglis, K. 1996. Parliamentary speech. *Australian Journal of Law and Society* 12: 147–62.

Marr, D. 2013. Ashbygate. *Guardian Australia* 12 July.

Milne, G. 2010. 'Exclusive: Oakeshott makes a bid for Speaker', *The Drum Opinion*, 15 September.

Murray, J. 2002. The role of the Speaker and political reality. *Conference of Association of Clerks at the Table*. July, Brisbane.

Quick, J. and Garran, R. 1976 (1901). *The annotated constitution of the Australian Commonwealth*. Sydney: Legal Books.

Remuneration Tribunal 2012, 2013. Report no. 1 of 2012; Determination no. 13 of 2013.

Snedden, B. 1980. Ministers in parliament — a speaker's eye view. *Politics* 15(2): 68–85.

Wright, B. 2013. *Hung parliaments — are they good for parliament?* ASPG Victorian Chapter Seminar. Canberra.

.

Part III: The content of rhetoric

9. 'The maximum of good citizenship': Citizenship and nation building in Alfred Deakin's post-Federation speeches

Mark Hearn and Ian Tregenza

By general consensus Australia's second prime minister, Alfred Deakin (1856–1919), was the most significant political leader in the decade following Federation. A major architect of the movement towards Federation, Deakin also drove many of the key reforms and policy initiatives of the post-Federation liberal, nation-building project, including immigration restriction, industrial arbitration and tariff protection. His achievements are all the more remarkable considering the general political instability he faced where fluid and volatile party allegiances and minority governments were the norm. Despite these obstacles, the support Deakin was able to gain for these initiatives owed much to his capacity to persuade.

Deakin's rhetorical ability was one of the most commented upon features of his public life, which stretched from 1879 to 1913, and across colonial politics in Victoria, the 1890s debates over Federation, and the decade following the inauguration of the Australian nation in 1901. Though, as his biographer John La Nauze notes, Deakin privately wished that 'journalists would say less about his oratory and more about his legislative record' (1965: 408), it was Deakin's power to communicate through the spoken word as much as any of his legislative achievements that established his reputation. Deakin was widely recognised as an outstanding figure in an age that placed great value on speech as performance. In Joy Damousi's phrase he 'was a product of the world in which he spent his formative years before the turn of the century; a world that was shaped and governed by the Victorian oral culture of listening and speaking' (2010: 172). According to La Nauze, 'Deakin possessed most of the attributes of the traditional orator: a handsome presence, a manner that could range from passionate earnestness to light humour without loss of dignity, a rich musical voice best described as light baritone. His speaking was extraordinarily rapid ... but his articulation was always perfect; he never hesitated for a word' (1965: 245–46).

In Australia and abroad, Deakin's oratory attracted considerable attention. After meeting Deakin at the 1887 Colonial Conference in London, the British liberal politician Sir Charles Dilke described him as 'the man of greatest promise in all of Australia ... a great administrator, a man of extraordinary eloquence and charm' (La Nauze 1965: 91). Deakin's reputation in Britain was only enhanced two decades later by his visit as Prime Minister to the Imperial Conference (1907) where the former secretary of state for the colonies, Joseph Chamberlain, remarked that 'Mr. Deakin has been the hero of the conference, and his speeches produced a great affect on the public mind' (*Kalgoorlie Western Argus* 1907). After hearing Deakin speak in London in 1907 Fabian Ware, the editor of the *Morning Post* (for which Deakin was the anonymous Australian correspondent for 13 years), was moved to write that 'Those who were privileged to hear him speak … will never forget the profound impression he created … Those were indeed stirring times when faith seemed to have been restored to politics in England, and great intellects were willing to bow to the inspiration of an ideal' (La Nauze 1965: 508). And yet another: 'If you will give us Mr. Deakin, you may have all our leaders' (*Lone Hand* 1907). A similar estimation of Deakin's eloquence was widely held in Australia. For example, the *Townsville Bulletin* in August 1907 declared:

> Mr Deakin is a man for whom Australians of all political parties had much admiration before his recent representation of the Commonwealth at the Imperial Conference. His policy might be condemned; but he always evidently believed wholeheartedly in it, and his skill in supporting it by argument in Parliament or from the platform was ever a delight to the lover of an intellectual contest. He has the oratorical gift more than any living Australian.

A key element in this oratorical gift, according to the *Townsville Bulletin*, was Deakin's sincerity:

> Mr Deakin's oratory carries an audience away, because his hearers feel sure that the man so eloquently addressing them thoroughly believes that his proposals are necessary for his country's salvation. They come away from the experience, either stimulated to assist him in his political propaganda or weakened in opposition to it by the doubt which its advocacy by so obviously able, honest and earnest a man raises.

Deakin's post-Federation eloquence drew much of its strength from his determined and passionate advocacy of proposals he believed vitally 'necessary for his country's salvation', reform measures that would bind Australians more closely to the emerging nation and which would maximise their good citizenship: encouraging their productive participation in the economy, and their willingness to accept the need for preparedness for war, and the sacrifices that war might demand.

In the decade following Federation, Deakin served as attorney-general and then three times as prime minister. While he had long been recognised as a great orator, the speeches he gave during this decade, on immigration restriction, the establishment of the High Court, industrial arbitration, tariff protection and defence were profoundly influential in shaping Australia's cultural and institutional development in the early twentieth century. Collectively, they may be the most influential series of speeches in Australian political history.

These reforms contributed to what is now referred to as the Australian settlement, the liberal, nation-building project of which Deakin was a significant architect, and which has attracted considerable research interest.[1] The literature on the Australian settlement constitutes a recently constructed narrative of twentieth century Australian history, which tends to emphasise the building of a protected and regulated Australian state — a 'fortress Australia'. This chapter suggests that this view fails to capture an important dimension of Deakin's vision, as much concerned with building the character of citizens as it was with building strong institutions. Indeed these were two sides of the same project of building the new Australian nation.

Deakin's narrative of character and citizenship

Deakin well understood that self-government brought a range of challenges that could only be met by expanding the capacities of its citizens. This may seem paradoxical: 'the language of citizenship' was, as Alison Holland observes, largely absent from the constitution of the Commonwealth of Australia adopted in 1901. Yet, as Holland adds, the language of citizenship 'was not insignificant in broader social and political disputes of the period', and informed the nation-building project that followed Federation (2005: 155–56).[2] Whereas the constitution could rest on defining Australians as British subjects, the active process of constructing government that followed Federation required an active conception of civic participation. From 1901 Deakin appealed to citizenship — which he emphasised as certain qualities of character, rather than a series of rights and entitlements — as the foundation of national strength and ultimately national freedom. While the challenges Australia faced were shaped by the rapid industrial, technological and military developments then taking place within the global order, the qualities of character that Deakin appealed to were ancient ones, namely those civic and masculine virtues of discipline, self-reliance, and readiness to take up arms to defend 'hearths and homes' (Australia, Parliament 1907: 7510). Nothing short of this was necessary for the establishment of a

---

1   See, for example, Birrell 2001; Fenna 2012; Kelly 1992; Lake 2003; Marsh 2001; Roe 1976; Sawer 2003; Stokes 2004.

2   See also Chesterman and Galligan 1999; Davidson 1997; Galligan and Roberts 2004.

'free people'. This is perhaps no more succinctly stated than in his 1907 speech regarding defence, wherein he urged the establishment of compulsory military training:

> What we aim at is the maximum of good citizenship, with the spirit of patriotism as the chief motive power of a civic defence force. For always, behind the weapons, behind the organization, behind the gun, there is the man. It is in the character and capacity of its manhood that the real strength and energy of resistance of a people must be found. (Australia, Parliament 1907: 7510)

The masculine nature of the emergent Australian nation is a well-researched theme (Lake 1992).[3] Marilyn Lake has emphasised Deakin's attraction to the republican ideal of manhood and self-reliance that he saw embodied in the American nation and in some of its great literary figures such as Ralph Waldo Emerson and Henry David Thoreau (2007a). Moreover, Lake has suggested that the 'capacity for great oratory was one of the masculine virtues Deakin associated with the nation builders of "the great republic"' (2007b: 50). There is no great surprise in this, since the links between citizenship and oratory have been a feature of the civic republican tradition since ancient Greece and Rome. Lake describes Deakin's and his (male) contemporaries' high estimation of rhetoric as a 'fantasy of male power'. Lake might be right to describe this as a fantasy, but if so, it is a fantasy with an ancient pedigree.

There is no doubt that a central theme of the public culture of Victorian-era Britain and Australia concerned the links between oratory and masculine virtue. Oratory was a vital part of the armoury of the 'public moralists' of the period, who were determined to promote both individual and national 'character', which in turn was understood principally in masculine terms — a masculinity in service to civic responsibility.[4]

Reflecting on the art of public speaking in 1904, Deakin observed the close relationship between speech making and individual character. In so doing, Deakin provided an insight into how he privileged sincerity, the desire to honestly express deeply held convictions, to lend power to his political narrative and provide the basis of a persuasive civic participation. Indeed, in the art of speech making, what counted above all else was character: 'It seems, and is a hard saying, but it is profoundly true, that character is the greatest of all sources of influence in speech as in act' (Deakin 1904: 162). Practice and preparation are undoubtedly necessary for any form of speech making, but

---

3   See also Stokes 2004: 12–13; Hearn 2006.
4   The relationship between manliness and character is discussed at some length in Stefan Collini's *Public moralists: Political thought and intellectual life in Britain, 1850–1930* (1991). See also Mangan and Walvin 1987; Roper and Tosh 1991.

in the end, following rules or precepts has limitations and an over-reliance on such diminished effective speech making: 'Imitation and rule can only make a mechanical and jejune speaker'. Moreover, 'A sermon or speech of eminent quality cannot be "prepared," in the deepest sense of the word, at the time; it is the flower of a life of thought and feeling'. As it was 'the man behind the gun' who mattered in the defence of the nation, likewise in oratory, 'It was the man behind the words that gave them their impact' (Deakin 1904: 161–63).

Deakin identifies some notable figures whose speeches reflect their individual characters. About the great nineteenth century British statesman and Prime Minister William Gladstone, Deakin wrote that his speeches compelled due to the 'personal magnetism in his eloquence, and the tremendous motive power of heartfelt belief'; the eighteenth century parliamentarian and philosophic Edmund Burke was the great exemplar of 'literary oratory and philosophic statesmanship'; the British liberal politician William Harcourt is described as the greatest remaining 'pillar … [of] the classic school of Parliamentary oratory — dignified but effective, magisterial, courteous, overflowing with the stored knowledge of the student and the man of the world'; Deakin's Victorian mentor George Higinbotham was said to have 'had the grand style, great elevation of thought, and a superb delivery reminding me of Gladstone, and, like him, able to sustain flights of impressive potency utterly impossible to lesser men'. The English bishop Charles Gore, whom Deakin heard at Westminster Abbey, though in some respects awkward and stiff, nevertheless possessed 'tremendous earnestness' and 'transcendent sincerity' which 'swept all those hindrances out of mind, and at last left the congregation rapt and overwhelmed …' (Deakin 1904: 162–63). Another who impressed Deakin at first hand was the American preacher Henry Ward Beecher who could speak at great length with few notes: 'There was no trace of repetition by rote — all was spontaneous; yet there was no flaw in the sermon delivered to 3000 people, who listened to it with an eager silence, rippled only now and then in response to his touches of naïve humour' (Deakin 1904: 165).

Deakin admired the oration of these figures because their words reflected their admirable if diverse characters. They embodied *ethos*, or character, which, along with *pathos* and *logos*, was one of the key ingredients that Aristotle identified as vital to the art of rhetoric.[5] As many of the witnesses to his oratory attest, Deakin likewise was an exemplar of this quality. Deakin's post-Federation speeches reveal how one of Australia's most important public figures drew upon his character, as expressed in the performance of public speaking, to help shape the terms of the emerging nation.

---

5   These three modes of persuasion (*pisteis*) can be defined in the following way: *ethos* — the character of the speaker; *pathos* — the emotional state of the audience; *logos* — the argument of the speech. See Aristotle 1991: 1356a. For further discussion see Rapp 2010.

Deakin's nation-building narrative

James Curran has observed the role of recent Australian prime ministers in defining a sense of national identity and purpose (2004). Deakin's role in establishing a national narrative is now neglected and since the publication of La Nauze's 1965 biography, research on Deakin has often focused on his formative experiences and inner life.[6] Yet public narrative fulfils a vital function in the formation of action and identity. Margaret Somers and Gloria Gibson argue that '… stories guide action … people construct identities (however multiple and changing) by locating themselves or being located within a repertoire of emplotted stories; that "experience" is constituted through narratives.'[7] On behalf of the Australian people, Deakin engaged in an elaborate sense-making narrative that validated new policy measures: establishing their relationship with key notions of Australian nation-building and the freedom of citizens of the new Commonwealth, binding subjects to a 'truth' of the nation they shared together as an imagined community (Anderson 1991: 6–7).

In the context of late-nineteenth century liberalism, freedom was, as Patrick Joyce describes, 'a formula for exercising power', 'the active and inventive deployment of freedom as a way of governing people'. Liberalism cultivated subjects who were 'reflexive and self-watching', who constantly monitored 'the very civil society and political power that are at once the guarantee of freedom and its threat' (Joyce 2003: 4). As Deakin's extensive personal papers attest, the prime minister was both the subject and a key interpreter of the liberal rule of freedom in Australia, monitoring his own public conduct and ideals as he helped to define and construct a nation-building project that required the citizen to be active in the organic development of their own government. The subject would be governed not by rigid direction but by the indirect techniques of liberalism, the cultivation of 'some authority of independent minds' that would respond to the 'ever-changing, ever developing needs and forms of unfoldment in society', as Deakin explained when introducing the conciliation and arbitration legislation to Parliament in 1903 (Australia, Parliament 1903: 2863).

Deakin's reference to 'some authority of independent minds' echoed the influence of the thinkers who influenced him, and whose work he voraciously read, including the American philosopher and psychologist William James (Hearn 2008: 204). In *The Pluralistic Universe* James argued that '[t]he pluralistic world is thus more like a federal republic than like an empire or a kingdom.

---

6 La Nauze 1965; Gabay 1992; Rickard 1996; Hearn 2008; Brett 2012.
7 Cited in Joyce 1994: 153. On narrative identity see also Somers 1997; White 2000; Kerby 1991; Poiana 1999.

However much may be collected, however much may report itself as present at any effective centre of consciousness or action, something else is self-governed and absent and unreduced to unity' (1996: 321–22).

This is the dynamic at the heart of Deakinite liberalism, and is reflected in his speeches. Liberalism seeks to create that 'absent' space for self-government, but in doing so generates ambiguity and tension; as Nikolas Rose observes, in liberalism 'governable subjects' must govern themselves, guided only by limited interventions from the state (1999: 42–43). Like many liberals of the period, Deakin was aware of the dangers of overly interventionist legislation, and the way government action could hinder as much as it could enhance the character of its citizens. Echoing the concerns of another mentor, Charles Pearson, Deakin wrote in 1893 that he feared 'State socialism … mainly because of the weakness of the social idea in us & run by selfishness nothing could exceed the corruption likely to be bred under a system of State Socialism'.[8] Despite these dangers Deakin, like Pearson, was resigned to the need for more rather than less state socialism at this time.

The character of the emerging nation and its citizens were governed, in Deakin's mind, by clear demarcations of gender and race. Industrial relations policy and tariff protection would allow Australian industry to flourish within the young nation, while maximising the productive output of the male workforce: Deakin was concerned to mobilise manhood in order to protect and develop the nation. Defence policy would help police the perimeter of a vulnerable Commonwealth, while disciplining its male citizens to the task of nation-building. 'It is in the character and capacity of its manhood that the real strength and energy of resistance of a people must be found', Deakin told Parliament in 1907. In his defence statement Deakin marginalised the role of women. Women might train as nurses, Deakin conceded, but they were primarily required in the home, as a source of 'patient loving kindness' in support of their spouses and sons (Australia, Parliament 1907: 7535). Despite the introduction of a universal franchise in 1902, women were significantly excluded from parliamentary politics and workforce participation (Grimshaw 1996: 196–97, 207–08). In Commonwealth policy, women would be relegated to the home to foster their maternal role and on behalf of the nation, a task addressed by the new conciliation and arbitration system under the direction of Justice Henry Bournes Higgins who, in a series of decisions between 1907–20, enforced wage discrimination against women to discourage their participation in the paid workforce (Hearn 2006; Ryan and Conlon 1989).

Deakin sought an idealised unity in his conception of the Commonwealth, a space where white men and women could enact the freedom of self-government, guided by restrained state intervention. Yet his idealised space was colonised by

---

8   Deakin cited in Walter and Moore 2006: 21.

the anxieties that had helped to shape it, and which Deakin called the citizens of the new Commonwealth to observe and guard against. It was a problem of managing space and population, as Deakin stressed in the immigration restriction debate in 1901 and the Ballarat election address of 1903. Deakin returned to these themes in the defence statement of 1907, when he identified the need to defend Australian territory through compulsory military training and the establishment of an Australian navy.

As Deakin explained in his Ballarat speech, the idea of a white Australia did not simply involve the immigration restriction of undesirable aliens, but represented a far broader and inclusive — for white Australians — conception of 'protection' and security: 'A white Australia does not by any means mean just the preservation of the complexion of the people of this country. It means multiplying our homes so that we may be able to defend every part of our continent. It means the maintenance of conditions of life fit for white men and white women. It means equal laws and opportunities for all, it means protection against the underpaid labour of other lands. It means the payment of fair wages. (Cheers.)' (*Sydney Morning Herald* 1903: 7). Moreover, white Australia was a fundamental precondition for securing the unity of the liberal nation, which in Deakin's mind would also promote a unity of character, as he explained when introducing the immigration restriction legislation in Parliament in 1901:

> The unity of Australia is nothing, if it does not imply a united race. A united race means not only that its members can intermix, intermarry and associate without degradation on either side, but implies one inspired by the same ideas, and an aspiration towards the same ideals, of a people possessing the same general cast of character, tone of thought … Unity of race is an absolute essential to the unity of Australia. It is more, actually more in the last resort, than any other unity. (Australia, Parliament 1901: 4807)

The unity of white Australia can be expressed as a problem of 'security, territory, population' (Foucault 2007: 108), which animated Deakin's conception of nation-building. Michel Foucault described 'governmentality' as having '… knowledge as its target, political economy as its major form of knowledge, and apparatuses of security as its essential technical instrument' (2007: 108). As a form of knowledge, Foucault observed that the word economy originally identified a patriarchal figure who provided 'wise government of the family', and political economy took up the idea of governing the state as attentively '… as that of a father's over his household and goods' (2007: 108). A code of masculine and patriarchal protection runs through Deakin's national narrative, preoccupied with securing the exposed territory of the Australian nation in order to protect the 'hearths and homes' of its citizens, so that they could harmoniously 'intermix, intermarry and associate without degradation on either side'. 'Unity of race' was an 'absolute' essential to securing the population, yet in his Ballarat address Deakin reminded his audience that the territory of Australia was dangerously exposed:

> A continent of 3,000,000 square miles, containing nearly 4,000,000 of people, scattered in a fringe upon its outer rim — a country whose increase in the matter of population is extremely small — a country whose birth rate at present is low — a country which we hold, but of which we only occupy a fraction, and of which we as yet use but a minute fraction — these are the fundamental facts to be burnt into our memories and maintained there for the purpose of interpreting what the Commonwealth is and suggesting what Australia ought to be. (*Sydney Morning Herald* 1903: 7).

Within the zone protected by the apparatus of security provided by immigration restriction and stronger defence measures, Australians could exercise their self-governance, which paradoxically they would be compelled to do by government edict. As Deakin declared in his defence statement: 'We are a free people, with political equality and sole authority in a country where all have the opportunity to possess homes of their own. Our position as free men in a free country casts on all the responsibility of undertaking our own defence' (Australia, Parliament 1907: 7528). In words that civic republicans through the ages would have appreciated, Deakin declared 'the best results from military training are to be obtained in a citizen army exactly in the proportion in which it is a citizen army. When men rally around their hearths and homes simply to safeguard them and those they love, they discharge a duty'. Failure to respond to this call is to risk much more than material possessions:

> If we lost the whole of our financial possessions we should miss them much less than if we were robbed of our liberty, constitutional freedom, civilization, and social status … None of us can conceive Australians in serfdom, or subject to an alien rule … we can never forget that what we have most to defend first and last is our national life and ideals more precious than life of the breathing frame. (Australia, Parliament 1907: 7510)

As in policy on conciliation and arbitration and white Australia, liberal self-government and freedom apparently had to accommodate some forms of formal restriction and compulsion.

The regulation of work was also a key site of the tension between self-governance and government intervention, and formed the defining code and hence the most contested space of the political economy of the post-Federation nation-building project. The liberal Australian state had sanctioned, through formal recognition of trade unions and universal democratic franchise, the right of the working class to industrial and political mobilisation. As Foucault has argued, however, '[t]he freedom of workers must not become a danger for the enterprise and production'. So, while '[l]iberalism must produce freedom', it must also establish '… limitations, controls, forms of coercion, and obligations relying on threats' (Foucault 2008: 64–65). 'Biopolitics' makes population 'a political problem', which modern government has solved through a network of interventions (Foucault 2003: 243–47).

As the leader of minority ministries reliant on Labor Party support in Parliament to remain in office, Deakin's administrations introduced instruments of restriction and compulsion to secure Labor support while preserving the essential structure of capitalist enterprise and liberal polity: restriction of non-white immigrants, compulsory dispute resolution imposed on employers and unions, and tariffs — at times at prohibitive levels — on imported products to protect local production and employment. The young nation would develop as a closed economy and culture, within an 'apparatus of security', as Foucault characterised this form of liberal governance (Foucault 2007: 108).

In recent decades compulsory arbitration has come to be seen as one of the pillars of the Australian settlement, which has been unravelled as the Australian state has undergone a series of liberalising reforms. Seen through the neoliberal lens, the institution of compulsory arbitration and centralised wage fixation is viewed as an excessive form of state paternalism (Kelly 1992). What is often missed in this analysis is the particular understanding of freedom and civic virtue that was central to the new liberal reforms and is reflected in Deakin's 1903 speech introducing the conciliation and arbitration legislation. Reflecting the tension between liberal freedom and rule identified by Joyce and Rose, for Deakin the extension of the rule of law into the realm of industrial arbitration undoubtedly involved greater state coercion, but it also represented an extension of the realm of freedom. He famously claimed that this legislation marked 'the beginning of a new phase of civilization' that would substitute the reign of law for the reign of violence in industrial affairs. The 'People's Peace' that it would usher in was akin to the medieval transformation of civil society that occurred when warring barons came to recognise the authority of the 'King's Peace' (Australia, Parliament 1903: 7510).

Historians have rightly linked the principles underlying the Commonwealth Court of Conciliation and Arbitration to the critique of 'freedom of contract' that was a feature of the new liberal thought of the period, stemming in particular from the idealist philosopher T.H. Green.[9] Also worth emphasising

---

9   Green's essay 'Liberal legislation and freedom of contract' (1881) is the seminal work. Deakin was well acquainted with this tradition of thought. He was a long-term friend of the leading American idealist Josiah Royce (see Lake 2007a). In August 1908 Deakin attended a lecture given by the Welsh idealist Henry Jones, followed by lunch the next day with the Victorian Governor Sir Thomas Carmichael and Henry Laurie,

here, however, are the civic republican features of Green's thought, which ties freedom as civic virtue to the restraint of arbitrary power. Citizens can only realise their full capacities, or achieve freedom in the positive sense, when they enjoy the security that comes from restricting the exercise of arbitrary power. Deakin's project of extending the realm of law into industrial arbitration can be understood in these terms as it entailed the substitution of 'a new *régime* for the reign of violence by endowing the State — which in itself possesses a strength greater than that of either or both of the contestants — with power to impose within the limits of reason, justice, and constitutional government, its deliberate will upon the parties to industrial disputes' (Australia, Parliament 1903: 2868). It would be, he urged, 'a distinct gain to transfer to the realm of reason and argument those industrial convulsions which have hitherto involved, not only loss of capital, but loss of life, liberty, comfort, and opportunities of well-being' (Australia, Parliament 1903: 2864). This was a political manifestation of Green's idea of freedom as:

> a power which each man exercises through the help or security given him by his fellow-men, and which he in turn helps to secure for them. When we measure the progress of society by its growth in freedom, we measure it ... by the greater power on the part of the citizens as a body to make the most and best of themselves. ... the mere removal of compulsion, the mere enabling a man to do as he likes, is in itself no contribution to true freedom. (1986: 199)[10]

According to Deakin in 1907, the process of nation-building was 'compelled by the circumstances of our time and situation', and it required a renovation of space and time in order to adjust the Australian community, and the terms of the new nation, to the productive demands of the rapidly modernising early twentieth century (Australia, Parliament 1907: 7510). The demands of modernity intensified anxieties over population, productivity and identity, which the liberal, nation-building project strove to address.

New technologies and the accelerating production of *fin de siècle* industrial modernity intensified the threat of danger that found a focus in defence policy, expressed in the dilemma of time and situation that Deakin posed before parliament in December 1907: how, with apparently little time before the prospect of war must be faced, and with limited available defence resources, could such an exposed and vast space as the Australian continent be defended?

---

professor of philosophy at the University of Melbourne. Deakin also replied enthusiastically to a review that Walter Murdoch wrote on J.H. Muirhead's *The Service of the State* in 1909 with the following: 'Bravo! again — Muirhead admirable — Jones 'Idealism as a practical Creed' — (his Sydney lecture) says the same thing ... tho' he derives direct from Hegel & not apparently from Green' (La Nauze and Nurser 1974: 36–37, 43; see also Sawer 2003: Chpts 1 and 3).

10   For discussion of the relationship between Green's thought and contemporary republican theory see Tyler 2006.

Deakin insisted Australia 'must keep step' with the 'feverish haste' with which the world's 'leading nations are arming' (Australia, Parliament 1907: 7511; Chandler 1990; Ledger and Luckhurst 2000). Just as other nations equipped themselves with intimidating new military and naval technologies — the battleship, the submarine, the machine gun — so must Australia.

Deakin also observed the intensifying 'commercial competition' that was accelerating between rival nations, requiring tariff protection to allow white nationhood to flourish in Australia: 'We protect ourselves against armed aggression; why not arm ourselves against aggression by commercial means. We protect ourselves against undesirable coloured aliens. Why not protect ourselves against the products of the undesirable alien labour? (Cheers.)' (*Sydney Morning Herald* 1903: 7).

'Aggression', and the fear of it, reflected the competitive, 'feverish haste' of industrial modernity, as Peter Gay has observed: aggression channelled into industrialisation, and manifested in the identification and exclusion of 'convenient others', which in the Australian context in the period could be the hordes of Asia against whom Australians must arm themselves (1995: 68, 447). Aggression provided a key metaphor of Deakin's speeches, overtly addressed in defence policy but also colonising policy in trade, immigration and work. Aggression reached into the productive demands made of men and the discriminations enacted against women, identified as 'gentle invaders' of the paid workforce who must be 'driven' back to the home (Hearn 2006: 15–20). Deakin masked this aggression under the rubric of 'the People's Peace', which he said would follow the implementation of the conciliation and arbitration Act. The aggression of industrial competition and class conflict would be suppressed — or at least contained — by the elimination of strikes through the intervention of the court, although as Erik Eklund and others have documented, unions continued to resort to strike action following the passage of the Act in 1904, and employer aggression was manifested in lockouts of workers, resistance to union activism and wage claims — including resorting to High Court appeals against industrial awards granted by the Court of Conciliation and Arbitration, a successful tactic that significantly restricted the court's power in the first decades following Federation (Eklund 2001; Markey 2012: 122; Cockfield 1998). The workplace, the most contested terrain of Australian political economy, was the space Deakin's nation-building project was least successful in securing.

Aggression was also an underlying theme within the republican tradition which tied civic virtue to the duties involved in maintaining self-government, foremost among them the readiness to respond to conflict and aggression. Like Machiavelli, for whom *virtù* consisted in those masculine qualities that enabled rulers to take control of fortune (*fortuna*) and pursue the actions demanded by the situation (*necessità*), Deakin well understood that particular measures and qualities of citizenship in the new Australian nation were not optional but were 'compelled by the circumstances of our time and situation'.[11]

Conclusion

At the end of his essay 'Public speaking and public speakers', Deakin observed that the public speaker invariably reveals his inner personality. 'Consciously or unconsciously,' he mused,

> a speaker is always revealing himself to those who care to analyse him. He cannot help it. What he says, and how he says it, his arguments, his line of thought, and the motives to which he appeals declare his nature and ideas with trumpet tongue. His voice, his manner, even his choice of words, draw aside the veil of personality in spite of himself. (1904: 165)

The speaker is engaged in what Hannah Arendt termed an act of self-disclosure: 'In acting and speaking, men show who they are, reveal actively their unique personal identities and thus make their appearance in the human world … This disclosure of "who" … somebody is — his qualities, gifts, talents, and shortcomings, which he may display or hide — is implicit in everything somebody says or does'. For civic republican Arendt, political action — the distinctive form of human freedom — is bound up with the ability to communicate through speech. In the realms of 'labour' and 'work', governed by biological and economic necessity, speech is incidental. But in politics, which assumes plurality among human beings, action and speech are inseparable:

> the actor, the doer of deeds, is possible only if he is at the same time the speaker of words. The action he begins is humanly disclosed by the word … it becomes relevant only through the spoken word in which he identifies himself as the actor, announcing what he does, has done, and intends to do. (1958: 179)

Deakin's willingness to disclose himself helped to make him one of the most persuasive advocates of the nation-building mission in post-Federation Australia.

---

11 We do not suggest that Deakin had an intimate knowledge of Machiavelli or that the Australian Federation was a continuation of what John Pocock described as the 'Machiavellian moment'. Nevertheless we do know that Deakin had a profound knowledge of classical literature and his famous appetite for reading developed at a young age. According to La Nauze, although Deakin never mastered Latin or Greek he 'read, in translation, more Greek and Latin literature than most of his contemporaries who performed creditably in classics' (1965: 1: 18–19). Perhaps the more immediate Italian influences were the founders of the Italian nation, Giuseppe Garibaldi and especially Giuseppe Mazzini, who inspired Deakin in his younger days. See the discussion in Hirst (2000: 7–11). The American republic, as Lake (2007a) has emphasised, was also for Deakin a guiding ideal. In other words, the republican resonances in Deakin's speeches had multiple sources.

In Arendt's phrase, this was 'the enacted story' (1958: 181) that Deakin guided. Without the component of personality revealed on the public platform, and at least some measure of intimacy shared with his audience, his capacity to frame an effective message would have been seriously diminished.

Despite his eloquence and command of detail, that message did not always persuade; Deakin often faced intractable political resistance. Fighting always from the corner of minority government, by 1910, Deakin was no longer able to fashion an electorally effective coalition behind his leadership. With the advent of a decisively elected majority Labor government under Andrew Fisher in April 1910, the Deakin era was effectively closed. Deakin's last significant political performances were made as leader of the opposition, in resistance to a nation-building initiative proposed by Labor — the Fisher government's 1911 referendum proposal to extend Commonwealth legislative power over industrial relations, trade and corporations — the key contested areas of Australian political economy. Deakin's oratory helped defeat Labor's referendum proposals by appealing to a negative instinct: denying the expansion of Commonwealth power — an expansion he had often championed, and that had been periodically frustrated by High Court veto of his government's legislative initiatives. By 1911 Deakin summoned the spirit of liberalism as a warning against the excesses of government power. If Labor's constitutional amendments were carried, the Commonwealth would '… exercise a despotic control over every commercial or manufacturing undertaking in Australia' (Hearn 2005: 87.4). The nation-building project, in Deakin's conception, had its limits, and he did not share Labor's conviction that government should intervene more directly to ease the burden of economic disadvantage experienced by the Australian working class.

Deakin evidently hoped that his oratorical skills would help preserve his reputation as a significant figure in Australian political history. Many great public speakers from the past, as well as contemporaries from across the sea, Deakin observed, can 'so often come to seem familiar friends … There are few historical personages better known, or at all events more easily knowable, than those to be found in the long line of descent from Demosthenes and Cicero to Gambetta and Castelar' (1904: 165). Deakin was a worthy successor to this line of descent. By examining Deakin's key speeches from the post-Federation decade we can learn much not only about the early national project, but much of the character of 'the man behind the words' who did so much to shape that project.

References

Anderson, B. 1991. *Imagined communities*. London: Verso.

Arendt, H. 1958. *The human condition*. Chicago and London: University of Chicago Press.

Aristotle 1991. *The art of rhetoric*. H. Lawson-Tancred ed. London: Penguin.

Australia, Parliament of 1901. *Commonwealth parliamentary debates: Senate and House of Representatives*.

—— 1903. *Commonwealth parliamentary debates: Senate and House of Representatives*.

—— 1907. *Commonwealth parliamentary debates: Senate and House of Representatives*.

Birrell, B. 2001. *Federation, the secret story*. Sydney: Duffy & Snellgrove.

Brett, J. 2012. Alfred Deakin's childhood: Books, a boy and his mother. *Australian Historical Studies* 43(1):61–77.

Chandler, A. 1990. *Fin de siècle* industrial transformation. In M. Teich and R. Porter eds. *Fin de siècle and its legacy*. Cambridge: Cambridge University Press.

Chesterman, J. and Galligan, B. 1999. *Defining Australian citizenship*. Carlton: Melbourne University Press.

Cockfield, S. 1998. McKay's Harvester Works and the continuation of managerial control. *Journal of Industrial Relations* 40(3): 383–400.

Collini, S. 1991. *Public moralists: Political thought and intellectual life in Britain, 1850–1930*. Oxford: Clarendon Press.

Curran, J. 2004. *The power of speech*. Carlton: Melbourne University Press.

Damousi, J. 2010. *Colonial voices: A cultural history of English in Australia 1840–1940*. Cambridge: Cambridge University Press.

Davidson, A. 1997. *From subject to citizen: Australian citizenship in the twentieth century*. Cambridge: Cambridge University Press.

Deakin, A. 1904. Public speaking and public speakers. *Life* 15 February.

Eklund, E. 2001. From patriotic interest to class interest: Employers and Federation, 1890–1912. In M. Hearn and G. Patmore eds. *Working the nation, working life and Federation 1890–1914*. Sydney: Pluto Press.

Fenna, A. 2012. Putting the Australian settlement in perspective. *Labour History* 102: 99–118.

Foucault, M. 2003. *Society must be defended*. London: Penguin Books.

—— 2007. *Security, territory, population*. Basingstoke: Palgrave Macmillan.

—— 2008. *The birth of biopolitics*. Basingstoke: Palgrave Macmillan.

Gabay, A. 1992. *The mystic life of Alfred Deakin*. Melbourne: Cambridge University Press.

Galligan, B. and Roberts, W. 2004. *Australian citizenship*. Carlton: Melbourne University Press.

Gay, P. 1995. *The cultivation of hatred*. London: Fontana Press.

Green T.H. 1986 (1881). Liberal legislation and freedom of contract. In P. Harris and J. Morrow eds. *Lectures on the principles of political obligation and other writings*. Cambridge: Cambridge University Press.

Grimshaw, P. et al. 1996. *Creating a nation*. Ringwood: Penguin Books.

Hearn, M. 2005. Examined suspiciously: Alfred Deakin, Eleanor Cameron and Australian liberal discourse in the 1911 Referendum. *History Australia* 2(3): 87.1–87.20.

—— 2006. Securing the man: Narratives of gender and nation in the verdicts of Henry Bournes Higgins. *Australian Historical Studies* 127: 1–24.

—— 2008. A transnational imagination: Alfred Deakin's reading lists. In D. Deacon, P. Russell and A. Woollacott eds. *Transnational ties: Australian lives in the world*. Canberra: ANU Press, pp. 197–211.

Hirst, J. 2000. *The sentimental nation: The making of the Australian Commonwealth*. Melbourne: Oxford University Press.

Holland, A. 2005. The common bond? Australian citizenship. In M. Lyons and P. Russell eds. *Australia's history, themes and debates*. Sydney: UNSW Press.

James, W. 1996. *A pluralistic universe*. Lincoln: University of Nebraska Press.

Joyce, P. 1994. *Democratic subjects*. Cambridge: Cambridge University Press.

—— 2003. *The rule of freedom*. London: Verso.

Kalgoorlie Western Argus 1907. 23 July: 34.

Kelly, P. 1992. *The end of certainty*. Sydney: Allen & Unwin.

Kerby, A.P. 1991. *Narrative and the self*. Indiana University Press.

Lake, M. 1992. Mission impossible: How men gave birth to the Australian nation — nationalism, gender and other seminal acts. *Gender & History* 4(3): 305–22.

—— 2003. White man's country, the trans-national history of a national project. *Australian Historical Studies* 34(122): 346–63.

—— 2007a. 'The brightness of eyes and quiet assurance which seem to say American': Alfred Deakin's identification with Republican manhood. *Australian Historical Studies* 38(129): 32–51.

—— 2007b. Sounds of history: Oratory and the fantasy of male power. In J. Damousi and D. Deacon eds. *Talking and listening in the age of modernity: Essays on the history of sound*. Canberra: ANU Press.

La Nauze, J. 1965. *Alfred Deakin: A biography*. Melbourne: Melbourne University Press.

La Nauze J.A. and Nurser, E. 1974. *Walter Murdoch and Alfred Deakin on books and men. Letters and comments 1900–1918*. Clayton: Melbourne University Press.

Ledger, S. and Luckhurst, R. 2000. Introduction. In *The fin de siècle, a reader in cultural history, c. 1880–1900*. Oxford: Oxford University Press.

Lone Hand 1907. 2 September.

Mangan, J.A. and Walvin, J. 1987. *Masculinity and morality: Middle-class masculinity in Britain and America, 1800–1940*. Manchester: Manchester University Press.

Markey, R. 2012. The significance of the Fisher Labor government. *Labour History* 102: 119–29.

Marsh, I. 2001. The Federation decade. In J.R. Nethercote ed. *Liberalism and the Australian Federation*. Sydney: The Federation Press.

Poiana, P. 1999. Narrative identity. *Literature and aesthetics* 9.

Raap, C. 2010. Aristotle's rhetoric. In E.N. Zalta ed. *The Stanford encyclopedia of philosophy*. URL: http://plato.stanford.edu/archives/spr2010/entries/aristotle-rhetoric/. Consulted 19 August 2013.

Rickard, J. 1996. *A family romance: The Deakins at home*. Carlton: Melbourne University Press.

Roe, J. 1976. Leading the world? 1901–1914. In J. Roe ed. *Social policy in Australia*. Sydney: Cassell Australia.

Roper, M. and Tosh, J. eds. 1991. *Manful assertions: Masculinities in Britain since 1800*. New York: Routledge.

Rose, N. 1999. *Powers of freedom: Reframing political thought*. Cambridge: Cambridge University Press.

Ryan, E. and Conlon, A. 1989. *Gentle invaders, Australian women at work*. Ringwood: Penguin Books.

Sawer, M. 2003. *The ethical state? Social liberalism in Australia*. Melbourne University Press.

Somers, M.R. 1997. Deconstructing and reconstructing class formation theory: Narrativity, relational analysis, and social theory. In J.R. Hall ed. *Reworking class*. New York: Cornell University Press

Stokes, G. 2004. The Australian settlement and Australian political thought. *Australian Journal of Political Science* 39(1): 5–22.

Sydney Morning Herald 1903. The federal campaign. 30 October: 7–8.

Townsville Daily Bulletin 1907. 23 August: 4.

Tyler, C. 2006. Contesting the common good: T.H. Green and contemporary republicanism. In M. Dimova-Cookson and W.J. Mander eds. *T.H. Green: Ethics, metaphysics, and political philosophy*. Oxford: Oxford University Press.

Walter, J. and Moore, T. 2006. State socialism in Australian political thought: A reconsideration. *Australian Journal of Politics and History* 52(1): 13–29.

White, G. 2000. Histories and subjectivities. *Ethos* 28(4): 493–510.

10. The rise and fall of economic rationalism

Geoffrey Stokes

Introduction

The term economic rationalism is one of political categorisation, commendation and criticism. Although economic rationalist thought and policy were part of a broader international trend, the term itself represents a particularly Australian contribution to political rhetoric. First deployed in the 1970s to commend the 'economic rationality' of Gough Whitlam's Labor government, the term came to increasing prominence in the late 1980s and early 1990s to disparage market-oriented economic policies, economics and economists. During this later period, advocates and opponents of the economic reforms of the successive Labor governments of Bob Hawke and Paul Keating (1983–96) often argued their case within the language of economic rationalism. Perhaps more than at any time in recent Australian history, these debates brought economic policy regularly, even obsessively, to the forefront of public attention. As a result, government ministers, journalists, commentators and ordinary citizens became accustomed to using a new rhetoric that included references to 'competition', 'level playing fields', 'price signals' and 'picking winners'. Advocates of 'markets' often singled out their capacity to 'discipline' or 'punish'.

Disputes over the term and the phenomena it described provoked a wide range of responses that included: accusations of dogma, appeals to history, claims about human nature, as well as the advocacy of competing social and moral religious values. At times, the debates were bewildering because participants on all sides regularly made accusations of irrationality against the arguments of their opponents (e.g. Stilwell 1989; Hyde 1993a, 1993b; Makin 2013). Even though the term has largely been abandoned by academics, in favour of the more conventional term 'neoliberalism', it still appears sporadically in the media (Gittins 2011; Edwards 2013; Makin 2013), historical accounts, and retrospective analyses (e.g. Kelly 1992, Bell 1998, Nevile 1998; and Megalogenis 2012). It is also referred to in everyday political discussions among educated citizens. This chapter sketches the evolution of the content of the rhetoric, indicates a select range of arguments over it, and discusses its political significance since the 1970s.

Intellectual and political contexts

The rhetoric of economic rationalism originally offered a shorthand way of understanding and criticising fundamental shifts in Australian policy that were initiated by federal Labor governments. Over time, however, the term was also deployed to criticise those who championed free market ideas. Pertinent examples include business associations, such as the Australian Chamber of Commerce (from 1992 it became the Australian Chamber of Commerce and Industry), neoliberal theorists, such as Friedrich Hayek, and think tanks, such as the Institute of Public Affairs and Centre for Independent Studies. For some, therefore, economic rationalism was the trimmed down rhetorical successor to that of the 'New Right'. There are, however, no clear lines of *historical* demarcation between the New Right and the onset of 'economic rationalism'. One of the last books on the New Right in Australia (Coghill 1987) was published four years into the Hawke government and the contributors were overwhelmingly members or supporters of the Australian Labor Party (ALP).

The New Right is a term drawn from British politics and applied to criticise the ideas and policies of the Liberal and National Party governments of 1975–83, led by Malcolm Fraser (see Sawer 1982). The term was applied to those such as British Prime Minister Margaret Thatcher (1979–90) and US President Ronald Reagan (1981–89). These leaders pursued a combination of radical free market economic policies and conservative social policies, along with a belief in the value of a strong state over democratic participation. Economic rationalism of the Labor variety generally supported a strong welfare state and did not promote an unduly conservative social agenda. Nonetheless, observers of the Hawke government pointed out how during that period social security policies moved away from the principles of universalism and towards those of targeting and selectivity, as well as encouraging the privatisation of certain kinds of welfare provision (Gibson 1990: 184). Nor was Labor expressly anti-democratic, though some critics discerned such tendencies.

In its simplest formulation, economic rationalism was a label applied to the philosophy of government action that gave greater priority to encouraging market forces. The advocates of economic rationalism wanted to reduce direct government intervention in the economy with the aim of increasing the role that markets, economic competition, and prices could play. In practice, this entailed policies to: (1) limit or reduce government spending and lowering taxes; (2) privatise and corporatise the public sector; and (3) deregulate the economy. The latter included removing controls on the exchange rate, and deregulating financial and labour markets. Such policies were intended to reduce constraints upon markets and capital, and promote economic productivity and growth. It has to be said, however, these policies had uneven and unanticipated outcomes, and were not always successful in achieving their objectives (See e.g. Quiggin 1997; Fenna and Tapper 2012).

The core principle and associated economic policies had their intellectual origins in neoclassical economic thought. In its later versions, economic rationalism was based on a combination of the macroeconomic and microeconomic theories of the 'Chicago School' (see Quiggin 1997: 2). These theories emphasised the merits (efficiencies) of economic competition and the drawbacks (inefficiencies) of government intervention to correct market failures. Because of the centrality of neoclassical economic thought to the mainstream of the economics discipline in Australia, professional economists were generally regarded, sometimes erroneously, as the standard-bearers of economic rationalist ideas. It is also important to note that the debates over economic rationalism mapped onto the longer conflict between the advocates of a more radical Marxian political economy and orthodox, liberal economists working within university economics departments. The political economists, many of whom worked in other disciplines, were among the notable critics of economic rationalist ideas and policies (see e.g. Rees et al. 1993).

Since colonial times, there have been many debates over economic policy and the best means for governments to promote economic development (See e.g. Butlin et al. 1982: 10–28; Head 1986; Horne 1976). Arguments about the relative priority that should be given to state intervention and free markets has a long history in which Australians and their governments widely accepted that markets ought to be subordinated to contemporary social values and national imperatives (e.g. Melleuish 1990). Such conclusions were later buttressed by Keynesian arguments about the role of government in the economy. The apparent incapacity of Keynesian policies to address inflation and other economic problems, however, led to a fracturing of the post-World War II consensus on economic policy in Europe and Australia. The practical problems of economic growth, inflation, 'stagflation', unemployment, and taxation, created a space for alternative ideas and models of economic reform.

In Australia, this space opened up with the end of the 'long boom' and the increase in unemployment during the Whitlam Labor government (1972–75). Under this government, economic rationality came to be considered a virtue when compared with previous policy traditions that justified and institutionalised economic inefficiency. Donald Horne appears to have been the first to use the term when he referred to those 'economic rationalists', among them Whitlam, 'who wanted to restore certain market conditions that they thought would lead to a more rational allocation of resources' (1976: 164). Thus the reformers pursued efficiency through policies that promoted 'economic rationality'. For

Horne, such an approach took account of both the limits of markets and the necessary role of government. For this reason, Horne saw economic rationality as 'the most subtle theoretical compromise of the mixed economy era' (1976: 244).

A.S. Watson used the term 'economic rationalism' to describe 'Labor thinking on agricultural policy' that embraced the new tendency to reduce assistance to producers and promote market forces in the sector (1979: 164). Similar to Horne, John Quiggin comments on the distinctiveness of this early approach: 'The views of the first generation of economic rationalists were generally in the economic mainstream of the period — Keynesian in macro terms and supportive of the "mixed economy" in micro terms' (1997: 2). Adherence to this first version among 'Labor' economists was evident in later debates. The promise of rationality and efficiency also gave economic rationalism its positive normative tone.

Barry Hughes applied a slightly problematic and more pejorative meaning to the term when he called attention to Labor Treasurer Bill Hayden's 1975 budget, which he saw exemplifying the 'new view of "economic rationalism"' (1980: 114). For Hughes, however, the political rhetoric surrounding this budget endorsed a *departure* from Labor's previous Keynesian expansionist policies that had aimed to promote full employment, along with the adoption of policies that aimed to reduce protection and combat inflation. Hughes, who later worked as an adviser to Keating during his term as Treasurer, used the term 'economic rationalism' to label this shift in the priorities of the federal Labor government, though he pointed out that the budget reality did not match the supporting rhetoric.

Glenn Withers referred to the term disapprovingly in the context of debates over labour market deregulation (1986: 23, 32). For Withers the 'economic rationalists', who he also called 'neoliberals', were pitted against the 'economic realists' who opposed deregulation and the 'neo-corporatists' who supported the Labor Accord between the government and the trade union movement (1986: 23, 32). Withers criticised those economists (proposing deregulation) who engaged in 'rationalism', by which he meant using an '*a priori* method', and deducing their conclusion from general (neoclassical) economic principles with little reference to empirical evidence (1986: 24). With this rendition we may see the shift to a criticism of not only the policies, but also the theory and methods used by some economists to support them.

With Brian Head's article on the topic, economic rationalism assumed the status of an 'ideology' characterising the era of economic reform that began with the election of the Hawke Labor government in 1983. Taking up, and giving content to, the issue of method, Head wrote:

> The ideology of 'economic rationalism' derives from *a priori* assumptions of neo-classical economic theory. In particular, it assumes that *market*

forces typically unleash growth, innovation and efficiency, whereas *governmental* regulations and expenditures typically impede growth, stifle productivity and entrepreneurship, and generate inefficiencies in both the public and private sectors. (1988: 466)

Harking back to an earlier political critique, Head also distinguished a more 'bellicose form propounded by New Right ideologues' that represented the market as a 'cargo cult' whose benefits will only be delivered if its opponents, such as 'strong unions, high taxes, big government', were defeated (1988: 466).

Two years later, Greg Whitwell (1990) considered it fitting to announce the 'triumph of economic rationalism', which he largely attributed to the economic ideas and political power of the Australian Treasury Department, especially under the leadership of its Secretary John Stone (1979–84, later National Party Senator for Queensland).[1] Thus the rhetoric of economic rationalism came to be used critically to denote a new national doctrine of formidable ideological and institutional power.

The term took on a more explicit derogatory tone after the publication of Michael Pusey's *Economic rationalism in Canberra* (1991). This book provided an account of how those in the senior ranks of the Commonwealth Public Service had come under the influence of a new ideology that pushed the previously dominant one of nation-building to the margins. In Pusey's account, these officials subscribed to a free market agenda that broke with previous Keynesian and social democratic ones that gave priority to meeting social needs. Pusey's language was colourful and apocalyptic, provoking immediate robust responses from both supporters (e.g. Emy 1992; Leach 1991) and critics (e.g. Blandy 1992; Stone 1992). Even though Pusey (1991: 1) did not define clearly the 'locus strike' of economic rationalism, his book depicted a significant problem in the national bureaucracy and was a timely catalyst for opposition to these trends.[2] (It was published in the same year that the government began the first stage of selling off the Commonwealth Bank in a public float.) As a consequence, references to 'economic rationalism' proliferated, and supplied the rhetoric through which much Australian public debate on the role of government in the economy was conducted.

Just as important, the term economic rationalism became a category for organising subsequent historical reflection upon such debates and policies. For example, Paul Kelly's influential book on Australian politics in the 1980s argued that the Hawke/Keating Labor governments had instigated a remaking of the

---

1 Neil Johnston's commentary on Whitwell's paper reflects the meaning evident in the mid-1970s. He writes about 'the emergence of a new paradigm of economic rationalism which advances the market approach to allow for market imperfections' (1990: 141).
2 Even those sympathetic to the book observed numerous flaws. For a good overview see Bell (1993).

Australian political tradition.[3] In this account, the older ideas and policies of the 'Australian settlement' that had been formed in the early years of Federation, were replaced by new ones, proposed by what he calls the 'internationalist rationalists'. Kelly saw 'Hayden's economic rationality' (1992: 19) as a precursor to the 'economic rationalism' of the Hawke/Keating governments (1992: 32). Nonetheless, Kelly also viewed economic rationalism as an element of the New Right movement that he saw as a group committed to deregulation of the labour market and radical reform of the Australian system of industrial relations (1992: 269). In his closing chapter, Kelly equated economic rationalism with market-based reforms, and refers to 'free market rationalism' (1992: 684, 686).

By 1992, two clear political and normative *uses* of the term economic rationalism were current, largely linked to the role of the state in the economy. With the first use, economic rationality, rationalism, and rationalists were usually expressions of commendation, primarily used with reference to Labor government policies that promoted economic efficiency in support of the larger national interest. For some advocates (e.g. Garnaut 1983: 161), support of free trade symbolised a stronger commitment to internationalism. Economic rationality was the general principle guiding a modernising Labor that sought to overcome the 'sentimentalism' and 'traditionalism' (Kelly 1992: 2) that legitimated economic inefficiencies, and supported sectional interests. In this use, it was understood that government was not abandoning its central role in regulating the economy, but simply opening up sectors to market forces where it was judged it would lead to greater public good.

On the other hand, economic rationalism also became a term of historical censure that signified a dangerous break with previous Australian social and economic traditions. In later reflection on these shifts, Lindy Edwards drew out their significance:

> The Australian Settlement was embedded in our social values and was a coherent part of our cultural system. Economic rationalism is not ... Our social values dictate that government is the centre of our collective efforts to manage ourselves. It is strong and proactive. It negotiates social conflict and protects the vulnerable. (2002: 151–52)

In this view, the state had played, and ought to continue to play a major role, not just in setting the economic rules and parameters, but also in intervening directly in the economy by various means. Famously, the latter included the large national public sector trading corporations, such as the Commonwealth Bank, Australian Airlines, Qantas, Telecom (later Telstra), and other public utilities. It is this second dimension that set the tenor of criticism after 1991,

---

3   See Stokes (2004) for a critique of Kelly's arguments.

and to which the advocates of market imperatives were pressed to reply. In so doing, an ideology of economic rationalism emerged, as well as a defence of the discipline of economics.

Methodological considerations

Although the title of economic rationalist came to have pejorative connotations, there were a few who adopted it as a badge of honour (e.g. Harper 1993; Hyde 1991; James et al. 1993: xxi–xxiv). Nonetheless, many of those accused of being economic rationalists refused to accept what they saw as a simplistic label, or else contested aspects of the explicit and implicit content (e.g. Brennan 1993; Blandy 1993). None formulated a systematic doctrine. Furthermore, some commentators applied the category loosely to the New Right movement (including Pusey 1993), and to political figures who would not have been familiar with the term. George Megalogenis, for example, recruits Thatcher as an economic rationalist (2012: 124).

These features of the debate created difficulties for the task of critique, which usually begins with trying to understand what the advocates of a line of thought say or write in support of it, and then evaluating the quality of the arguments, and the various consequences. That is, the critic asks: are the claims true, coherent, or plausible, and will the measures proposed lead to the intended outcomes? Because the character of economic rationalism relies a great deal upon what its *critics* say about it, this approach is problematic. What tended to occur was that the critics produced an ideal model or extreme position that had a particular coherence, but to which few academics, public servants, or political leaders held unqualified allegiance.

Possibly the best example of this extreme came from Pusey, who articulated in stark terms what he saw as the key propositions of neoclassical orthodoxy:

It's *always* necessary to cut public spending.

Wages and salaries are *always* too high and we must *always* redistribute the nation's income upwards away from wage and salary earners …

Welfare spending is *always* too high.

It's *always* a good idea to move the burden of taxation away from inputs on business and onto consumers … and/or wage and salary earners.

We must *always* accept ever higher levels of unemployment.

> We must *always* deregulate the private sector and remove public controls over business. (1992: 65)

Elsewhere, Pusey writes in a similar manner: '"Economic rationalism" is a doctrine that says that markets and prices are the *only reliable* means of setting a value on anything, and, further, that markets and money can *always*, at least in principle, deliver better outcomes than states and bureaucracies' (1993: 14).[4]

Whatever the evidence for such views in the higher echelons of the public service of 1985, it is not clear that any reputable economist would have espoused all such claims, especially those that did not differentiate between levels or sectors of the economy. Nonetheless, such models served the purpose of demonstrating what the critics saw as a number of the main tenets of a major doctrine that both described and justified a significant change in governmental policies and practices. It also specified the intellectual sources of the doctrine, as well as the officials and institutions that supported it. The political base of the new policy trend was located in the central public service economic agencies of Treasury (see Whitwell 1986), and Finance, along with their ideological allies in the Industry Commission that was established in 1990.

Pusey's book (1991) on the topic was not a study of political thinkers, but of the emergence of a new culture among the senior public servants of Canberra. It is arguable, therefore, that economic rationalism may be understood as a form of critical political rhetoric, which points to a set of 'ideas embedded in practice' (see Stokes 1994: 246–48). These ideas 'operate to set the practical terms of government debate and action' (Stokes 1994: 247) and do not exist in explicit doctrinal form. Once they are given attention, however, both the critics and supporters are prompted to search for doctrinal support and inspiration. This quest for antecedents and doctrine leads directly to scrutiny of the ideas of leading economists and the discipline of economics itself.

Overall, the critics of economic rationalism tended to see it as a more or less coherent — even utopian (Melleuish 1998: 79) — philosophy of the role of government in economy and society. For J.W. Nevile, economic rationalism is not driven by economics but by 'social philosophy' (1998: 173, 179). When looked at this way, economic rationalism takes a stronger shape and historical agency, somewhat akin to the political ideology (see Battin 1992 and Edwards 2002: 36). In this form, it allows a critique that is wider and more multidimensional than would perhaps normally be directed towards a shift in bureaucratic culture and

---

4   See also Tim Battin who defines economic rationalism as 'the belief that the market is the only legitimate allocator of goods and services in *society* at large not just in the *economy*' (1991: 296).

government policy. By drawing out the particular political logic of this position and the criticisms of it, one may better understand a few of the key issues at stake within the rhetoric of economic rationalism.[5]

Debates over ideology, economic history, society and democracy

The critics of economic rationalism ranged over a number of economic, political and social themes. It is not possible to canvass all of them, nor all those who have contributed to the debates. I have therefore selected exemplars and where necessary included my own reflections. I have not pursued the technical debates on specific economic policies, such as the role of the public sector, labour markets, financial deregulation, and international trade, but focused on a selection of larger, more general issues.

Ideology and social science

One of the major criticisms of economic rationalism was that its advocates claimed it was a value free and neutral form of social science when, in reality, it was an ideology, in the sense of a dogma that largely disguised specific value commitments. Further, these values were those of an individualist, competitive and libertarian kind that conflicted with the 'social' values of equality, cooperation, and concern for the public good. More specific to Australia, such economic rationalist dogmas were seen to undermine longstanding national commitments, such as those to full employment, wage justice and social equity.

Ian Harper subscribed to the neutrality claim when he wrote: 'The fact is that so-called "economic rationalism" is the attempt to apply (reasoned, logical) economic principles to the formulation of public policy which has as its ultimate aim the improvement of living standards for all Australians' (1993: 23). Stone rejected the allegation of ideology to write: 'economic rationalism is not basically about political ideology at all (and hence not basically about cultural and moral positions either), but chiefly about *what works*' (1992: 27). For Tony Makin, economic rationalism is 'a synonym for using time tested economic principles to improve policy outcomes' (2013). Geoffrey Brennan tried to clarify the claim by saying: 'economics appeals to a "rationalist" method in the sense that it presupposes a distinction between ends and means, ... and is concerned with the relation between means and ends rather than the appropriateness of those ends' (1993: 5). The ends or values, he argued, are not specified by economics.

---

5   On this topic see Edwards (2002).

Nevertheless, it is hard to avoid the observation that for economic rationalism the primary means or instruments to achieve social 'ends' were markets, in which particular economic principles hold, or ought to hold, sway. From the critics' perspective, two values were central. First, in assessing efficiency, markets were believed to be the most efficient means for achieving a variety of ends. Second, markets both required and inculcated particular values, such as those of self-reliance and a competitive and possessive individualism. The critics' argument would be that the raised scientific status accorded to economic principles overruled other, less 'scientific' social or political principles, such as social equity or democratic participation, that would support government-directed or corporatist economic planning. Essentially, the latter values were regarded as 'sentimental' and 'nostalgic'.

For many critics, the claims to science also effected a closure on empirical analysis, and particularly on what can be counted as evidence. Thus economic rationalists failed to appreciate that some relevant factors could not be quantified, and were often ignored. The criteria of 'relevance' may also be contested from different value perspectives. Although deductive logic may be value neutral, there are no neutral means for collecting facts or neutral techniques for organising them. Values of an epistemic *and* ethical kind influence the selection of variables to be assessed and the empirical facts to be collected, as well as for assessing their significance. That is, there was no unmediated empirical base or 'raw data' against which to test economic propositions: their selection and interpretation required normative judgement. Nevile explains: 'This judgement is heavily influenced by the values of the person making the judgement' (1998: 175). Such are the kinds of theoretical and empirical arguments that Hugh Stretton (e.g. 1969; 1987) formulated over a long period. So troubled was Stretton by the general direction of the teaching of economics that he spent many of his early 'retirement' years writing a massive 852-page alternative, introductory textbook to the discipline (Stretton 1999). This issue of values and the selection of facts became relevant in assessing the trajectory of Australian economic history.

Australian economic history and causation

The economic rationalism narrative drew upon a reinterpretation of the history of Australia's economic performance, its rates of economic growth and standard of living. Key parts of this story can be attributed to journalists such as Max Walsh (1993) and specific reforming/rationalist authors, such as Ross Garnaut, who became senior economic adviser to Hawke from 1983–85 (see Beeson and Stone 2013). On the rationalist account, Australia went from being an 'open' economy in the 1870s, when there were few restrictions on international trade, to a closed one with numerous barriers, notably tariff protection. Kym Anderson and Garnaut, amongst others, argued that protection brought less economic growth in Australia when compared to other less protectionist economies (1987: 12–17). On their historical evidence Australia had declined in its world ranking from 3rd in GDP per capita in 1950 to 14th in GDP per capita in 1980, and much of that decline was attributed to its high rates of protectionism. They showed that by 1984 the Australian economy had become less open to foreign trade, when most other major economies were becoming more open, particularly in trade of manufactures. Australia was experiencing a decreasing share of not only world trade, but also trade in manufactures. In addition, our living standards had declined to 15th in the world.

The causes of these problems were primarily attributed to industry protection, which led to lack of competition and low productivity (see also Anderson and Garnaut 1986). In this oft repeated account, the economic consequences of tariffs brought higher costs to the 'efficient' export industries of farming and mining, and therefore made these sectors less globally competitive. In addition, the higher prices for consumers had caused most harm to the poorest Australians.

Other factors were thought to contribute to decline. The high wages brought about by centralised arbitration conducted behind the 'tariff walls' of protection prevented employment of more workers and led to higher unemployment. It was also claimed that the deficit budgets required by social security and industry support sapped entrepreneurial initiative. Government regulations also added higher costs to production than were necessary. The rationalists argued further that it was politically difficult to resolve such problems because Australian governments were overly influenced by special interests, namely, trade unions, manufacturers and, in the past, the farm lobbies. For some commentators, all this was leading Australia down the 'Argentinian road' to economic and political decay. In 1986, Keating's reference to the potential for Australia to become a 'banana republic' dramatised a particular economic assessment (Kelly 1992: 196–97), and symbolised a crisis that had to be addressed.

Such accounts of Australian economic history were challenged by those on the left and right. Colin White, for example, argued that league table comparisons of standards of living were an inaccurate guide to Australian achievements (1992a; 1992b). Given the size of the possible statistical errors, they offered little proof of economic decline. White made the contrary positive argument that our economic history represented a series of triumphs over the adversities of climate, geography, distance and small domestic markets. In this more heroic narrative, the state was crucial in fostering diverse forms of economic development and overcoming high levels of risk. Cooperation between government and business was also vital. For White, and others, one of the major social outcomes of previous policies was a more egalitarian class structure, an achievement that was now under threat.

White also offered an alternative explanation for current economic problems, arguing that they arose from the very policies designed to overcome the previous problems (1992a: 34–36). For example, lower protection reinforced the trends towards de-industrialisation and financial deregulation helped created other difficulties, such as a massive increase in the overseas debt that it was supposed to solve. Indeed, the nature of the debt also changed from direct investment towards more speculative finance. Nor were the costs of the economic transition taken into account. Ian McLean's (2012: 10) book *Why Australia prospered* largely confirms White's arguments that Australian Government economic policies were 'rational' and successful: 'At the core of our story lies a policy and institutional adaptability in the face of markedly changed economic conditions that ensured enhanced living standards for a rapidly expanding population over most of the past two centuries' (2012: 10).

Interestingly, White's argument found an ally in C.D. Kemp, one of the founders of the Institute for Public Affairs. In the ironically titled article 'Those terrible 80 years' (1991), Kemp repudiated the historical interpretation of the years since Federation and criticised the views of John Hyde and Garnaut. He too claimed that the facts did not support the claims of policy mistakes, and the statistics did not allow conclusive international comparisons to be made about standards of living. For Kemp, protection was essential for establishing new industries. He drew attention to the postwar achievements of full employment for 25 years and rising standards of living.

Like White, Kemp gave different explanations of the economic problems of the 1980s. He pointed to foolish public *and* private sector decisions on large projects, many of which he suggested had led to increased overseas debt and the chronic weakness in the nation's balance of payments. Perhaps more telling, Kemp criticised extreme market philosophies that enthroned the values of greed and self-interest. In his view, business had relinquished its responsibility for the whole society, and for economic and social progress and stability. In the late 1990s Malcolm Fraser (e.g. 1997a; 1997b; 1998) joined the debate to criticise economic rationalism and celebrate its eventual demise.

Human nature, community, and society

At the heart of these debates were ethical concerns, not only about the negative consequences of economic rationalism, but also values, and assumptions about human nature. For the critics, economic rationalists understood individuals primarily as rational agents and creators of their own destiny. To draw on an older formulation from C.B. Macpherson (1962), possessive individualism lay at the heart of economic rationalism. Individuals were essentially 'liberal economic subjects' and largely defined by their possessive capacities, particularly those to possess property (see e.g. Marginson 1988). As the critics saw it, economic rationalism relied on a conception of human nature in which people were generally motivated by self-interest, and in which the (a)morality of greed and pursuit of financial reward were central. Where such values dominated, it is argued, they tended to overwhelm collectivist and altruistic ones, and damage community. In these circumstances, the state was essential as a protector of community, the weak and the vulnerable.

Whereas Michael James among others denied that the promotion of markets necessarily entailed a morality of 'greed', he did propose that individuals were 'rational actors' who had particular ends, and were generally motivated by self-interest, which he claimed was not necessarily the same as 'selfishness' (1993: 162). Accordingly, individuals can choose rationally the best means to realise those ends or values. Human beings are maximisers of personal utility, which when pursued freely will create greater economic and public good. In this view, markets are the best facilitators of both individual utility *and* good communities.

Such claims were evident in John Hewson's electoral manifesto *Fightback!* (Liberal Party of Australia 1991). When Hewson became Liberal Leader of the Opposition he made the values of economic rationalism the foundation of his electoral tilt at the prime ministership: 'Because markets are based on voluntary cooperation and decentralised decision making, they also create the only conditions in which a moral community can emerge' (Liberal Party of Australia 1991: 27). For the economic rationalist, people were essentially consumers, customers, or clients, bent on getting the best that the market(s) can offer. Any behaviour that did not fit this rational actor model would be deemed non-rational or 'irrational'. Yet, as James demonstrated, markets do rely upon a more expansive range of 'elementary virtues', such as 'honesty, fairness, truth-telling, responsibility, reliability and promptness', many of which are supported by law (1993: 163).

Hyde took up these issues to affirm that indeed, economic rationalism and classical liberals 'believe that a civil order based as much as possible upon voluntarism is more just, more stable and more efficient than one based unnecessarily on authority' (1991: 27). Such a liberal order was not anarchy, but one in which 'the rules of social interaction are relatively few, certain and maintained by governments that do not enter the game on behalf of individual players'. For Hyde, therefore, economic rationalism opposed economic discrimination, favouritism, and privilege, which he saw as able to be checked by impersonal markets, as well as other political checks and balances that 'disperse authority' (see also Hyde 1993a). Yet, true to an older classical liberalism, there were few references to democracy.

Democracy

For some critics, economic rationalism was an attack on political democracy. Yet, avowed economic rationalists made claims to advancing democratisation. Wolfgang Kasper, for example, argued that open market competition could promote autonomy and freedom and overcome the anti-democratic features of Australian government (1991: 31):

> Australians — at least those living north of Victoria — now realise that the institutions and policies that gave us a comfortable, if inefficient, regulatory order have failed. Our economic system needs transformation as urgently as that of Eastern Europe. Government of the people, by the bureaucrats, for the rent seekers is in disrepute. Instead people want more autonomy, less government intrusion, lower taxation and are less supportive of institutions that seek and grant privileges by regulation, central wage-fixing, comprehensive welfare and bipartisan politicking.

At the heart of this view is the repeated claim that government had been captured by special interests, such as trade unions, corporations, and sectional community groups, who, in addition to imposing extra tax burdens on the rest of the citizens, also prevent them from fulfilling their personal goals.

Complementing this assumption was that of the 'entitlement consensus', which describes the view that 'all members of the community have a right to certain entitlements including, amongst other things, a free education, free medical treatment, and protection of employment' (Valentine 1996: 9). The rationalist criticism was that little attention is given to assessing whether society had the economic means or resources to pay for such entitlements. Thus the rights of citizenship needed to be subject to a rigorous cost benefit analysis. On the other hand, it is argued by some economic rationalists that markets actually enhanced democracy and citizenship by expanding individual choices and strengthening civil society (Rutherford 1993).

The critics of economic rationalism also noted political events in New Zealand, where Roger Douglas, the finance minister in the Labour Government from 1984 to 1988, had become a convert to free market principles, but had not publicised the fact before assuming office (Bromby 1993). Douglas also espoused the view that it was often politically unwise to engage in much discussion of radical reforms before embarking upon them, lest they be derailed by 'special interests'.

With such claims in mind, the critics expressed concern about the power of elites, the narrowing scope for political decision-making, and the reduction in the domain of citizenship. The first concern derived from Pusey's depiction of an elite of economic bureaucrats that determine economic policy in Canberra. As John Carroll described it, a 'new mandarin caste' of 'econocrats', specialists in a particular type of economics, have taken over key positions of economic policy advice (1992: 13). Where Treasury was the main power base (Whitwell 1986; 1990), the economic ideas had spread to other Commonwealth agencies and public service departments. Often explicit, or at least implied, in these analyses was the view that government was controlled by unelected technocratic elites.

Peter Brain regarded economic rationalism as an 'undemocratic doctrine' because its

> ... central proposition is that the community should not extend its control into many areas that are important to community welfare. Implicitly, economic rationalism endorses the primacy of established private interests over future private interests, as well as over current and future collective community interests. (2001: 300)

Brain's solution was to strengthen representative democracy through the breakdown of party discipline and/or the two party system (2001: 317–18). Battin adopted a similar line of criticism in arguing that economic rationalism presented the economy as the embodiment of the general interest and thus excluded as partisan any views or interests that challenged it (1992: 16). Problems of allocation and distribution were not regarded as subject to political negotiation, but reduced to an economic calculus or technique.

From a social democratic perspective, the critique of economic rationalism offered the opportunity to recommend a democratisation of the economy. Geoff Dow (1992) and others (e.g. Rees et al. 1993) saw potential for creating institutions to enable wider participation in formulating economic policy. Generally, this meant encouraging formal involvement in policy making from those outside the political and bureaucratic elites, such as trade unions and business. For others, such models of economic policy making drew upon the incipient Australian tradition of corporatism evident in the early institutions of arbitration and conciliation. Pusey argued a similar line with reference to the social democratic models in Western European countries (1992: 65–66). For Michael Muetzelfeldt economic rationalism reduced citizenship to the, albeit greater, active participation in markets, rather than as a passive claimer of rights to social security (1992: 194). James Walter argued further for an active citizenship that would serve as a check upon both the state *and* the market (1996: 108).

Politics and rhetoric after economic rationalism

It is arguable that the dispute over economic rationalism had a number of consequences for Australian politics and political rhetoric. First, the political momentum for economic reform slowed somewhat with Hewson's 1993 loss of the 'unlosable election' to Keating.[6] Staking all on maintaining reform through his electoral package of policies, Hewson put economic rationalism on the electoral agenda. For many critics, *Fightback!* was the radical extension of what had come before, and the epitome of economic rationalism (see e.g. Melleuish 1998: 80– 81). *Fightback!* set out an individualist, social and economic philosophy (e.g. Liberal Party of Australia 1991: 26), but among the microeconomic policies was a new consumption tax. This was a bridge too far at the time and Labor under Keating was able to exploit these commitments for electoral advantage.

It could also be ventured that economic rationalist policies were partially responsible for the upsurge in populism, as exemplified in electoral support for Pauline Hanson's One Nation movement from 1997. Those damaged or threatened by economic reform and rapid shifts in global markets sought populist electoral remedies. The One Nation rhetoric picked up the critique of elites, their lack of respect for 'ordinary Australians', and encouraged them to punish governments (Stokes 2000).

At the other end of the political spectrum, however, the decline in the language of economic rationalism corresponded with a revived national concern with citizenship (*Whereas the people* 1994; Walter 1996: 105; Hudson and Kane 2000). It seemed as if the discursive conflicts and political divisions stimulated by economic rationalism required soothing with talk of rights and responsibilities. The Keating government established programs to promote citizenship and civic education throughout the country, with a view not only to encourage political knowledge and participation, but also to promote both difference and inclusivity. These programs continued under the ensuing Howard government, but with a shift in the terms of reference to the subject of democracy (see e.g. Hirst 2002). The rhetoric of citizenship and democracy was also part of a wider trend to renovate Western liberal democracies in the wake of the collapse of the Soviet Union after 1989.

With the arrival of globalisation discourse in the mid-1990s, and debates over the effects of trade and economic policies, the dominant political rhetoric changed again, but it carried a more neutral and determinist tenor. For its uncritical enthusiasts, globalisation described an empirical phenomenon that had to be both understood and accepted (see Stokes 2009). Global economic determinism replaced the normative determinism of economic rationalism. In this context, the agency implied in active citizenship remained an important political resource for confronting the rhetoric of determinism.

---

6 According to Quiggin, however, there was simply a change in government strategy towards a more elitist and technocratic approach, such as that implemented through the national agreement on the National Competition Policy (2005: 29). See discussion below.

Within Labor thinking, the focus shifted towards that of how to absorb and shape globalisation. The departure from the past lay first in wider acceptance that freer global markets and more open international trade were of universal benefit. The second difference was the expression of stronger doubts about the relative value of government intervention in the economy. Mark Latham's *Civilising global capital* (1998) represented a mix of the old and new Labor thinking on the Australian economy and society. Dispensing with economic rationalism in a few pages, Latham set Australian social democratic thought squarely within the context of the challenges of globalisation (1998: 37–42). Along with likeminded others around the world, he embarked on a quest for a 'third way' between capitalism and socialism, one that was to be based on new forms of citizenship and social cooperation (1998: 325).[7] These ideas paralleled those formulated by the sociologist Anthony Giddens (1998) and taken up by the UK Labour Prime Minister Tony Blair (1998), which became part of the rhetoric of New Labour. In 2003, Latham became the federal Labor Leader of the Opposition, but resigned from parliament after losing the 2004 federal election.

As the rhetorical and analytical importance of globalisation grew in significance, 'economic rationalism' began to disappear from the critical discourse, to be replaced by the more conventional and universally accepted terms 'market liberalism', 'economic liberalism' and, eventually, 'neoliberalism'. The latter appeared with a vengeance in an essay on the 2007 global financial crisis, written by then Prime Minister Kevin Rudd (2009), which attracted wide attention in Australia and internationally. The language of Rudd's critique of market failure was reminiscent of that directed at economic rationalism, but now placed in a global context. Although the term economic rationalism has fallen out of favour, much of its supporting rhetoric has remained current.

More important perhaps than the residual rhetoric, the policies and practices of economic rationalism have continued to be implemented. For example, various institutions have been established to promote its values, such as 'competition', and to extend microeconomic reform. The National Competition Policy (NCP), which was agreed upon by the Council of Australian Governments in 1995 and continued until 2005, instigated new principles and extended revised federal trade practice laws to the conduct of publicly owned trading enterprises at federal, state, territory and local levels of government (National Competition Policy 2007). Overseen by the National Competition Council, the new laws aimed at reducing 'barriers to competition' and had a profound impact on state-owned business enterprises that had previously enjoyed monopoly status in sectors such as the provision of water, energy, transport and communications. Because

---

7   Barry Hindess (personal communication) argues that the quest for a 'third way' has a long history in social democracy, beginning with Eduard Bernstein and continuing through the work of Anthony Crosland's *The Future of Socialism* (1956).

these entities could no longer maintain their monopolies unless there was a clear 'net public benefit', they had to open their markets to competitors. Most were also 'corporatised', meaning initially that they were bound to embrace the governance models and management practices of private enterprise. Many such business enterprises have been partially or wholly transferred to private ownership. Such transfers generated $61 billion in proceeds for state and Commonwealth governments from 1990–97 (Reserve Bank of Australia 1997: 1). One innovative, hybrid funding model has been the introduction of 'public private partnerships' to undertake large infrastructure projects whose value is in excess of $50 million. Also created in 1995, the mission of the Australian Competition and Consumer Commission (2012) has been to promote 'competition and fair trade in markets', and administer the *Trade Practices Act*.

Governments and business organisations still pursue 'flexible labour markets', and the institutions of wage arbitration, bargaining, and conciliation have been transformed to implement this concept. Under Keating, the Labor government established the Australian Industrial Relations Commission (AIRC), which promoted decentralised 'enterprise bargaining' over centralised wage fixing. The ensuing Howard government continued this trend with its 'WorkChoices' laws and, in 2006, established an Australian Fair Pay Commission, that had a more limited remit than its predecessor the AIRC. The quest for greater 'productivity' is enshrined in the Productivity Commission (successor to the Industry Commission), established in 1998. Its economic models are informed by neoclassical economic theory, and their reports are widely regarded as authoritative.

Whereas privatisation has mostly run its course at the federal level, due to the inevitable reduction in the number of existing public sector trading corporations, the NCP has ensured that this practice has maintained momentum at the state level. The corporatisation of public services has also proceeded apace with greater use of private sector management techniques, such as employment contracts and performance bonuses, as well as the 'outsourcing' of services, implementing 'user pays' policies, and budget requirements for 'efficiency dividends'.

The deregulation of financial markets has brought new public actors and styles of rhetoric into economic reporting in the mass media. Global financial credit ratings agencies, for example, deliver regular updates on whether governments have 'AAA credit ratings' or lower. This rhetoric has a hard edge to it, however, as low rankings can penalise poorly performing governments and constrain their access to credit and loan funds. In this way, a key accountability mechanism has evolved outside parliaments and beyond national borders.

More broadly, the substantive ideas of the early debates have persisted without reference to 'economic rationalism'. In May 2013, on the 70th anniversary of the founding of the Institute of Public Affairs, Rupert Murdoch, the Chairman and CEO of News Corporation, delivered a stirring address on the morality of markets. The speech was an unqualified paean to the virtues of markets and capitalism. Murdoch argued how free markets advanced not only freedom and individualism, but also justice and fairness (2013). In this exercise of 'soft power' the tougher rhetoric of 'discipline' and 'punishment' was notably absent. The speech marked out the rhetorical requirements for success in the contest of ideas over the respective roles of governments and markets.

Conclusion

Throughout the rhetoric and critical commentaries may be observed at least four analytical *meanings* of economic rationality and rationalism. In the first broad sense, as described by Quiggin, it referred to 'policy formulation on the basis of reasoned analysis, as opposed to tradition, emotion and self-interest' (1997: 2). This had its antecedents in the Weberian concept of instrumental rationality, understood as action oriented towards a goal. In the second meaning, economic rationalism refers generally to 'economic efficiency', however that is determined by economic theory, and in which markets are the optimum means of attaining the designated goal. A third meaning can be discerned, namely that of the use of argument based upon an *a priori* method, or deduction from abstract general principles or self-evident assumptions (Withers 1986: 24; Quiggin 1997: 2). Again, the assumptions and principles relate to the ideal working of markets, rather than being drawn from empirical observation and testing. A fourth meaning draws on these dimensions, but conceives economic rationalism as a world view or ideology that encompasses, but extends beyond, economic theory. When combined, as they were in the minds of most later critics, these elements comprised a social and political doctrine, one of whose distinguishing features was its dogmatism.

In each of these forms, the language of economic rationalism enabled those who used it to criticise or commend those political, economic and social agendas that appeared to break with tradition. The rhetoric helped distinguish between political friends and foes, make judgements on economic history, specify the causes of contemporary predicaments, and propose alternative strategies for the future of Australia. As outlined above, both the normative assessment and substantive content of the rhetoric evolved over time. Where its earliest use was mostly one of approval, it later became largely a vehicle of condemnation. From being used as a simple pointer to economic efficiency in specific sectors, it came to represent an all-encompassing ideology that applied to all aspects of economy and society.

Economic rationalism is but one among a number of forms of rhetoric that, since the 1970s, have served to frame, criticise, and defend government economic policy. Perhaps more important, with the rise of economic rationalism as both an ideology and a government practice, it is arguable that the language of Left critique changed from that of Marxist political economy and socialism to that of mainstream economics and liberalism. In this way, the more radical critiques from political economy that relied upon concepts such as capital and class lost rhetorical power. Economic critique thus became conducted mostly in the Weberian and reformist terms that generally accepted the imperatives of capitalism. It has to be said, however, that, whatever the socialist rhetoric, the mainstream of the ALP had always operated on this political terrain.

References

Anderson, K. and Garnaut, R. 1986. Australia: Political economy of manufacturing protection. In C. Findlay and R. Garnaut eds. *The political economy of manufacturing protection: Experiences of ASEAN and Australia.* Sydney: Allen & Unwin.

—— 1987. *Australian protectionism: Extent, causes and effects.* Sydney: Allen & Unwin.

Australian Competition and Consumer Commission 2012. URL: http://www.accc.gov.au/about-us. Consulted 19 October 2013.

Battin, T. 1991. What is this thing called economic rationalism? *Australian Journal of Social Issues* November: 294–307.

—— 1992. Economic rationalism and ideology. *Journal of Australian Studies* 33: 12–18.

Beeson, M. and Stone, D. 2013. The changing fortunes of a policy entrepreneur: The case of Ross Garnaut. *Australian Journal of Political Science* 48(1): 1–14.

Bell, S. 1993. Weak on the state: Economic rationalism in Canberra. *Australian and New Zealand Journal of Sociology* 29(3): 387–401.

—— 1998. Economic restructuring in Australia: Policy settlements, models of economic development and economic rationalism. In P. Smyth and B. Cass eds. *Contesting the Australian way: States, markets and civil society.* Cambridge: Cambridge University Press.

Blair, T. 1998. *The third way.* London: Fabian Society.

Blandy, R. 1992. Multiple schizophrenia: Economic rationalism and its critics. *Australian Quarterly* 64(1): 101–07.

—— 1993. Economic rationalism and prosperity. In S. King and P. Lloyd eds. *Economic rationalism: Dead end or way forward?* Sydney: Allen & Unwin.

Brain, P. 2001. The Australian Federation 2001: Political structures and economic policy. In Australian Broadcasting Corporation. *The Alfred Deakin Lectures: Ideas for the future of a civil society.* Sydney.

Brennan, G. 1993. Economic rationalism: What does economics really say? In S. King and P. Lloyd eds. *Economic rationalism: Dead end or way forward?* Sydney: Allen & Unwin.

Bromby, R. 1993. Rogernomics persists in one dimension. *Australian* 22 December: 11.

Butlin, N., Barnard, A. and Pincus, J.J. 1982. *Government and capitalism.* Sydney: George Allen & Unwin.

Carroll, J. 1992. Economic rationalism and its consequences. In J. Carroll and R. Manne eds. *Shutdown: The failure of economic rationalism and how to rescue Australia.* Melbourne: Text.

Carroll, J. and Manne, R. eds. 1992. *Shutdown: The failure of economic rationalism and how to rescue Australia.* Melbourne: Text.

Coghill, K. ed. 1987. *The new right's Australian fantasy.* Fitzroy/Ringwood: McPhee Gribble/Penguin.

Douglas, R. 1993. *Unfinished business.* Auckland: Random House.

Dow, G. 1992. The economic consequences of economists. *Australian Journal of Political Science* 27(2): 258–82.

Edwards, L. 2002. *How to argue with an economist: Reopening political debate in Australia.* Port Melbourne: Cambridge University Press.

—— 2013. Clashes over ideology key to Labor's ructions. *Age* 3 April. URL: http://www.theage.com.au/opinion/politics/clashes-over-ideology-key-to-labors-ructions-20130402-2h4vu.html. Consulted 1 May 2013.

Emy, H. 1992. Michael Pusey's *Economic rationalism in Canberra. Quadrant* 36(7/8): 57–61.

Fenna, A. and Tapper, A. 2012. The Australian welfare state and the neoliberalism thesis. *Australian Journal of Political Science* 47(2): 155–72.

Fraser, M. 1997a. Not by fiscal control and deregulation alone. *Australian* 13 August: 13.

—— 1997b. Who's steering this ship, then? *Australian* 27 August: 15.

—— 1998. Neglected bush must be won back. *Australian* 15 July: 13.

Garnaut, R. 1983. Protection, structural adjustment and development. In J. Langmore and D. Peetz eds. *Wealth poverty and survival: Australia in the world*. Sydney: George Allen & Unwin.

Gibson, D. 1990. Social policy. In C. Jennett and R.G. Stewart eds. *Hawke and Australian public policy: Consensus and restructuring*. South Melbourne: Macmillan.

Giddens, A. 1998. *The third way: The renewal of social democracy*. Cambridge: Polity.

Gittins, R. 2011. Politics of self-interest feeds the inner beast. *Sydney Morning Herald* 7 September. URL: http://www.smh.com.au/opinion/politics/politics-of-selfinterest-feeds-the-inner-beast-20110906-1jvs4.html. Consulted 1 May 2013.

Harper, I. 1993. Long live the rationalists. *Australian* 1 February: 23.

Head, B. 1986. Economic development in state and federal politics. In B. Head ed. *The politics of development in Australia*. Sydney: Allen & Unwin.

—— 1988. The Labor government and 'economic rationalism'. *AQ* 60(4): 466–77.

Hirst, J. 2002. *Australia's democracy: A short history*. North Sydney and Carlton: Allen & Unwin and the Curriculum Corporation.

Horne, D. 1976. *Money made us*. Ringwood: Penguin.

Hudson, W. and Kane, J. eds. 2000. *Rethinking Australian citizenship*. Oakleigh Vic: Cambridge University Press.

Hughes, B. 1980. *Exit full employment: Economic policy in the stone age*. Sydney: Angus & Robertson.

Hyde, J. 1991. The case for rationalism. *Weekend Australian* 21 September: 27–28.

—— 1993a. Economic irrationalists fly in the face of reason. *Australian* 8 October: 15.

—— 1993b. An irrational tag in the name of reason. *Australian* 19 November: 13.

James, C., Jones, C. and Norton, A. eds. 1993. *A defence of economic rationalism*. Sydney: Allen & Unwin.

James, M. 1993. Markets and morality. In C. James et al. eds. *A defence of economic rationalism*. Sydney: Allen & Unwin.

Johnston, N. 1990. Commentary. *Australian Journal of Public Administration* 49(2): 140–43.

Kasper, W. 1991. The revolution we have to have. *Weekend Australian*, 12–13 October: 31.

Kelly, P. 1992. *The end of certainty: The story of the 1980s*. St Leonards: Allen & Unwin.

Kemp, C.D. 1991. Those terrible 80 years. *Quadrant* 35(11): 17–22.

King, S. and Lloyd, P. eds. 1993. *Economic rationalism: Dead end or way forward?* Sydney: Allen & Unwin.

Latham, M. 1998. *Civilising global capital: New thinking for Australian Labor*. St Leonards: Allen & Unwin.

Leach, B. 1991. Review of M. Pusey, *Economic rationalism in Canberra*, 1991. *Social Alternatives* 10(4): 61–62.

Liberal Party of Australia. 1991. *Fightback! It's your Australia*. Canberra.

Liberal Party of Australia. 1992. *Fightback! Fairness and jobs*. Canberra.

Macpherson, C.B. 1962. *The political theory of possessive individualism: Hobbes to Locke*. Oxford: Clarendon Press.

Makin, T. 2013. Economic irrationalism has guided policies of the il-literati. *Australian* 1 July: 10.

Marginson, S. 1988. The economically rational individual. *Arena* 84: 105–14.

McLean, I. 2012. *Why Australia prospered: The shifting sources of economic growth*. Princeton: Princeton University Press.

Megalogenis, G. 2012. *The Australian moment: How we were made for these times*. Camberwell Vic: Penguin/Hamish Hamilton.

Melleuish, G. 1990. 'Keeping the shutters firmly closed': The social laboratory, liberal intellectuals and the growth of the 'protectionist mentality'. In G. Melleuish ed. *Australia as a social and cultural laboratory*. St Lucia: Australian Studies Centre.

—— 1998. *The packaging of Australia: Politics and the culture wars*. Sydney: UNSW Press.

Muetzelfeldt, M. 1992. Economic rationalism in its social context. In M. Muetzelfeldt, ed. *Society, state and politics in Australia*. Leichhardt: Pluto Press.

Murdoch, R. 2013. Markets radiate morality. *Weekend Australian* 6–7 April: 19.

National Competition Policy. 2007. URL: http://ncp.ncc.gov.au/. Consulted 19 October 2013.

Nevile, J.W. 1998. Economic rationalism: Social philosophy masquerading as economic science. In P. Smyth and B. Cass eds. *Contesting the Australian way: States, markets and civil society*. Cambridge: Cambridge University Press: 169–79.

Pusey, M. 1991. *Economic rationalism in Canberra: A nation building state changes its mind*. Port Melbourne: Cambridge University Press.

—— 1992. What's wrong with economic rationalism? In D. Horne ed. *The trouble with economic rationalism*. Newham Vic: Scribe, pp. 63–69.

—— 1993. Reclaiming the middle ground … from new right 'economic rationalism'. In S. King and P. Lloyd eds. *Economic rationalism: Dead end or way forward?* Sydney: Allen & Unwin, pp. 12–27.

Quiggin, J. 1997. Economic rationalism. URL: http://www.uq.edu.au/economics/johnquiggin/JournalArticles99/econrat99.html. Consulted 12 May 2013.

—— 2005. Economic liberalism: Fall, revival and resistance. In P. Saunders and J. Walter eds. *Ideas and influence: Social science and public policy in Australia*. Sydney: UNSW Press.

Rees, S., Rodley, G. and Stilwell, F. eds. 1993. *Beyond the market: Alternatives to economic rationalism*. Leichhardt: Pluto Press.

Reserve Bank of Australia. 1997. Privatisation in Australia. *Reserve Bank of Australia Bulletin*. December.

Rudd, K. 2009. The global financial crisis. *The Monthly* February: 20–29.

Rutherford, T. 1993. Democracy, markets and Australian schools. In C. James et al. eds. *A defence of economic rationalism*. Sydney: Allen & Unwin.

Sawer, M. ed. 1982. *Australia and the new right*. Sydney: Allen & Unwin.

Smyth, P. and Cass, B. eds. 1998. *Contesting the Australian way: States, markets and civil society*. Cambridge: Cambridge University Press.

Stilwell, F. 1989. Economic rationalism is irrational. *Arena* 87: 139–45.

Stokes, G. 1994. Conceptions of Australian political thought: A methodological critique. *Australian Journal of Political Science* 29(2): 240–58.

—— 2000. One Nation and Australian populism. In M. Leach, G. Stokes and I. Ward eds. 2000. *The rise and fall of One Nation*. St Lucia: University of Queensland Press.

—— 2004. The 'Australian settlement' and Australian political thought. *Australian Journal of Political Science* 39(1): 5–22.

—— 2009. Neoliberal hyperglobalism in Australian political thought. In H. Löfgren and P. Sarangi eds. *The politics and culture of globalisation: India and Australia*. New Delhi: Social Sciences Press.

Stone, J. 1992. Kind hearts and conservatism: The mistakes of mis-defining economics. *Weekend Australian* 25–26 January: 27.

Stretton, H. 1969. *The political sciences*. London: Routledge.

—— 1987. *Political essays*. Melbourne: Georgian House.

—— 1999. *Economics: A new introduction*. Sydney: UNSW Press.

Valentine, T. 1996. Economic rationalism vs the entitlement consensus. *Policy* Spring: 3–10.

Walsh, M. 1993. The demise of protection. In C. James et al. eds. *A defence of economic rationalism*. Sydney: Allen & Unwin.

Walter, J. 1996. *Tunnel vision: The future of political imagination*. St Leonards: Allen & Unwin.

Watson, A.S. 1979. Rural policy. In A. Patience and B. Head eds, *From Whitlam to Fraser: Reform and reaction in Australian politics*. Melbourne: Oxford University Press, pp. 157–72.

Whereas the people: Civics and citizenship education, Report of the Civics Expert Group 1994. Canberra: Australian Government Publishing Service.

White, C. 1992a. Mastering risk: The story of Australian economic success. In J. Carroll and R. Manne eds. *Shutdown: The failure of economic rationalism and how to rescue Australia*. Melbourne: Text.

—— 1992b. Fuel for the fire in rationality debate. *Australian* 23 September: 11.

Whitwell, G. 1986. *The Treasury line*. Sydney: Allen & Unwin.

—— 1990. The triumph of economic rationalism: The Treasury and the market economy. *Australian Journal of Public Administration* 49: 124–40.

Withers, G. 1986. Economic rationalism and wage fixation. *Economic Papers* 5: 23–34.

11. Languages of neoliberal critique: The production of coercive government in the Northern Territory intervention

Melissa Lovell

A critical approach to the study of rhetoric can help us to better understand the patterns of political discourse that normalise coercive approaches to government. This critical approach is especially necessary for the study of the governance of Australian Aboriginal Affairs. Historically, representations of Aboriginal peoples as uncivilised, violent and irrational have played a crucial role in the legitimation of colonialist policies. The work of postcolonial scholars has led to a growing acceptance among academic circles of the *constructed* nature of our knowledge about culture and identity. Furthermore, we can understand the process of identity construction — of ourselves and other groups — as a social process that is 'bound up with the disposition of powerlessness in each society' and which therefore has an impact on 'the legislation of personal conduct, the constitution of orthodoxy, [and] the legitimization of violence' (Said 2003: 332).

The study of political rhetoric clearly needs to take into account the way that the subjects of government policy — including Aboriginal people — are represented within political discourse. Scholars of rhetoric have long grappled with the relationship between rhetoric and knowledge. In general, scholars have been divided between those who define knowledge as 'justified true belief', and those with a less positivist orientation who have sought to understand the way that knowledge is socially created (Foss and Gill 1987: 385). The latter group often uses the work of Michel Foucault to develop analyses of the role of rhetorical frameworks — or *discursive formations* — in the production of knowledge and representation (Biesecker 1992; Cooper 1988; Foss and Gill 1987: 392; McKerrow 1989). As Raymie McKerrow explained in his influential 1989 article, a critical rhetoric seeks to understand the way that the normalisation of language is used to maintain the status quo and to structure power relationships. McKerrow argues that 'the initial task of a critical rhetoric is one of re-creation — constructing an argument that identifies the integration of power and knowledge and delineates the role of power/knowledge in structuring social practices' (McKerrow 1989: 102–03).

It is this critical approach to rhetoric that I adopt in this chapter. In particular, I seek to examine the relationship between the production of knowledge and the legitimation of coercive public policy approaches in the field of Aboriginal Affairs governance. My analysis focuses on the formal political debate over the introduction of Australia's Northern Territory Intervention, which was designed to protect Aboriginal children from widespread abuse and neglect in remote NT communities (Howard and Brough 2007). Often linked to a neoliberal economic development paradigm, the Intervention was the target of much criticism (Concerned Australians 2010: 8; Dodson 2007; Tangentyere Council 2007). Many people were concerned that the Intervention was a strike against the political and group rights of Aboriginal people, and saw the policy as an assimilationist, paternalist and colonialist development in Australian Aboriginal Affairs policy (Conor 2007; Macoun 2011; Manderson 2008; Mazel 2009). Federally, however, there was general consensus within the major political parties over both the necessity of the policy and its more coercive elements. My analysis focuses on this parliamentary discourse, as well as other political speeches that sought to justify coercive approaches to Aboriginal Affairs governance. I argue that the legitimation of coercive governance depended upon the development of new forms of knowledge about both Aboriginal people — as the objects of governance — and the limitations of alternative techniques for Aboriginal governance. Neoliberal conceptions of good governance and the ideal citizen were employed to produce new forms of knowledge about the field of Aboriginal Affairs governance.

Coercion and neoliberal government

A critical rhetoric attends to the 'discourses of the dominant'. It creates a space to problematise these discourses and open up 'spaces of invention' for those who read them (Phillips 2002: 342). Drawing on Foucault's scholarship, critical rhetoric scholars make discursive practice the locus for investigation of social processes. In particular, they consider the way that knowledge and power relations are closely interwoven (Cooper 1988: 10–15). In this chapter, I ponder the question of whether, and in what manner, the knowledge produced in debates over the NT Intervention might be linked to identifiably neoliberal politics. Furthermore, I consider whether it is reasonable to suggest that this neoliberal paradigm is responsible for the recent normalisation of coercive approaches within Aboriginal Affairs governance.

I derive the above questions from the particular situation of my case study, rather than from broader theoretical principles. There are two relevant contexts. The first of these is the idea — common among scholars of Australian and Aboriginal Affairs policy — that Australia has shifted toward a neoliberal policy paradigm in recent decades. Neoliberalism is commonly understood as an elite ideology whose proponents have sought to permanently transform Australian government.

Proponents of neoliberal politics are hostile towards an 'interventionist' welfare state, which they see as both economically inefficient and morally damaging to citizens because it encourages a culture of dependency on government services (Rose and Miller 1992: 198). Neoliberals adopt a utopian conception of capitalism; they see liberty as a condition that individuals can best pursue through ordinary participation within a free market (Cahill 2007: 228). The NT Intervention has been described as part of a broader ideological shift within Aboriginal Affairs policy towards a neoliberal policy paradigm (Altman 2007: 2; Hinkson 2007: 6; Walter 2010: 126–27). This paradigm has been characterised by antipathy toward elements of a rights-based policy agenda, such as the recognition of native title and Aboriginal self-determination. It sought to bring legislation, policy and the institutional framework in line with the government's broader neoliberal agenda by emphasising the principle of mutual obligation as a replacement for the principle of self-determination (Anderson 2008: 766).

The second relevant context is the increasing normalisation of coercive approaches to governance in Aboriginal Affairs policy. When I describe the Intervention as coercive, I mean that the federal government used its authority to compel Aboriginal people to act in particular ways and to substantially reform the institutional and administrative structure of remote Aboriginal communities. The early stages of the NT Intervention, which drew on the language of military intervention and deployed Australia's military to occupy remote NT Aboriginal communities, was a potent display of state power and of the federal government's ability to coerce Aboriginal citizens (Rundle 2007: 37, 43). Once established, the Intervention encompassed most aspects of daily life in NT Aboriginal communities. It was described by then Prime Minister John Howard as 'radical, comprehensive and highly interventionist' and as a 'sweeping assumption of power and a necessary assumption of responsibility [by the federal government]' (Howard 2007: 70). Some key measures — outlined in three parliamentary Acts — included the compulsory acquisition of Aboriginal townships by the government through five-year leases; the dismantling of the permit system for townships on Aboriginal land; and income management reforms that prescribed the way that Aboriginal people spent their incomes, and which linked social security payments to children's school attendance. There were also a number of important measures linked to the government's law and order agenda. These included the application of heavy penalties for use of alcohol and pornography, the removal of customary law and cultural background as considerations during bail and sentencing, and an increased police presence in Aboriginal communities (Parliament of Australia 2007: 23). With the initial 'stabilisation' phase of the Intervention complete, the program has moved into a long-term 'development' phase known as Stronger Futures in the Northern Territory (Australian Government 2011). The Stronger Futures legislation firmly entrenches many of the coercive elements of the original intervention in Australian social security policy.

We would intuitively expect these two contexts to be related in some way. Many critics of neoliberal ideology would be unsurprised at the idea that a neoliberal politics could restructure the relationship between governments and Aboriginal peoples towards a more coercive set of power relations. Indeed they might find this idea self-evident, and further explanation of this relationship to be redundant. I believe, however, that it is important to drill down into the detail of the relationship between neoliberal government and the normalisation of coercive government in Aboriginal Affairs policy. Describing policies as neoliberal has provided critics with a mechanism for linking particular examples of governance to a broader nationwide, or even global, system of ideological hegemony and political domination. The process of connecting policy to global hegemonies can, however, make the case for coercive government appear more coherent than it really is. This is because we come to understand the politics of the NT Intervention as part of a global system of power, which because of its size and influence, is virtually unassailable.

I reorient the discussion of the intervention to focus on the ways in which the broader tropes of neoliberal governance have been incorporated into the legitimising discourses surrounding the intervention in specific ways. As pointed out by Kendall Phillips, discursive formations are riddled with incoherence and contingency, but they work to give the overall impression of 'authority and absoluteness' (2002: 333). It is the 'contradictions' within discourse that provide a space for freedom — in the Foucauldian sense — as an opportunity for dissension and, consequently, the development of new kinds of knowledge, subjectivity and power relations (Phillips 2002: 336–37). In the remaining sections of this chapter I sketch out two examples of the ways in which common neoliberal tropes have been actively reworked in order to produce new types of knowledge. The knowledge produced in this manner positions Aboriginal people as deficient and, therefore, as appropriate targets for intensive government. This analysis is informed by Foucault's later work on liberal governmentality, which understood government as any deliberate attempt to systematically shape human conduct (Dean 2010: 18). I also explain why the production of this kind of knowledge might have contributed to the normalisation of coercive power relations.

Neoliberal subjects: A summary of politicians' statements about desirable attitudes and conduct among Aboriginal people

Many people are familiar with Foucault's work on the production of the subject, including his arguments about the relationship between knowledge and disciplinary forms of power in the early modern period (1977). His later work built on these ideas and focused on government as a new form of power that had 'population as its target, political economy as its major form of knowledge, and apparatuses of security as its essential technical instrument' (2008: 109). Existing alongside earlier forms of power, such as sovereignty and discipline, government sought to 'conduct ... the conduct of men' and applied a new body of social scientific knowledge about economics, society and populations to the management of the whole social body (Foucault 2007: 107–08; 2008: 108, 86). The concept of governmentality is a useful one because it provides a means of connecting the production of knowledge about populations — as the subject of attempts to govern — to discourses about what constitutes good and effective government. In the case of the NT intervention, I show that legislators borrowed familiar tropes about, first, the capable neoliberal subject and second, about the failures of the welfare state. Legislators employed these tropes to produce knowledge about Aboriginal communities. In this section I look at parliamentarians' statements about Aboriginal people. I argue that these statements draw on a broader neoliberal conception of the capable subject to produce knowledge about the deficiencies of Aboriginal people.

First, I need to outline what I mean by the capable subject and how this is related to neoliberal forms of reasoning or governmentality. Since there is no universal standard by which we can judge conduct, it is necessary to acknowledge that there are a multiplicity of rationalities — or governmentalities — which draw on, and produce, different kinds of knowledge in order to develop different understandings about what constitutes good and effective government (Dean 1999: 19). Against this general background, scholars of governmentality have sought to understand how different strands of liberal thought employ different understandings of effective government, individual liberty and the appropriate relationship between the individual and state (Dean and Hindess 1998: 12). For instance, welfarist rationalities for political rule arose as a formula for liberal government that sought to guarantee individual wellbeing against the vagaries of a market system, while simultaneously securing the liberties required for capitalist enterprise. This mode of *social* government incorporated a variety of programs and technologies of government including tax regimes, social insurance, employment agencies, and state intervention in the economy (Rose 1993: 291–93). In contrast, neoliberal rationalities of government seek to liberate populations from dependency on state welfare and public services. While neoliberals deplore 'big government', scholars of governmentality have pointed out that neoliberalism is not necessarily any less interventionist than other forms of liberal government. Neoliberals often emphasise the need to construct the artificial, but nonetheless necessary, conditions that make the market, and good outcomes, possible (Donzelot 2009: 28–30; Watson 2004: 587–88). For instance, many neoliberal programs attempt to deliver health, employment, education and similar services via market arrangements rather than through social technologies such as nationalised health (Hindess 2002: 140).

The above examples of governmentalities are only general types, and there is much variation on these basic themes. Nonetheless, a focus on these broad types can help us to identify how proponents of different strands of liberal thought have developed different and competing conceptions of the ideal citizen. Welfarist rationales for rule have generally focused on the ideal of a national community of 'thrifty, industrious and socially responsible' male breadwinners and female domestic workers. In contrast, neoliberal forms of rationality shift the target of government intervention toward the production of active, autonomous and entrepreneurial individuals. The capable neoliberal citizen is primarily a responsible individual who manages risk by purchasing private insurance against unemployment, ill health or disability, and who actively develops their human capital in ways that will help them to compete in the labour market and optimise the quality of life for themselves and their families (Donzelot 2009: 29; Larner 2000: 13; Rose 1993: 296; Rose and Miller 1992: 192–200). It is this second set of capabilities that structured discourse about Aboriginal people during the NT Intervention debates.

This discourse took three main forms. First, legislators argued that Aboriginal people should adopt the attitudes and behaviours that are necessary for success in a free market economy. Country Liberal Party MP David Tollner illustrates this idealisation of the free market economy when he argues that Aboriginal Australians need to have access to 'real property rights' so they can 'buy a home … own a piece of land … [and] start businesses'. His ideal also incorporates a vision of small-scale entrepreneurship in which every community includes 'a market garden, a greengrocer, a hairdresser, a restaurant, a clothing shop, a shoe shop, a bakery or a butcher shop' (Parliament of Australia 2007: 96–97). When the Labor Minister for Indigenous Affairs, Jenny Macklin, speaks of Aboriginal parents being 'the best role model possible' for their children she is clearly referring to the role they should play as participants in a mainstream economy and labour market (Macklin 2009a). On a separate occasion, Labor Prime Minister Julia Gillard made a 'call for changes in behaviour' and urged Aboriginal people to behave in responsible ways. She asked Aboriginal people to 'take care of your children; to take a job when you find one; to create a safe environment; to send your kids to school, pay your rent, save up for a home; to respect good social norms and to respect the law' (Karvelas 2011). The behaviour outlined here bears a close resemblance to the neoliberal conception of the responsible citizen.

Second, the discourse emphasised the deficiencies of Aboriginal people. A closer examination of one aspect of the NT Intervention, the Income Management (IM) regime, reveals the strength of the view that Aboriginal people were irresponsible and incapable of managing their own affairs. The IM regime diverted 50 per cent of individuals' regular fortnightly social security payments, and 100 per cent of all lump sum payments such as the Baby Bonus, to a special management account. This allowed government to direct Aboriginal individuals' expenditure, including the type of items individuals could buy — for example, food, beverages, clothing, household items, housing, and childcare — and where they could buy them (Human Rights and Equal Opportunities Commission (HREOC) 2008: 270). According to Liberal Party MP David Fawcett, IM was developed in 'recognition that there is a small subset within our community who, for whatever reasons, have not developed the life skills, the motivation or the ability to manage their own circumstances and the circumstances of those whom they have responsibility for' (Parliament of Australia 2007: 111). IM received almost universal support from parliamentarians, suggesting that Fawcett's views were unexceptional. Indeed, IM featured as a prominent aspect of later Labor government policy in the Northern Territory, where it was seen as necessary to prevent the purchase of harmful substances, such as alcohol (Macklin 2009b).

The final aspect of the discourse on the NT's Aboriginal population focused on the idea that Aboriginal culture was an obstacle to development and probably responsible for the deficiencies of Aboriginal individuals. This type of justification was most explicit among politicians of the Liberal–National coalition. Former Liberal MP Barry Haase, for instance, problematised Aboriginal culture by making explicit comparisons between an Aboriginal and mainstream 'style of life'. He argued that some of the 'cornerstones of our mainstream society', including respect for education, the rule of law, and an acceptance of personal responsibility, were non-existent in many Aboriginal communities (Parliament of Australia 2007: 102–03). Minister for Indigenous Affairs Mal Brough also focused on the social context of problems in Aboriginal communities. He argued that 'normal community standards and parenting behaviours' had broken down in some remote Aboriginal communities. He attributed this breakdown to the lack of economic activity and the availability of 'free money' in the form of welfare (Parliament of Australia 2007: 2). Labor parliamentarians also employed this rationale for the Intervention. For example, Prime Minister Kevin Rudd referred to the 'manifest failures on the part of [Aboriginal] individuals and communities' and to the 'dysfunctional culture of violence and neglect that blights some communities' (Rudd 2009). This type of analysis associates the problems in Aboriginal communities with wider cultural and behavioural norms.

Taken together, these three elements of discourse contributed to the view that Aboriginal people fall below socially acceptable norms of behaviour. This way of representing Aboriginal people incorporates elements of recognisably neoliberal reasoning — namely, its view of desirable capabilities and behaviour — but the use of these ideas to position Aboriginal people and culture as deficient is a product of the particular discourse of the intervention itself. This is not the first time that free market ideology has been used to position Aboriginal people in this way. Scholars have previously noted the way that neoliberal free market ideology had already 'infiltrated' the 'fabric of Indigenous life'. In the past this has seen many attempts to normalise the Aboriginal population by replacing concerns for 'custom, kin and land' with 'individualist aspirations of private home ownership, career and self-improvement' (Hinkson 2007; Walter 2010: 121–23).

Neoliberalism and the problematisation of Aboriginal land tenure and employment projects

The justifications for the NT Intervention not only involve the production of new knowledge about Aboriginal people's capacity for responsible behaviour, but also a critique of former approaches to Aboriginal governance. In this section I analyse parliamentarians' statements about two areas of policy: the land tenure system and Community Development Employment Projects (CDEP). I argue that the policies of the pre-Intervention period were associated, in the minds of many politicians, with an increase in welfare dependency among Aboriginal people, and with poor economic and social outcomes for Aboriginal people. This narrative of policy failure draws on the neoliberal critique of welfarist government and is used by politicians to explain the lack of steady progress in Aboriginal Affairs policy. This narrative results in the classification of past policy approaches, including rights-based approaches, as obstacles to Aboriginal welfare.

Before looking at specific policies, I note the general narrative about the failure of past policies in Aboriginal Affairs policy. Brough summarised the situation of the NT Intervention in the following manner: 'When confronted with a failed society … [d]o we respond with more of what we have done in the past? Or do we radically change direction with an intervention strategy matched to the magnitude of the problem?' (Parliament of Australia 2007: 10). This rhetorical question demonstrates that the Intervention was understood as part of a deliberate and necessary shift in policy approach. For Brough and his parliamentary colleagues, these major reforms removed artificial obstacles to development in Aboriginal communities. In his words, the Intervention was designed to 'break the back of violence and dysfunction' and 'allow us to build sustainable, healthy approaches in the long term'. The NT Intervention was compared to an 'emergency surgery' that was required after a long period of ineffective 'bandaid' solutions (Parliament of Australia 2007: 12). Labor politicians were less focused on the narrative of policy failure but nonetheless tied their support of the Intervention to the poor conditions in Aboriginal communities (Parliament of Australia 2007: 107–08). Bipartisan support for the Intervention suggests that earlier approaches to Aboriginal Affairs were considered problematic by members of both the Coalition and Labor parties.

Land tenure and rights

Politicians demonstrated particular antipathy to recognition of Aboriginal difference, including departures from conventional conceptions of economic development. Aboriginal land rights were directly linked, in the political discourse, with poor economic development in Aboriginal communities. The *Aboriginal Land Rights (Northern Territory) Act* of 1976 allows for the communal freehold ownership of land by Aboriginal groups who can demonstrate a traditional and ongoing connection to that land. The Act guarantees Aboriginal participation in decisions about land use — such as mining and other industry on Aboriginal land — and gives Aboriginal owners control over access to their land through a system of permits administered by land councils (Central Land Council).

These land rights, particularly the permit system, were seen as problematic by Brough and his parliamentary colleagues. Brough argued that the land tenure system on Aboriginal lands was an obstacle to the development of a 'real economy' (Parliament of Australia 2007: 11). His analysis of the situation was as follows:

> Banks will not lend money to start up small businesses because a committee [i.e. the Land Council] decides what tenure arrangements will apply. People cannot even borrow to buy their own home because they cannot own or lease a block of land. And to cap it all off, these towns have been closed to outsiders because of the permit system (Parliament of Australia 2007: 11–12).

Tollner developed a similar critique of land rights that described the Act as being about the 'preservation of culture' rather than 'good land management, land administration or planning for the future exploitation and productivity of the land' (Parliament of Australia 2007: 96–97). Like Brough, Tollner understood the land rights system as detrimental to Aboriginal people's economic prospects. Aboriginal control of land use had, according to Tollner, 'reduced Aboriginals to a welfare dependency status'. He argued that a powerful Aboriginal elite dominated decision-making in Aboriginal communities and distributed funds to 'select groups and individuals on a grace-and-favour basis, with little flowing down to those at the bottom' (Parliament of Australia 2007: 97).

Communal ownership and management of resources by Aboriginal people was, therefore, viewed as inherently problematic. They not only reduced the prospect of Aboriginal individuals engaging in a market economy but, according to the logic of Brough and Tollner, made this type of engagement practically impossible for individuals living on Aboriginal land. The distinctiveness of Aboriginal land tenure and, related to this, community governance arrangements, was a problem for politicians of all major parties. Both Coalition and Labor MPs repeatedly emphasised that their goal was to transform Aboriginal communities into normal suburbs. For instance, in June 2007, Howard declared that 'normalisation' was one of the main goals of Commonwealth involvement in Aboriginal communities, and there are references in the parliamentary debates on the NT Intervention to 'normal community standards' and 'normal suburbs' (Howard and Brough 2007; Parliament of Australia 2007: 2, 14, 74). In 2009, Macklin summarised the Labor government's goals for Aboriginal communities in the following terms:

> Our benchmark will be to progressively deliver in communities or townships the facilities and services you would expect in an Australian town of the same size. The same infrastructure and services that support and sustain healthy social norms so people can reach their potential and businesses can thrive. So children grow up safe and healthy and go to school; where they have the best role model possible — a parent who goes to work each day. So children see their parents taking responsibility for the family's economic security and planning and providing for the future (Macklin 2009a).

This type of statement suggests that the future of Aboriginal communities should, in all important respects, be identical to that of non-Aboriginal Australians.

The NT Intervention included a number of measures designed to counter the power of land councils. The legislation for the Intervention dismantled the permit system for townships on Aboriginal land and roads into towns (though not for uninhabited Aboriginal land). It also included a measure for compulsory leasing of Aboriginal towns to the Commonwealth Government so that government agencies could deliver services without negotiating leases with land councils (Hinkson 2007: 1–2; Parliamentary Library 2007). By February 2008 these leases applied to a total of 64 communities (Department of Families 2009). These communities were managed in accordance with the community governance provisions outlined in the NT Intervention legislation. For example, government business managers were appointed to manage government-funded social and building programs, and there was a new prohibition on alcohol and pornography (Yu, Duncan and Gray 2008: 25).

CDEP versus 'real jobs'

Like land rights, the CDEP program, which had existed in various incarnations since 1977, came under fire for being part of a failed policy approach. The scheme straddled the divide between welfare and work by enabling Aboriginal groups to employ Aboriginal individuals to work part-time on projects of importance to local Aboriginal people. Individuals were paid a wage equivalent to the Commonwealth social security benefit, to which they would have been entitled if they were unemployed (Sanders 1997: 2–3). The abolition of CDEP and the transition to 'real jobs, training and mainstream employment services' was an important aspect of the NT Intervention legislation (Parliament of Australia 2007: 7).[1] Brough justified the abolition of CDEP by arguing that, while CDEP had been a significant source of funding for Aboriginal communities, it had 'not become a pathway to real employment'. He argued that CDEP was 'another form of welfare dependency for many people' (Parliament of Australia 2007: 7). CDEP was therefore understood as an obstacle to Aboriginal individuals' participation in a mainstream labour market.

CDEP was also viewed as a structural problem that was preventing Aboriginal people developing the capabilities necessary for a good life. Haase and National MP Ian Causley both defined Aboriginal people's success in life in terms of their suitability for and engagement with the employment market. Haase argued that CDEP was a sort of 'furphy' employment, which was contributing to social problems in Aboriginal communities (Parliament of Australia 2007: 102–03). He suggested that 'real' employment would benefit Aboriginal people because it would foster individual skills and attitudes, such as a sense of responsibility, financial independence and self-esteem (Parliament of Australia 2007: 102–03). Causley provided a similar analysis when he argued that the problems in Aboriginal communities could be attributed to unemployment, and that Aboriginal people lacked the education and skills to find employment (Parliament of Australia 2007: 104–05). Indeed, for both Causley and Haase the employment market was considered a site for training Aboriginal people. The availability of real employment was crucial, from their perspective, because it could help individuals build the capabilities for engagement in the economic

---

1   The transition to mainstream unemployment services, such as work for the dole, was meant to be complete by July 2008, however, the CDEP scheme was maintained by a Labor government until July 2013, when the Remote Jobs and Communities Program (RJCP) came into operation (Department of Education 2011: 3–4).

system as well as develop proper attitudes, such as a respect for education, a sense of personal responsibility and respect for the rule of law (Parliament of Australia 2007: 102–05).

The welfare state critique

Both CDEP and land rights were viewed as part of an earlier political paradigm that had focused on Aboriginal self-determination as an essential prerequisite for Aboriginal wellbeing. By 2007, however, there was strong antipathy toward this policy approach. The problematisation of this earlier policy approach often required a retrospective redefinition of the purposes of legislation so that it could be deemed a failure. For example, the Land Rights Act had been developed with the objective of maintaining the spiritual link between Aboriginal people and their land, and was never expected to ensure the economic development of Aboriginal people.[2] The focus on the economic development of land, on individual rather than communal land ownership, and on access to 'real' rather than CDEP jobs stemmed from an increasingly narrow conception of development, which focused on the centrality of the market economy to the production of capable citizens and functional communities.

The political discourse on the NT Intervention — including the critique of land rights legislation and CDEP — drew upon the now-familiar neoliberal critique of the welfare state. The accusation that former approaches to Aboriginal government contributed toward welfare dependency and social disorder is a distinctive component of neoliberal criticisms of welfare. Parliamentary critique of earlier approaches to policy had much in common with the views of free market think tanks, such as the Centre for Independent Studies (CIS). The CIS has long campaigned for the end of so called 'separatist' policies in Aboriginal Affairs governance. Its campaign involved arguments for closing down 'unviable [Aboriginal] communities', replacing communal forms of land ownership and management with individual freehold property rights, and removing CDEP and other 'pretend jobs' (Hudson 2009; Hughes and Hughes 2010; Hughes, Hughes and Hudson 2010; Walter 2010: 126–27). In the remainder of this paper I consider how the problematisation of both Aboriginal behaviour and past Aboriginal Affairs policy contributed to bipartisan support for the more coercive measures of the NT Intervention.

---

2   For instance, the 1974 royal commission on land rights acknowledged that white Australians had already settled on most arable land and that land available to be claimed by Aboriginal people was economically unproductive (Woodward 1974: 2, 9–10).

Coercive governance and Aboriginal Affairs policy: A new norm?

Previous scholarship on the NT Intervention addressed its neoliberal character but did not consider the important issue of how coercive government was justified by political elites. Given the bipartisan support for the Intervention, and the continuation of many of the coercive measures of the NT Intervention as part of the Stronger Futures scheme, it is important to consider the process of political reasoning that has made coercive policies acceptable to recent governments. My goal in this chapter has been to deepen our understanding of the way in which knowledge and power are linked in recent discourse on the NT Intervention. I have been concerned with the role of neoliberal tropes, such as responsible citizenship and the dangers of the welfare state, in the production of knowledge about Aboriginal people and Aboriginal community governance. I conclude this chapter with a few comments about the relationship between this discourse and the normalisation of coercive approaches to governance in this field. I suggest that justifications for coercive government employed aspects of neoliberal reasoning and governmentality, but that this reasoning was incorporated in an incomplete and patchy manner. This has meant that the NT Intervention relied on an incoherent and contradictory logic.

My explanation for this claim depends, once again, on the concept of governmentality. There are two relevant points here. The first relates to the nature of freedom and coercion in liberal government. Foucault argued that good government, from a liberal perspective, is government that manages the conditions of liberal freedom and fosters these conditions among the population (Foucault 2008: 61–68). This means that liberty is understood in functional rather than doctrinal terms, and only has value where it secures rather than inhibits prosperity and wellbeing. Since liberty is seen as a prerequisite for good outcomes, it makes sense that desirable liberties should be developed wherever they are seen to be lacking. Scholars of governmentality have pointed out that both facilitative and coercive forms of government are applied to the task of shaping individuals so they can govern themselves. For instance, the task of helping people get 'job ready' may involve facilitative skills-development programs run by government or non-profit organisations, as well as more coercive, involuntary programs which oblige unemployed people to contribute time and labour to approved organisations (Dean 2002: 38–41). In this context, we should understand coercion as a common technique for the production of capable liberal subjects.

The second relevant point is that coercive techniques of government have historically been applied in an uneven manner. Liberals have a tendency to draw upon coercive techniques of government where populations are perceived to lack the capabilities required for self-discipline, or where facilitative approaches to government are considered unlikely to be successful. In general, social scientific and other forms of expert knowledge are used to group liberal subjects according to their capacities for autonomy. The most autonomous individuals require little active government because their capacity for self-discipline allows them to conduct themselves appropriately within society and the economy. Other individuals, such as the unemployed or children, require help to acquire the necessary skills and capabilities for autonomous living (Dean 2002: 48). Historicist views, which see Indigenous people as falling below widely accepted norms for development, have increased the tendency to classify Indigenous people as part of a broader population of people — including criminals, immigrant communities and the urban poor — who are deemed to be incapable of self-discipline. This type of classification supports claims that Indigenous people require additional help, either facilitative or coercive, to learn how to conduct themselves appropriately (Hindess 2001: 365–71; 2004: 28–31).

Justifications for coercive government, therefore, depend on two prerequisites; political discourse must position a particular population as incapable of self-discipline, and simultaneously explain why more facilitative approaches to government would be unlikely to succeed in the task of governing this population. My analysis in this chapter suggests that both of these conditions are present in the political discourse of the NT Intervention. Politicians made it clear that they viewed Aboriginal people's behaviour, attitudes and skills as deficient and below the minimum standards expected of autonomous neoliberal citizens. The problematisation of past policy approaches in Aboriginal Affairs — which I have compared to the neoliberal critique of the welfare state — led legislators to doubt the utility of more facilitative strategies of government. As I mentioned above, CDEP, community governance provisions, the permit system and Aboriginal people's discretion to spend social security income according to their own preferences were all considered to be impediments to economic development. Since the chance of gaining voluntary participation in the new political agenda was low, both the Coalition and Labor governments considered coercive forms of governance to be justifiable and necessary.

What are the implications of this analysis for our understanding of the relationship between neoliberal government and coercive strategies of government? Based on this case study alone, there is no compelling reason to consider neoliberalism as more innately coercive than other strands of liberal government. Neoliberal tropes were used selectively in the production of knowledge about Aboriginal people, and the broader context of governance, in the Northern Territory. It is possible that many other standards of ideal citizenship and good government could have been used in a similar manner to position Aboriginal citizens and their communities as deficient and in need of intervention. The exact nature of this critique would have been different, but the effect on the relationship between Aboriginal and non-Aboriginal peoples might have been similar. In some respects, the discourse of the NT Intervention merely reproduces a longstanding tendency to target Aboriginal people for intensive intervention and reform. Neoliberal forms of argument can take their place among many other historical justifications for colonial government.

This does not mean that the neoliberal discourses of the Intervention should not be interrogated. The primary implication of my analysis in this chapter is that critics of the current approach to Aboriginal Affairs governance should address ideas about the cultural deficiency of Aboriginal people and the particular language of policy failure that has become common in recent years. The representations of Aboriginal people produced by these discourses are widely accepted and are being used to structure power relations in such a way that the views of Aboriginal people are almost completely dismissed unless they accord with the current political agenda. The current discourse also positions Aboriginal culture as an obstacle to the development and wellbeing of Aboriginal people, thereby paving the way for the forceful assimilation of Aboriginal people into the Australian cultural and economic mainstream. In this context, it is possible to point toward some of the less coherent aspects or implications of the current discourse. To provide one example, it is illogical to conflate all former policy approaches in Aboriginal Affairs governance with a failed welfare state regime. As Tim Rowse has pointed out, the initial impetus for Aboriginal self-determination could itself be considered part of a neoliberal reform agenda (Rowse 1996).

Another incoherency that might be capitalised on by critics is the difficulty of producing viable strategies for government that are consistent with current definitions of the policy problem. There is no obvious method available, based on current discourse, for the actual production of capable citizens. Intensive forms of regulation, such as the IM regime, may discipline individuals and ensure they act in certain ways. They are unable, however, to bring about the substantive changes in attitude that would, presumably, be required to produce capable, fully functioning neoliberal citizens. The usual neoliberal techniques for achieving this are unlikely to work in Aboriginal communities. The construction of quasi-markets for the delivery of formerly public services has been one common way of helping to boost the capabilities of individuals in non-Indigenous contexts. For instance, the Australian Government replaced public job creation and employment services with a competitive market of private and community sector job placement enterprises in the mid-1990s. The ethos of this quasi-market based delivery of social services is that clients can learn the norms and values of the market — such as initiative, responsibility, and competitiveness — through the experience of choosing between a range of private service providers. They can then apply these skills in real job markets (Dean 2010: 187–89). In remote Aboriginal communities, however, it would be enormously difficult to develop such quasi-market schemes as there are too few private and community sector organisations to develop a competitive marketplace for the provision of social services. The current discourses about Aboriginal governance lead to no viable plan for producing the outcomes that proponents claim to be desirable and necessary, and this makes these discourses both unstable and vulnerable.

To conclude, coercive government is more likely in situations where individuals are understood to lack important capabilities for success, and where facilitative approaches to government are seen as unlikely to achieve governance objectives. In this chapter I have presented a critical analysis of the rhetoric of the NT Intervention with the goal of destabilising the authority of those discourses which legitimate and normalise coercive approaches to Aboriginal Affairs governance. Drawing on the concept of governmentality, I demonstrated that Aboriginal people were perceived to be incapable of living an autonomous existence because of a lack of personal responsibility and skills. Aboriginal communities were also seen as falling short of the norms of mainstream society, with parliamentarians producing a powerful narrative that conflated past policy approaches with the failed welfarist approach in public policy. This narrative created new knowledge about the social conditions in Aboriginal communities, including a view that Aboriginal communities were dysfunctional and provided an insufficient environment for the development of capable, independent individuals. In this context, coercive government was seen as a necessary aspect of the plan to remove obstacles to the development of market economies in Aboriginal communities. This detailed understanding of the operation of knowledge/power in current political rhetoric opens up opportunities for a more targeted critique of the coercive aspects of Aboriginal Affairs policy.

References

Altman, J. 2007. The 'National Emergency' and land rights reform: Separating fact from fiction. An assessment of the proposed amendments to the *Aboriginal Land Rights (Northern Territory) Act 1976*. Centre for Aboriginal Economic Policy Research (CAEPR), Canberra. URL: http://caepr.anu.edu.au/sites/default/files/Publications/topical/Altman_Oxfam.pdf. Consulted 28 November 2013.

Anderson, I. 2008. Indigenous Australians and health rights. *Journal of Law and Medicine* 15: 760–72.

Australia, Parliament of 2007. Parliamentary debates. *House of Representatives Official Hansard* 11 (7 August). Canberra.

Australian Government 2011. Stronger futures in the Northern Territory: Policy statement. November. Canberra.

Biesecker, B. 1992. Michel Foucault and the question of rhetoric. *Philosophy & Rhetoric* 25(4): 351–64.

Cahill, D. 2007. The contours of neoliberal hegemony in Australia. *Rethinking Marxism* 19(2): 221–33.

Central Land Council, The Aboriginal Land Rights Act, URL: http://www.clc.org.au/Ourland/land_rights_act/Land_rights_act.html. Consulted 24 September 2011.

Concerned Australians 2010. *This is what we said: Australian Aboriginal people give their views on the Northern Territory Intervention*. East Melbourne.

Conor, L. 2007. Howard's desert storm. *Overland* 189: 12–15.

Cooper, M. 1988. Rhetorical criticism and Foucault's philosophy of discursive events. *Central States Speech Journal* 39(1): 1–17.

Dean, M. 1999. *Governmentality. Power and rule in modern society*. London: SAGE Publications.

—— 2002. Liberal government and authoritarianism. *Economy and Society* 31(1): 37–61.

—— 2010. *Governmentality. Power and rule in modern society*. 2nd edn. Los Angeles: Sage.

Dean, M. and Hindess, B. 1998. Introduction: Government, liberalism, society. In M. Dean and B. Hindess eds. *Governing Australia. Studies in contemporary rationalities of government*. Melbourne: Cambridge University Press.

Department of Education, Employment and Workplace Relations 2011. The future of remote participation and employment servicing arrangements: Discussion paper. Canberra.

Department of Families, Community Services and Indigenous Affairs 2009. Five year leases on Aboriginal land. URL: http://www.fahcsia.gov.au/sa/indigenous/progserv/ntresponse/about_response/housing_land_reform/Pages/five_year_leased_aboriginal_land.aspx. Consulted 1 October 2010.

Dodson, P. 2007. An entire culture is at stake. *Age* (Melbourne) 14 July: 9.

Donzelot, J. 2009. Michel Foucault's understanding of liberal politics. In M.A. Peters, A.C. Besley and M. Olssen eds. *Governmentality studies in education. Contexts of education*. Rotterdam: Sense Publishers.

Foss, S.K. and Gill, A. 1987. Michel Foucault's theory of rhetoric as epistemic. *Western Journal of Speech Communication* 51(4): 384–401.

Foucault, M. 1977. *Discipline and punish*. London: Allen Lane.

—— 2007. *Security, territory, population. Lectures at the College De France 1977– 1978*. Basingstoke: Palgrave Macmillan.

—— 2008. *The birth of biopolitics. Lectures at the College De France 1978–1979*. Basingstoke: Palgrave Macmillan.

Hindess, B. 2001. Not at home in the Empire. *Social Identities* 7(3): 363–77.

—— 2002. Neo-liberal citizenship. *Citizenship Studies* 6(2): 127–43.

—— 2004. Liberalism: What's in a name? In W. Larner and W. Walters eds. *Global governmentality: Governing international spaces*. London: Routledge.

Hinkson, M. 2007. Introduction: In the name of the child. In J. Altman and M. Hinkson eds. *Coercive reconciliation. Stabilise, normalise, exit Aboriginal Australia*. Melbourne: Arena Publications.

Howard, J. 2007. To stabilise and protect — Little children are sacred, address to The Sydney Institute, 25 June, *The Sydney Papers* 19(3): 68–76.

Howard, J. and Brough, M. 2007. Joint press conference with the Hon. Mal Brough, Minister for Families, Community Services and Indigenous Affairs. *Prime Minister of Australia: Media centre*. URL: http://pandora. nla.gov.au/pan/10052/20080118-1528/pm.gov.au/media/Interview/2007/ Interview24380.html. Consulted 25 June 2008.

Hudson, S. 2009. *From rhetoric to reality: Can 99-year leases lead to homeownership for Indigenous communities?* St Leonards: Centre for Independent Studies.

Hughes, H. and Hughes, M. 2010. *Indigenous employment, unemployment and labour force participation: Facts for evidence based policy*. St Leonards: Centre for Independent Studies.

Hughes, H., Hughes, M. and Hudson, S. 2010. *Private housing on Indigenous land*. St Leonards: Centre for Independent Studies.

Human Rights and Equal Opportunities Commission (HREOC) 2008. *Social Justice Report 2007*. Sydney.

Karvelas, P. 2011. 'Gap won't close if you don't act': Julia Gillard. *Australian* 10 February. URL: http://www.theaustralian.com.au/national-affairs/gap-wont-close-if-you-dont-act-julia-gillard/story-fn59niix-1226003313411. Consulted 15 February 2011.

Larner, W. 2000. Neo-liberalism: Policy, ideology, governmentality. *Studies in Political Economy* 63: 5–25.

Macklin, J. 2009a. Importance of delivering remote Indigenous housing in an efficient and affordable way — Delivering Indigenous housing, Speech, 15 September. URL: http://www.jennymacklin.fahcsia.gov.au/speeches/2009/Pages/speech_indig_19aug09.aspx. Consulted 30 September 2010.

—— 2009b, Strengthening the Northern Territory Emergency Response. Joint Media Release with Warren Snowdon MP, Member for Lingiari. 25 November. URL: http://www.jennymacklin.fahcsia.gov.au/mediareleases/2009/Pages/strengthening_nter_25nov2009.aspx. Consulted 14 February 2011.

Macoun, A. 2011. Aboriginality and the Northern Territory intervention. *Australian Journal of Political Science* 46(3): 519–34.

Manderson, D. 2008. Not yet: Aboriginal people and the deferral of the rule of law. *Arena Journal* 29/30: 219–72.

Mazel, O. 2009. Development in the 'First World': Alleviating Indigenous disadvantage in Australia — The dilemma of difference. *Griffith Law Review* 18(2): 475–502.

McKerrow, R.E. 1989. Critical rhetoric: Theory and praxis. *Communication Monographs* 56(2): 91–111.

Parliamentary Library. 2007. *Northern Territory National Emergency Response Bills 2007 — Interim Bills Digest*. Canberra: Parliament of Australia. URL: http://www.aph.gov.au/binaries/library/pubs/bd/2007-08/08bd018.pdf. Consulted 28 November 2013.

Phillips, K.R. 2002. Spaces of invention: Dissension, freedom, and thought in Foucault. *Philosophy & Rhetoric* 35(4): 328–44.

Rose, N. 1993. Government, authority and expertise in advanced liberalism. *Economy and Society* 22(3): 283–99.

Rose, N. and Miller, P. 1992. Political power beyond the state: Problematics of government. *The British Journal of Sociology* 43(2): 173–205.

Rowse, T. 1996, 'Neo-liberal/Advanced liberal tendencies in contemporary Aboriginal Affairs', paper presented to Culture and Citizenship Conference, Griffith University, Brisbane, Australia, 30 September – 2 October.

Rudd, K. 2009. *Closing the Gap* Report. Media release, 26 February. URL: http://pmrudd.archive.dpmc.gov.au/node/5287. Consulted 14 February 2011.

Rundle, G. 2007. Military humanitarianism in Australia's north. In J. Altman and M. Hinkson eds. *Coercive reconciliation. Stabilise, normalise, exit Aboriginal Australia.* Melbourne: Arena Publications.

Said, E.W. 2003. *Orientalism.* London: Penguin Books.

Sanders, W. 1997. *Opportunities and problems astride the welfare/work divide: The CDEP scheme in Australian social policy.* Canberra: Centre for Aboriginal Economic Policy Research (CAEPR).

Tangentyere Council 2007. Work with us, not against us. Press release. URL: http://www.tangentyere.org.au/publications/#press_releases. Consulted 29 October 2010.

Walter, M. 2010. Market forces and Indigenous resistance paradigms. *Social Movement Studies: Journal of Social, Cultural and Political Protest* 9(2): 121–37.

Watson, V. 2004. Liberalism and advanced liberalism in Australian Indigenous affairs. *Alternatives: Global, Local, Political* 29(5): 577–98.

Woodward, A.E. 1974. *Aboriginal Land Rights Commission.* Second report. Canberra: The Government Printer of Australia.

Yu, P., Duncan, M.E. and Gray, B. 2008. *Northern Territory emergency response.* Report of the NTER Review Board. Canberra: Attorney-General's Department.

Conclusion

Studying Australian political rhetoric

John Uhr and Ryan Walter

This book arose from a conference at the School of Politics and International Relations at The Australian National University, held in May 2013, and supported by an Australian Research Council grant awarded to the editors to study Australian political rhetoric. The conference was conceived with one overarching aim in view: to demonstrate the centrality of rhetoric to democratic politics. If rhetoric is broadly conceived as persuasive language use, then it is a daily activity for politicians, who must constantly communicate, inform, persuade, attack and defend, cajole, scare, conceal, while performing many other actions besides. Language use represents the core of the politician's vocation, and following its rhythms and consequences is the constant task of journalists and commentators. Yet Australian political scientists give it little attention. Reviewing the papers in this collection makes clear how successfully the conference's aim was realised.

The chapters in Part I are concerned with the relationship between political speech and political behaviour. Stephen Mills shows that Kevin Rudd's apology to the Stolen Generations (2008), given while he was prime minister, was a case of national leadership. Rudd was thus performing two actions at the same time — apologising and leading — in an international context in which the act of apologising is 'a new instrument of public leadership'. As the holder of the pre-eminent representative office, the prime minister can claim to speak on behalf of a political community and, in doing so, supervene on its public memory with greater force than other public officers because, as Mills notes, 'attempted apologies by public officials below prime ministerial rank have tended to fail'. Mills's gambit is that interventions into national memory can have 'transformative' power because they shape imagined pasts and futures. John Howard's less committal prime ministerial expression of 'deep sorrow' and his Motion of Reconciliation (1999) might, therefore, be seen not as a stubborn refusal to apologise, but as a more cautious assessment of the intervention into public memory required of the prime minister.

Ryan Walter addresses the language–behaviour nexus through Quentin Skinner's notion of 'evaluative–descriptive' terms. In this case, politicians attacked and defended a certain governmental action, normally referred to as fiscal policy. Walter argues that the terms 'responsible economic management' and 'fiscal discipline' were used to legitimate action, while a negative appraisive vocabulary was used to expose 'irresponsible economic management' or 'fiscal recklessness' in the same piece of fiscal policy. The criteria that define when these terms can be used are weak, and this is part of their appeal, as Howard and Treasurer Peter Costello appreciated while in office. The Australian Labor Party's recent fiscal misfortunes in relation to declining federal revenues were exacerbated by its leaders' seemingly imperfect understanding of this rhetoric, as the claims to 'responsible economic management' were fused with a promise to deliver a surplus, and this summoned the divergent value of 'trustworthiness'. Labor was consequently obliged to make cuts to spending to try to achieve a surplus and so align its behaviour with its rhetoric — a painful exercise that could have been avoided if the relatively demanding rhetoric of trustworthiness and promise-keeping had never been deployed and only the accommodating 'responsible economic management' had been used. Here, then, is a clear case where language use constrained action.

Jennifer Rayner examines the language used to justify two high-stakes decisions to change prime minister, from Bob Hawke to Paul Keating, and from Kevin Rudd to Julia Gillard. One transition was successful in the sense that the new leader was unencumbered by the need to explain and defend the leadership transition; by contrast, 'the rhetoric of Gillard's ascension gave the public multiple reasons to question her right to the role'. Perhaps Gillard's greatest mistake was to describe herself as an unelected leader and link her legitimacy to the exercise by Australians of a 'birthright' to choose their prime minister. As Rayner describes, this course of legitimation was negative in character because it held Gillard's legitimacy in abeyance until the next election, when that legitimacy was disastrously complicated by a minority government alliance with the Greens, which saw the prime minister reverse an election promise not to tax carbon. Worse, this populist justification was at odds with the actual constitutional and parliamentary workings of Australian democracy, and therefore turned Gillard away from a positive justification grounded in Australia's political history.

The first of Barry Hindess's chapters examines the language–behaviour relation from the opposite side, by underlining not how language constrains, but how it enables. The language of the *'Little children are sacred'* report on sexual abuse in Aboriginal communities provided linguistic and intellectual resources for the Howard government to employ in legitimating its Northern Territory 'Emergency Response' intervention, a set of actions that are likely to have been at odds with the desired wishes of the report's authors. The lesson, in other words, is that 'political rhetoric may be either intended or unintended and that the latter may well be consequential'. Key here was the report's use of an opposition between modern and traditional ways of living, which invokes a powerful set of assumptions regarding the need for change in those communities portrayed as traditional. When this modern/traditional distinction was combined with the report's appeal for urgency, the call for consultation with Aboriginal groups was easy to ignore. Hindess's chapter, therefore, offers a case study of unintended consequences in the realm of rhetoric.

Dennis Grube's chapter returns to the theme of the constraining effects of political rhetoric by introducing the concept of path dependency. Politicians make 'rhetorical choices' and, in doing so, they may impose limits on 'the range of rhetorical options open to them for the future'. Successful rhetoric will be repeated and lock a politician into a certain course unless they are prepared to face the risk of 'looking inauthentic, inconsistent and untrustworthy', yet political life is full of nuance and contingency that prompts changes in position. This trade-off was faced by prime ministers Rudd and Gillard and then Leader of the Opposition Tony Abbott. Where Abbott modified his rhetoric on asylum seekers early and at low political cost, Rudd and Gillard paid high prices for their reversals on climate policy. Managing the trade-off between consistency and flexibility is a crucial skill for leaders, as illustrated by the fortunes of Rudd and Gillard. Once more, rhetoric, or language use, emerges as the key skill for politicians, at the heart of Australian political events.

The focus of Part II is those standards for political rhetoric that are 'internal' to politics, in the sense that they are historical, polemical, or institutional. The hope is that the essays of Part II point the way to an alternative, empirical approach to conceiving of standards of rhetoric, as against looking to sources 'external' to politics, especially philosophical reason, as found in Rawlsian and Habermasian formulations of 'public reason'. For, if it is true that politicians use rhetoric everyday, then we need to know how their rhetoric is regulated, if at all, by everyday mechanisms.

Some of the standards of Australian political rhetoric are endogenous and some are imported. Mark Rolfe's paper pierces the myth of a golden past when Australian political rhetoric was inspiring and informing by investigating the history of rhetorical standards and their deployment in political combat from the 1820s. The absence of a stable and objective standard for judging rhetoric has meant that 'creative imaginings of past leaders and their rhetoric have been essential standards for judging current leaders and their language'. The United States has long been an exporter of rhetorical standards to Australia, especially the anxiety that rhetorical decorum (and its absence) might be symptomatic of a politician's character. In this respect, the rise of the 'plain speaking' trope in Australian politics and its use by Robert Menzies and Howard was foreshadowed by developments in the United States.

Hindess's second chapter studies 'dog whistling', a term of abuse used in recent Australian politics. It entails the accusation that a politician has sent a coded message — typically of unsavoury character — that will be correctly perceived by only one part of the electorate. Leftist commentators in Australia have tended to use the term to accuse Howard and Gillard of covertly expressing racist and anti-immigration sentiments. From the perspective of political rhetoric, dog whistling should be seen as 'a sophisticated kind of rhetoric', since an audience can be segmented with the same piece of speech. What dog whistling in fact designates is, therefore, simply the omnipresent practice in politics of coded messaging, it is just the message that is under attack. Hindess colourfully concludes that 'the concept of dog-whistle politics is hardly worth the napkin it was probably first scribbled on'. A different issue arises for the user of this attack term, that '[h]owever one reads the charge of dog whistling, the implied description of those who respond to its call is distinctly unflattering', while those who can perceive the coding behaviour 'constitute an observant, morally superior elite'. In Australia, at least, the accusation of dog whistling is normally a dog whistle itself.

The final chapter relating to standards of rhetoric is John Uhr's account of recent virulent debate over the role of the Speaker of the House of Representatives, including contributions from the three Speakers who held office during the Gillard minority government. The Speaker is one of the few offices prescribed in the Australian constitution as a regulator of parliamentary proceedings according to rules authorised by the House, but the exact role is underspecified, except on the point that the Speaker's deliberative voice is silenced. Uhr's account offers two conclusions. First, that 'independence' is the best candidate for an accepted principle that should guide the Speaker in Australia, but this principle does not 'confer a substantial positive role to determine positive standards of orderly conduct', and the Speaker's task is limited to disciplining disorderly conduct. Second, and despite the bipartisan acceptance of independence as the relevant principle to be invoked and denied in debates over the role of Speaker, the office of Speaker is not immune from party interests. In other words, the Speaker is the official regulator of democratic speech, but the nature of the Speaker's official duties is the subject of open-ended political contest.

This last point should be viewed with the earlier claim regarding the capacity for language use to constrain and enable action, because what emerges is a view of politics in which partisan contest is primarily linguistic in nature. This claim is balanced by the import of the final group of papers, where attention turns to the substantive content of political speech; political speech is not solely used to legitimate behaviour and attack opponents, but it is also used to set out normative visions, shape the behaviour of others, and produce policy. Mark Hearn's and Ian Tregenza's analysis of Alfred Deakin's post-Federation speeches, which are normally associated with nation-building and the idea of an 'Australian settlement', reveal that alongside Deakin's concrete policies on immigration and industrial policy sat a focus on citizenship. The nerve of Deakin's rhetoric was that Australian citizens would need to cultivate certain qualities if the nation-building enterprise was to succeed. Discipline, self-reliance, and patriotism took centrestage, and it was hoped that a citizenry that displayed these qualities would lend the fledging polity the unity needed for a safe future. The anxiety over national unity combined with Deakin's awareness of international competition in commerce and arms, and impelled his burdensome prescriptions for institution-building.

The nation-building enterprise that marked Australia's early history was perceived to have been attacked by 'economic rationalism', the topic of Geoffrey Stokes's chapter. Yet one of Stokes's findings is that this reproving use of the term worked alongside commendatory and categorical uses, and the phrase began life in the 1970s as praise for the Labor government of Gough Whitlam. As the intensity and volume of the debate over the role of economic reasoning in national life increased in the 1980s under the Hawke and Keating governments, the uses of the idea of economic rationalism came to diverge and, combined with the failure of John Hewson's explicitly reform-based election campaign in 1993, the term's prevalence in public life declined, even as the role of economic expertise gained acceptance. In other words, linguistic innovation and evanescence is an index to political–economic change.

Continuing the chronological development through Australia's policy history, Melissa Lovell studies how tropes of neoliberal discourse have been used to justify interventionist governmental techniques in the Northern Territory. In this respect, her chapter fits with the theme of Part I. Yet her major concern is to show how neoliberal tropes, such as the capable citizen and the failures of the welfare state, were used to produce governmental knowledge of Aboriginal people. Aboriginal people were distinguished as a segment of the Australian population by being attributed with two qualities. First, forms of personal comportment that fell below the standard of the autonomous neoliberal citizen. Second, substandard social and economic outcomes that were partly a result of this first quality, but which also flowed from the policy failures of communal land tenure and community employment programs. This specification of a sub-population was a necessary precondition for the legal apparatus that was applied to this population as the target of intensive government known as the Northern Territory Intervention.

Perhaps the overriding lesson from Lovell's chapter is that political speech is intimately involved in knowledge production and the work of governing. This point leads back to the original premise underlying the conference: language matters. It matters because using language is what politicians do, because it constrains, enables, and programs their governmental actions, even as those constraints can be mediated and shifted by further language use. The fact that political speech is not subject to stable, philosophical standards recalls John

Kane's opening comments on the perennial tension between the aspirations that have always been held for rhetoric and the disappointments that it routinely engenders. This, too, must be an ingredient in the study of political rhetoric.

www.ingramcontent.com/pod-product-compliance
Lightning Source LLC
Chambersburg PA
CBHW041119280326

41928CB00061B/3407